Taijiquan

Cultivating Inner Strength

Taijiquan

Cultivating Inner Strength

C.P. Ong

Bagua Press

DEDICATION

To my dearest Mahla,
and our children,
Thida and Mingwei.

ACKNOWLEDGMENTS

This book came to be written after hundreds of hours spent with each of the Grandmasters Chen Zhenglei, Chen Xiaowang and Zhu Tiancai over a decade. I am indebted to them for their generosity in sharing their knowledge, without which it could not have been written. I also would like to acknowledge two other masters, Zhang Zhijun and Chen Yu, who have also helped me gain insights of the art, and also Chiang Yun-chung who first taught me Taijiquan.

I would like to thank my friends and Taijiquan enthusiasts, Mary Anna Cirlot, Margery Gerard, Gary Lee and Lorraine Noval, and my son, Mingwei Ong, for valiantly struggling through the early drafts and editing the book.

I would also like to thank Weerayuth Aerjaipra for the book cover and interior design, my brother, Chong-Hin Ong, for his contribution in the graphics illustrations, and my wife, Mahla Ong for taking the photos of the form postures.

Contents

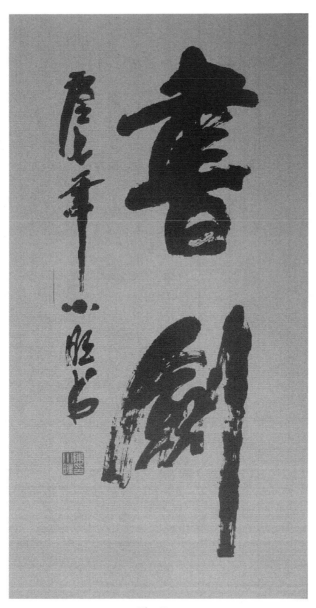

Shujian
(Book and Sword)
The pursuit of the literary and martial tradition

Calligraphy by Chen Xiaowang

Preface

The basic questions of Taijiquan—origin, *qi* (vital energy), *neijin* (internal strength), even what the art is—have no simple answers. The early Chinese literature on Taijiquan may give a fascinating account of the art, but they are written in terse non-vernacular classical verses and are couched in terms that are uniquely Chinese and specific to the art. The concepts are subject to interpretations. Furthermore, the narrative is often muddied with myths and legends that surround the art.

The Taiji concepts of yin and yang, *bagua* trigrams, and *wuxing* (five phases) are ancient and they permeate old Chinese thinking covering everything of "heaven, man and earth," but the development of Taijiquan is relatively recent—only three centuries old, during China's last Qing dynastic rule. The art and its derivations as practiced today were mostly standardized only in the 1920s, when followers began to cluster around their masters to form the various schools of Taijiquan. Then the story of Taijiquan took on partisan hues that would further cloud one's quest of the art. So controversies abound, but by keeping them in perspective, one can avoid from being entangled.

The approach in this book is guided by the central principle of Taiji balance—the balance of yin and yang. But yin and yang belong more to metaphysics than physical training. Ironically, the body relates to their manifestations readily. While Taiji balance may take a dissertation to explicate, the body builds a fluency of yin and yang and attains Taiji balance through practice.

The practice of Taijiquan is an arduous process of instilling the yin-yang principles in the body and mind through their representations. We study the yin-yang effects as expressed in the medium of the body, particularly, the musculo-skeletal structure. We superimpose physics and physiology onto the yin-yang framework to investigate Taijiquan motion. This approach deviates from traditional exposition, which shuns the mention of muscles.

Pragmatically, the art is to decipher and resolve excess or deficiency of yin or yang, thereby to reduce yin-yang imbalance towards Taiji balance. The rationale of practice is the same, whether one is a serious practitioner or a beginner, for martial arts or for health, only one's dedication and passion may vary.

The thesis of this book is that Taiji motion—motion in accord with Taiji principles—gives rise to *neijin* or internal strength. In other words, the practice of Taijiquan is a cultivation of inner strength, hence the subtitle of the book.

Science explains the power of *neijin*, but the yin-yang framework trains the body to produce the power of *neijin*. While physics defines force as a vector of direction and magnitude, Taijiquan generates a highly refined strength called *jin* (synonymous to *neijin*) that manifests the yin-yang duality in the *rou* (soft) and *gang* (hard) of *jin*. In usage, the rou-soft accords change and agility, and the gang-hard, power, and integral to the concept of *jin* is the liveliness of interchange between *rou* and *gang*, which is key to the marvel of *jin* in martial applications.

This *rou-gang* duality is seen in the frame structure of the body in its soft and hard attributes, as a representation of yin and yang (Chapter 6). With this representation, the muscle actions underlying the frame structure literally give meat to the Taiji metaphysical framework, and yin-yang imbalance can be deciphered as excessive or deficient muscle actions in the support of the frame structure.

Taijiquan resolves imbalance of muscle actions by the relaxation methodology of *fangsong*. The *fangsong* process nurtures qi. In time, as qi develops, the practitioner learns to use qi to comprehend the *fangsong* mechanism. Then the process of deciphering and resolving yin-yang imbalances meld into one of nurturing qi towards Taiji balance. The practice then elevates to the internal phase of using qi to drive motion, which leads to the actualization of the yi-qi-motion paradigm: *yi* (mind) initiates and activates qi, qi stirs and directs motion. The practice of Taijiquan thus can be described as nurturing qi and cultivating *neijin* in the development of Taiji balance.

An immediate import of Taiji balance is body balance. The resolution of muscle imbalances eases motion and qi flow at the joints, thus enlivening the dynamics within the frame structure to adjust to maintain balance. That is to say, a body tempered with Taiji balance responds with natural ease to keep balance—even when pushed suddenly from behind or in an accidental slip (Chapter 7).

From another standpoint of health, the regulation of qi flow with regard to Taiji balance, builds a holistic balance of the organ systems, which defines health in Traditional Chinese Medicine. Thus Taijiquan is commonly prescribed as a preventive medicine. Also, the *fangsong* process induces a discipline of meditation necessary to sharpen the mind at the higher levels of practice. This quiets the mind, and develops a harmony of the heart and mind (Chapter 10).

From a martial viewpoint, the core strength of *neijin* is the basis of Taijiquan's fascinating kungfu skills. Fascinating because there appears to be no exertion of strenuous efforts—the hallmark of *neijin*. So it seems that "the weaker is overcoming the stronger and the slower beating the faster," as exemplified in the skill of "four ounces repelling a thousand pounds" (*si liang bo qian jin*). *Neijin* kungfu techniques rely primarily on the leverage of coiling motion, called *chanrao*. *Chanrao* power derives from the body's rotational motion and is trained by the silk-reeling methodology (*chansi gong*) (Chapter 8).

This book introduces qi as it is experienced by the practitioner. However, Taiji theory posits a cosmic qi that regulates the universe and the intercourse of heaven, earth and man. Scholars of old might have explained natural disasters and the periodic dynastic upheavals as transgressions of the yin-yang order of the cosmic qi, but the practice of Traditional Chinese Medicine is pragmatically grounded on qi coursing the network of meridians interconnecting the organ systems, not the cosmic nature of qi. Likewise, Taijiquan training is not preoccupied with cosmic qi nor with qi flow in the Taoist "small or large orbits." Taijiquan training is driven by the development of qi to actualize the yi-qi-motion paradigm to break through at the joints, particularly, at the *kua* (pelvic) joints—the *kua* junction controls the motion between the upper and lower body.

The full development of qi in Taijiquan culminates in the formation of the central status of the *dantian* (Chapter 7), which is another manifestation of Taiji balance, and the body realizes Chen Xiaowang's Principle of Motion:

Yi dantian wei hai xin 以丹田为核心
Yi dong quan shen bi dong 一动全身必动
Jie jie guan chuan 节节贯穿
Yi qi guan tong 一气贯通

Establish the central status of the *dantian*
One part moves, the whole body moves
Qi energy threads through every joint
And fills the body unobstructed as one.

C.P. Ong
Potomac, Maryland.
Sep 1, 2013

Note: Taijiquan is the *pinyin* spelling of Tai Chi chuan. Throughout the book, the *pinyin* spelling is used, but in some cases the familiar common spellings of the Chinese terms are retained, such as kungfu (*pinyin gongfu*), Tao (*Dao*), and so on. Also, please read the pronouns of he, him or his used in the book as gender-neutral unless they refer to specific persons.

1
Allure of Taijiquan

You see the aesthetics in the grace and balance, but there is serenity in the slow and gentle flow and harmony within the calm. There is something alluring about the art of Taijiquan. The practitioner is enviably soaking in a store of wellness in the tranquility of relaxation.

Taijiquan eludes a simple description. It is denominated by non-physical attributes. The slow motion that is so characteristic does not define the art. If it did, then one could easily create Taijiquan motion by slowing down the playback of any action with a remote control. Slow motion alone does not equate to Taijiquan motion any more than an acrobat's aerial jump does to a ballerina's *grand jete*.

Taijiquan seems to lack physical strength, but it is not devoid of exercise vigor. The motion is soft but not weak—it has integrity and cohesion. There is connectedness in the slow motion as in the drawing of silk from a cocoon without breaking.

Exercise for Old People

The soft nature of Taijiquan exercise appears physically undemanding, and so most suitable for senior citizens. Indeed, very often we see and admire the poise and confidence of old practitioners gliding about and hands waving in slow motion—an impressionable image as we wish we could move that gracefully in our own old age.

Many elderly people take up the exercise as a recreation in community centers, but very soon they may find themselves rejuvenated and are more agile in their movements. This benefit has been borne out by the pioneering research of Dr. Stephen Wolf on the effectiveness of Taijiquan as a balancing exercise for seniors.[1] The study concludes that, compared to other exercise regimens, the seniors who practice Taijiquan improved their balance significantly. This is crucial as improved balance prevents falls, and falling down in old age can be catastrophic.

It is the fear of falling that makes moving about most burdensome in old age. We are living longer, but the quality of life suffers if mobility is impaired, not to mention the cost of care. A careless slip can easily erode confidence in mobility. Taijiquan exercise instills confidence in motion. More than preventing falls, maintaining this confidence is a vanguard against the vicissitudes of old age—any injuries become debilitating.

Moving slowly in Taijiquan induces one to be attentive to movements and postures. The exercise builds body awareness of motion, which fosters balance and stability. By being aware, one can also adjust the physical demands of practice so as not to be overworked. One does not give up the practice of Taijiquan in old age; one ages gracefully with Taijiquan.

Wolf relates an anecdote of an 86 year-old participant, which is both memorable and telling. At the end of the experimental study he asked what the subjects could do now that they could not before. In response the octogenarian stepped forward, lifted up one leg, slightly bending, and took off his loafer while balancing on the other leg. A brief moment later, long enough for all to applaud his accomplishment, he proceeded to put the loafer back on, balancing all the while on the one leg.

Indeed, seniors practicing Taijiquan derive a host of other health benefits besides balance. As well suited as it is for seniors, to characterize Taijiquan as an exercise for the old, is far from what the art is.

New Age Influence 1990s

Taijiquan is often described as an ancient Chinese art form based on the principles of yin and yang; it nurtures an ethereal life-force energy called *qi*, and bestows wellness. That a concept so alien has been able to move into popular Western culture, is due largely to the influence of the New Age lifestyle in the 1990s.

The New Age movement embraces a broad spectrum of alternative practices drawn on both Western and Eastern traditions to seek spiritual succor, healing, health, and general well-being. Their eclectic practices include harmonizing one's environment with the aroma of incense and sounds of wind chimes, dabbling with mirrors to deflect bad energy and crystals to absorb good energy, as well paying homage to ancient sites, such as the Stonehenge.

New Age grew from the ashes of the subculture of hippies in the 60s and 70s. The kaleidoscopic culture swept across the college campuses: the psychedelic trappings, the pot, the protests, the anti-Vietnam war activism, the tear gas, the saffron-robed and shaven Hare Krishnas prancing about, chanting, and beating drums and cymbals, and Transcendental Meditation. The pop adulation of Hindu culture reached its symbolic zenith in 1968 when the Beatles in collarless shirts and loose pantaloons, decked with marigold garlands, sat with the

Maharishi on the front gate of his ashram in Rishikesh at the Himalayan foothills of India. Unlike the counter culture that affronted society, New Age crept in surreptitiously in the ensuing decades.

The Eastern practices of yoga, Taijiquan, qigong (practice of qi energetics), meditation, reiki, and so on, fit in snugly with the New Age lifestyle as an energy-attuning and mind-body exercise. The New Age advocacy has been instrumental in popularizing these practices. Purists of the orthodox systems may complain of the New Age encroachments and the superficial embrace of their arts, but New Age is to be credited for the activities showing up in the community centers across the country.

Taijiquan is Not the Same

A cursory investigation into Taijiquan through browsing the Internet or books on the art or visiting schools, is more likely to result in confusion than understanding. Taijiquan is not a single, standardized practice. It comes in many styles, and many versions of different styles, which besides the slow motion, may not look alike in their outward form, and are as diverse as are the many dialects of the Chinese language, which are incomprehensible between one another.

There are five major schools of Taijiquan: Chen, Sun, Wu, Wu (Hao), and Yang. Yang is the most prevalent among them. There is also the Wudang School, and to add to the confusion, under the same school label, there are sub-styles whose forms are also different.

Although the different schools subscribe to the same Taiji theory, you quickly sense the contention among them—each claims to be more authentic or legitimate than the others. Rather than be bogged down by the disputes, we leap forward to the 1950s to find a modern offshoot that the reader is also most likely to encounter, namely, the simplified 24-Form Taijiquan.

Simplified 24-Form Taijiquan

The 24-Form Taijiquan is an outcome of the modern revival of Chinese Martial Arts, also known as *wushu* 武术, during the twentieth century. Taijiquan is a part of wushu and shares the same historical heritage.

The People's Republic of China, founded after the end of the Chinese Civil War (1927-1949), staged the First National Exhibition and Competition of Chinese Sports in Tianjin, November 8 – 12, 1953. Though billed as a sports program, wushu took center stage occupying the bulk of the events. Masters of some 139 wushu styles, came from all over China, and put on a dazzling display of their amazing skills at the national forum.

This was not the first time that the Chinese government had taken a direct hand in promoting wushu. The preceding Kuomingtang Nationalist Government had organized a national martial arts event in 1928 and again in 1933. Wushu was called *Kuoshu* (*Guoshu* in pinyin) then, a more exalted name, which means "national arts." The Nanking Central Kuoshu Institute was established in 1928 in the new capital of Nanking, which marked the "golden period" of Kuomingtang Nationalist Party rule.[2]

Wushu went international when a Chinese wushu delegation gave an exhibition performance at the 1936 Berlin XI Olympic Games.[3] Fu Shu-Yun (1916 –), one of the nine members of the wushu team, reminisced that the wushu performances received the longest applause with encores, and her Taijiquan demonstration stole the show.[4] Unfortunately, despite wushu's early appearance in the Olympics, wushu has yet to win approval as an official Olympic event.[5]

Wushu consists of the characters *wu* 武, which means "martial," and *shu* 术, "art or techniques," so the term refers to all fighting arts including weapons. However, it connotes more. It embodies a discipline steeped in moral codes and chivalry. It has long been a part of Chinese culture, with a history spanning over two millennia.[6] While children in the West grow up with Superman, Batman, Wonder Woman, and other super-fiends or heroes in comic books and movies, their counterparts in the Far East find their fictional heroes and heroines in the genre of martial arts novels, called *wuxia xiashou*, which tell the tales of loyalty and treachery, revenge and betrayal, righteousness and corruption, interwoven with martial chivalry or wuxia. These themes were poorly portrayed in the early Hong Kong kungfu movies, until Bruce Lee burst onto the world scene with *Enter the Dragon* (Robert Clouse, 1973). The more current version of this genre was successfully exploited in the internationally acclaimed *Crouching Tiger, Hidden Dragon* (Ang Lee, 2000). Many great movies have come on the heels of this film, like *Hero* (Zhang Yimou, 2002), *House of Flying Daggers* (Zhang Yimou, 2004), and *Fearless* (Ronny Yu, 2006), and no doubt more will follow.

Chinese history and novels have long saluted martial heroes and heroines, but none personifies the martial ethos of chivalry, honor, valor, righteousness, and loyalty more than Lord Guan Yu (c. 160 – 210), the redoubtable general from the *Three Kingdoms*.[7] He represents the epitome of martial prowess: the dignified bearing of him on horseback wielding the "Green Dragon Halberd" inspired both fear and awe. While the tales of his heroism are still regaled in operatic epics, the hero Guan Gong, the venerated name for Guan Yu, has stood to the present day as a deity, worshiped at the altar of almost every Chinese home throughout the world. Wushu is very much set into the Chinese cultural mosaic.

The Tianjin wushu event in 1953 was a celebration of this cultural heritage in the new socialist China. Shortly after, the Institute of Physical Education and Sports was founded to oversee the organization of sports and wushu. Thus wushu became institutionalized, giving rise to modern wushu as a sport, of which Taijiquan is a part. The diverse styles of traditional wushu were streamlined into standard routines, for example, with *changquan*, representing the northern styles, and *nanquan*, the southern, as well as the many weapons forms. This has sparked an ongoing debate between modern and traditional wushu, and sport and martial wushu.

At this period of wushu, the Institute in 1956 tasked the choreography of a Taijiquan routine that would be more suitable for popular dissemination among the masses, in keeping with the government's egalitarian agenda. The traditional forms were just too long and time-consuming to practice, and the traditional methods too arcane and demanding for mass propagation. The challenge was to reduce the one hundred-odd movements of the traditional Yang Style Taijiquan, prevalent then, to its core, by removing the many repetitive movements as well as the less essential ones. Thus, the 24-Form Taijiquan set was created. Instrumental in this simplification effort was Li Tianji (1913 – 1996),[8] who had been appointed a wushu research fellow at the Institute.

Under official auspices, the 24-Form Taijiquan quickly became the standard form, taught throughout China as part of physical education curriculum in schools and colleges. It is perhaps the best known Taijiquan form in the world today. As widespread as it is, the 24-Form Taijiquan is at best an abridged version of the traditional Yang form, a synopsis of the art.

Taijiquan as a Health Exercise

Taijiquan is enthralling. Not long after you take up the exercise, you begin to enjoy a marked improvement in health and well-being, which motivates you to practice more. You may also likely hear of someone who has been cured of a chronic ailment by Taijiquan, attesting that it is a healing art.

When I first started Taijiquan in 1972 I was not looking for any healing or thinking of any health benefits, but was simply drawn to it.

Nevertheless, I was amazed that within weeks, I no longer had to fight insomnia and irregular bowels. After I was more acquainted with the school, Martin Lee, a senior student at the main branch of the school, was pointed out to me. His head was completely shaven, as were those of some other senior students, a mark of devotion to the master, whose head was a handsome bald. I was told of Martin's miraculous cure by Taiji. He was then a research physicist at the Lawrence Radiation Laboratory in Livermore, California, and had been suffering from acute allergy and asthma since his youth, an ailment that plagued him into his adult life. In springtime, he had to don a gas mask to be safe from pollen in the air. Still, mask and potent medications did not prevent him from allergic seizures, which had become a springtime ritual for the local ambulance emergency staff. At the end of his wits, with no options left, he swallowed his skepticism, and succumbed to his wife's entreaties to seek Chinese medical advice. He was then referred to Kuo Lienying, a Taijiquan and kungfu master in San Francisco, whose small store-front school faced the Portsmouth Square Park, where students could be seen practicing regularly in the early morning hours. After the first season of practice, Martin was able to move about without the unsightly gas mask, and after the second, he was fine with almost no medication. After the third, his allergy was entirely gone. To this day, he and his wife, Emily are devoted practitioners and teachers of Taijiquan. They have also written a book on the curative effects of Taijiquan.[9]

In post-dynastic China many people took up Taijiquan practice for health reasons. Chen Pan Ling (1891 – 1967), a wushu and Taijiquan enthusiast and a hydraulics engineer, wrote in his book,[10]

> "Around 1912, tai chi chuan [Taijiquan] became popular in Peking, because there were many professors and students who had contracted tuberculosis (in China then tuberculosis was an incurable disease). After they practiced tai chi chuan for a time, most of them recovered their health. So, the Pekineses gave a nickname to tai chi chuan: tuberculosis-curing technique."

That Taijiquan is a prescription for health is not surprising from the viewpoint of Traditional Chinese Medicine (TCM). The practice nurtures qi, and regulates its circulation to harmonize the yin and yang, which is the basis of good health in TCM theory. The stronger and the more balanced the qi flow is, the healthier the body. Conversely, a weak or stagnating qi flow is an indication of some sickness, caused by blockages or an imbalance of the body's physiological systems—too much yin or too much yang. That is, by TCM, the very practice of Taijiquan cultivating qi fortifies one's health and well-being.

To say that Taijiquan is an exercise therapy for health and healing is not wrong, but this aspect is only a byproduct of the art. Nevertheless, Taijiquan is best known to the world as a health exercise, and an overwhelming number of practitioners take it up for health reasons. In fact, quite a number of famous masters state in their biographies that they initially sought the art to improve their weak or sickly constitution. The health aspect is the universal appeal driving the growth of Taijiquan.

Although TCM commonly prescribes Taijiquan as a health therapy, the medical science behind it is still unclear. Western scientific research on the subject was scant, until the 1990s, when it became clear that more and more of the healthcare dollar was being spent on non-conventional medicine. More research dollars are now spent on TCM and alternative medicine. Many of the nation's prestigious universities have set up a sub-discipline of alternative cum complementary medicine to meet the challenge. It is no longer uncommon for mainstream physicians to refer patients to TCM or other alternative traditional medicine for treatment.

The growing acceptance of complementary and/or alternative medicine (CAM) is documented in the paper, *A Review of the Incorporation of Complementary and Alternative Medicine by Mainstream Physicians*,[11] which finds that 30% to 50% of the adult population in industrialized nations use some form of CAM to treat health problems. The significant patient crossover to CAM attests that healing is still very much an art, despite the gigantic leaps of advanced medical science.

The common ailments that beset everyday modern life have little to do with stem cell research or the latest discoveries in DNA medicine. The bulk of patient medical complaints to physicians—over 60 percent—are colds, flu, headaches, allergies, chronic pains, arthritis, high blood pressure, sleeping disorders, and so on. Many of these common illnesses are lifestyle or stress-related, where healing is more an art than a pathological science. This is where TCM with its basic thrust of nurturing qi and balancing holistically the functions of the organs to fortify the body's constitution and immune system, proves to be an effective alternative.

Indeed, medical research continues to validate Taijiquan practice over other regimens, as an effective therapy to alleviate or cure a range of ailments, as compiled in a 2009 article, *The Health Benefits of Tai Chi*. [12] Peter M. Wayne, director of the Tai Chi and Mind-Body Research Program at Harvard Medical School's Osher Research Center, says,

> "A growing body of carefully conducted research is building a compelling case for tai chi as an adjunct to standard medical treatment for the prevention and rehabilitation of many conditions commonly associated with age."

In particular, the practice of Taijiquan is endorsed by "The Arthritis Foundation" as a treatment for arthritis. [13] The pain relief can sometimes come miraculously fast even in just one session of practice as the slow-motion exercise induces relaxation of the joints. Dr. Paul Lam, a physician from Sydney, Australia, is a pioneer in promoting the Taijiquan treatment for arthritis. [14] His "Tai Chi for Arthritis" program first gained international recognition in 1997 when Arthritis Australia endorsed it. According to his biography, he cured his own osteoarthritis by the practice of Taijiquan.

Taijiquan as a Chinese Martial Art

Taijiquan as a kungfu art is tantalizing and confounding at the same time. How can the soft and gentle practice prepare one to meet the crushing knock-out punch of a Mike Tyson? The slow motion of Taijiquan is antithetical to the speed and power of a fighting art, which nevertheless, adds to its allure.

One might quickly dismiss it as a long-lost distant cousin of a kungfu art, like humans and rodents sharing a common ancestry. Unlikely as it may seem, Taijiquan is still very much practiced as a martial art. In fact, to a serious student of Oriental martial arts, the quest of the higher levels of combat skills leads to the "softness" principles of Taijiquan. The link between Taijiquan and kungfu is anything but tenuous. All the major schools of Taijiquan still teach it as a Chinese martial art, and in fact, tout their martial prowess as proof of their authentic teachings.

The martial arts of the Orient rely on the body's "inner strength" for high-level kungfu. This kind of strength is developed by cultivating the life-force energy qi (in Japanese martial arts, ki). Taijiquan training cultivates qi to build this inner strength called *neijin*. The remarkable kungfu feats of Taijiquan that one hears about is based on neijin. Not surprising then, kungfu peers regard Taijiquan as a highest form of martial arts.

Still, even to a kungfu practitioner, the art can be enigmatic as Taijiquan methods are diametrically opposite to the power training in karate, taekwondo, shaolin, and other kungfu systems. This is not a cultural anachronism as people in China are equally as puzzled by the incongruity between the softness of slow motion and the power-packed action of speed. It is no less a puzzle to an Oriental than an Occidental.

Taijiquan as a kungfu art is a riddle only because its slow-motion training is perceived as devoid of power. Strength is identified with muscles and, power with speed, both absent in Taijiquan training, thus the seeming paradox. Contrary to appearance, Taijiquan is not about how slowly or gently to move, but to cultivate qi to develop inner strength. The soft training is only a means to an end, to build a store of qi necessary for inner strength. The power of Taijiquan motion is there, like that of water pressure in a fireman's hose.

Taijiquan as a modern competitive sport shows more of its martial character. To appeal to the audience and judges, competitors perform the heel kicks vertically high, albeit in slow motion; the posture of "Snake Creeps Down" is crouched so low as to be almost touching the ground; and the leaps and jumps are acrobatically impressive.

The martial aspect is evident in the standardized Taijiquan 42-Form Competition Routine,[15] which was first introduced at the 1990 11th Asian Games in Beijing. This physically more demanding form is an amalgamation of movements from the five major schools of Taijiquan, choreographed with varying degrees of difficulty, many of which are kungfu-like. Ironically, the acrobatic and flowery movements that appeal to an audience do not translate to the high-order kungfu skills of Taijiquan. The stuff of neijin (inner strength) is not apparent to an untrained eye.

Good Taijiquan

The Taijiquan of a gold medalist, whose training is weighted towards wushu competition, is not necessarily good Taijiquan to a traditionalist. Although the aesthetics of good Taijiquan are universally appealing, that of competition Taijiquan may just be external, lacking in the substance of internal energy. Good Taijiquan exhibits both the fluidity of yin softness and the solidity of yang power, the dual character of neijin.

Good Taijiquan is recognized by the kungfu skills it manifests, that is, in actual combat. When Yang Luchan first came to Beijing in late 1850s, it was not the aesthetics of his form that impressed the people. He decisively defeated his challengers and earned the name, "Yang the

Invincible," which catapulted him to the top ranks of martial artists of his era, and thus the recognition of the art.

Good Taijiquan is about its training that develops neijin as the core strength. The strength of neijin, unlike the naked force of a muscular hulk, is not apparent but it can beat back a big bully with no visible effort, even in one's old age.

Good Taijiquan does not just produce excellent, but extraordinary kungfu skills—it makes a peerless hero, as conveyed in the verse of *Taijiquan Classics*,[16]

Ren bu zhi wo wo du zhi ren
人不知我我独知人
Ying xiong suo xiang wu di gai you ci er ji ye
英雄所向无敌盖由此而及也

I know the opponent's moves but he does not see mine
One becomes a kungfu hero, invincible with no peers.

Because the attributes of neijin are mainly non-physical, they often lead to misinterpretation. For example, it spawns a culture of disdain for physical force in Taijiquan. Indeed, some purists go as far as to argue that if muscular force is detected then it is not that of the ideal force of neijin. In Taijiquan push-hand matches, it is not good enough to push someone down, but that it be done without brute force, that is, with inner strength, and better still if it appears invisible. So the person floored might yet be the winner, if the opponent was deemed to have used sheer physical muscular force and is thereby penalized or disqualified, clearly turning the meaning of combat on its head.

The problem is that there is no clear articulation of what neijin is. The concepts and the principles of Taijiquan in the old texts are written in terse Chinese classical verses, expressed more for style than to elucidate, thus subject to interpretations. There is no disagreement that good Taijiquan training delivers high-level kungfu skills and that the basis of these skills is neijin. However, experts do not always agree on what neijin is, and differ on how best to train for it.

Unfortunately, the culture of secrecy in Chinese martial arts does not encourage an open exchange. Discussion of the art often reverts to the claims of authenticity of transmission based on a lineage chart that meticulously traces through the venerable masters of old to the current holder. It has long become customary to accept the prestige of a kungfu master by the lineage. This custom is unique to Chinese martial arts. Lineage pedigree does not count for much in the other traditional Chinese arts, such as calligraphy, painting, or music.

The currency of the lineage pedigree presumes that the "secret of the art" is passed down the line. It is believed that the real kungfu skills are highly guarded secrets, taught only within the family and rarely outside. Unfortunately, this custom has badly skewed the focus away from the substance of the art to the lineage pedigree, and to the masters themselves. These engender issues that cloud the quest for good Taijiquan.

Expert Opinions of Taijiquan

Expert opinions of what is good Taijiquan are not about subtle shades of gray, but can be like day and night. For instance, at the 1953 Tianjin wushu event, Chen Fa'ke, the 17th generation standard bearer of Chen Family Taijiquan, was one of the experts invited to give a performance. Fa'ke was a direct descendant of Chen Changxin who taught Yang Luchan the Chen family art, which Yang and his descendants would spread worldwide as Yang Family Taijiquan.

Wu Tunan (unrelated to the founders of the Wu and Wu-Hao schools),[17] a noted Taijiquan expert and a scholar, openly questioned whether Chen Fa'ke was performing Taijiquan, critiquing that the latter's form was not based on the Taiji principles of "thirteen postures" (*shisan shi* 十三势). Yet contemporaneous accounts put Chen Fa'ke's

Taijiquan kungfu skills at the rarefied heights that have not been rivaled in modern times. This illustrates dramatically how contentious it could be to define Taijiquan.

The strong differences are not as alarming as it seems, as even within the same style or system, not all the masters agree among themselves, nor do they teach the same things. To be sure, Wu Tunan's opinion was not shared by his peers and equally famous fellow masters.

Liu Musan was a Wu Style master with a following in Beijing, and Hong Junsheng (1907 – 1996) was one of his students. Hong had been a sickly youth and was advised to take up Taijiquan. He started learning Taijiquan from Liu Musan in 1930. Hong recounts his first encounter with Chen Fa'ke, which amplifies a similar misunderstanding of Taijiquan, in his book, *Practical Boxing Method of Chen Style Taijiquan.*[18]

A report in the Beijing *Xiao Shi Bao* newspaper at that time created a buzz in the kungfu circles about a Taijiquan master, Chen Fa'ke, from Chen Village. In China then, opera was the main entertainment and Yang Xiaolou was Beijing opera's superstar, like Tom Cruise and Bono rolled into one. An illness had stricken the celebrity and the fans sorely missed him on the stage. To the delight of the city, he recovered and resumed performing. He was cured by Chen Fa'ke's Taijiquan. The master was thus graced by the student's celebrity status in the newspaper report.

Liu and his students decided to invite Chen Fa'ke to be their teacher, eager to learn Taijiquan from its source. Chen gave them a demonstration which included some movements from the Chen Cannon Fist routine that were powerfully explosive. The power-packed action surprised them as the movements were unlike the even and gentle flow that they were accustomed to. They thought that the swift movements violated the principle of moving like "pulling silk," and the foot stamping loudly on the floor, which shook the tiles, did not seem to conform to the quiet "stepping like a cat." Liu and students were left wondering if Chen was doing Taijiquan.

Notwithstanding their doubts and out of propriety, they decided to learn from Chen on a trial basis. It did not take them long to be completely convinced of Chen's high-level kungfu skills. Hong recounts that the students were anxious to check out Master Chen, and asked him about neijin (inner strength). Instead of explaining, Chen pronounced that his neijin would propel Liu (who happened to be the master's push-hand partner) to land on a wooden chair about three meters away, and promptly proceeded to do so at will and with ease. The precision of the effortless throw so astonished them that Liu and his students immediately redoubled their efforts to learn from the master. Hong studied with Chen until 1944, when he left to work in Jinan, Shandong Province. He went on to become an accomplished master himself, and left behind a legacy of literature and many followers.

Two Titans of the Yang Style in the United States

We do not have to go to a distant past to see the differences in Taijiquan styles played out. The development of Taijiquan in the United States offers a study of the contrast in style and substance of two Yang sub-branches that have come to form the bedrock of the art in the country. These two Yang derivations came to the U.S. shores in the mid-1960s, one brought in by Cheng Manching (1901 – 1975) who spearheaded the effort in New York, and the other by Kuo Lienying (1897 – 1984) in San Francisco.[19] They loomed as titans in the world of Taijiquan and martial arts. Their legacies still cast a long shadow over the Taijiquan landscape in the country.

Although both were of the same 4th generation in the Yang lineage, their transmissions came down along different lines. Cheng learned the art around 1930 from Yang Chengfu (1883 – 1936), the grandson of the founder, Yang Luchan. Kuo began his Taijiquan in 1918 learning from Wang Jiaoyu, who acquired the art from Yang Banhou (1837 – 1892), the second son of the founder.

The Cheng and Kuo forms are quite different. No doubt, the backgrounds of the two masters shaped their perception and presentation of the art. Cheng was already a Chinese medical doctor and an artist when he took up Taijiquan to cure his debilitating lung ailment. An erudite scholar, he would later be proclaimed a master of the "Five Excellences" in the arts of painting, calligraphy, poetry, healing, and martial arts. He served as a member of the National Assembly in the Kuomingtang government. Kuo on the other hand was more down to earth, and lived by his passion for martial arts. He had studied Shaolin and other kungfu before Taijiquan, and also mastered the other internal martial arts of Xingyi, and Bagua. He was an officer in the Kuomingtang Army and like Cheng, Kuo too served in the National Assembly. With the take-over of China by the Communists, both fled with the Nationalists to Taiwan.

While Cheng was scholarly, Kuo was all kungfu. In 1951 Joe Louis, the boxing champion, visited Taipei, and the local press hailed him as the world's "King of the Fist." In his mid-fifties then, Kuo was at the prime of his martial skills, and so scoffed at the proclamation. He publicly challenged the champion boxer to a fight, creating a stir in the local media.[20] Kuo had said many times that he had no doubts that he would defeat the champion. Alas, the challenge was ignored, and the world was deprived of a would-be epic match between Kuo and Louis.

Cheng popularized a version of Yang Style, which he condensed from the traditional Yang to a 37-movement form. Kuo taught another Yang version consisting of 64 movements, known as *Guang Ping Yang Style*, so named to distinguish it from the other Yang Styles. Guang Ping is the name of the prefecture in Yongnian where the Yang family resided. Besides the similar names, the physical forms bear little resemblance. The Cheng movements are smaller and softer, and the stances are higher, compared to Kuo's, which are recognizably more martial in character. These two fourth-generation offshoots of the Yang lineage are quite different in flavor and substance.

Fig. 1.1 Cheng Manching (1901 – 1975)

Fig. 1.2 Kuo Lien-Ying (1895 – 1984)

Changes in the Physical Forms of Taijiquan

It does not take many generations of transmission for changes to occur in the Taijiquan forms. Cheng Manching's form was already different from that of the other earlier disciples of Yang Chengfu,[21] influenced perhaps by the master's presentation of the art in his later years. Followers grouping around the 4th generation successors would become more contentious after the demise of the master.

For instance, some followers would point out that Yang Zhengduo was only 10 when his father Yang Chengfu passed away, to imply that there could not have been anything substantive transmitted from father to son at that young age. The critique ignores the far more important factor of his own achievement under the Yang family training system.

The physical changes of the Taijiquan form had already occurred in the earlier three generations of Yang. The Yang legacy boasts of the "small frame" form of Yang Banhou, the second son of the founder, the "medium frame" of Yang Jianhou, the third son, and "the large frame" of Yang Chengfu, the grandson. The founder's own form had likely changed from that of his master's, Chen Changxin.

The physical differences in the form reflect mostly the body's comprehension of the art. They are a consequence of an individual's expression of the principles of Taijiquan as the practice matures. They are organic and greatly enrich the art.

Therefore, differences in the form cannot be a basis to distinguish between which is better or the more authentic. This is as it should be, given that the emphasis of the art is non-external. The irony is that we tell the forms of Chen, Sun, Wu, Wu (Hao), Yang, or a sub-style, by the physical appearance, that is, the movements and postures, and not by some internal characteristics.

With Saddhammaransi Sayadaw during a
meditation retreat in 1998 in Yangon.
Author practices *vippassana* insignt meditation.

On the grounds of the ruins of
Bagan, Myanmar

2
Evolution of the Major Schools

Founders of the Major Schools

Contrary to popular belief, Taijiquan is not ancient. The history of the art is relatively recent in the time-scale of Chinese civilization. Traced to the founders, the schools of Yang, Wu (Hao), Wu, and Sun began between mid-1800s and early 1900s, while the Chen style originated in the 1600s. Also, the many Taijiquan forms practiced today were standardized no earlier than the 1920s.

However, though not old, the history of Taijiquan is fogged by myths and legends. Myths can be inspirational, but more often than not, they shroud the art and engender controversies. Let us visit the founders in the backdrop of history.

Founders of the major schools of Taijiquan

Fig. 2.1 Chen Wangting (c. 1600 - 1680)
Founder: Chen School

Fig. 2.2 Yang Luchan
(1799 - 1872)
Founder: Yang School

Fig. 2.3 Wu Yuxiang
(c. 1812 - 1880)
Founder: Wu (Hao) School

Fig. 2.4 (Wu) Quan You
(1836 - 1902)
Founder: Wu School

Fig. 2.5 Sun Lutang (1861 - 1933)
Founder: Sun School

Wu Yuxiang (c. 1812 – 1880) Cast a Long Shadow

The art that has come to be known as Taijiquan was virtually unknown except in the isolation of Chen Village (Chenjiagou), Henan Province, its birth place. It had been practiced there for some two centuries and not taught to other than clan members until an outsider Yang Luchan (1799 – 1872) was initiated into it by Chen Changxing (1771 – 1853), the 14th generation patriarch of the Village art. Yang Luchan would introduce it to his native Yongnian County, Hebei Province, and from there it would spread.

Whatever students Yang had in Yongnian, none survived the march of time except Wu Yuxiang (c. 1812 – 1880). Wu not only perpetuated the art down a line of succession that bears his name, known today as Wu (Hao) Style Taijiquan, but played an instrumental role in the development of Taijiquan.

Wu came from a family of literati gentry. He had two older brothers who also shared his love of martial arts but perhaps not with the intensity of passion. Both his brothers attained the crown jewel of literary success, the *Jinshi* degree, earning them high official positions in the Qing government. Wu himself did not achieve anything notable in his time, literary or otherwise. While his brothers were praised to the skies as the pride of Yongnian in the local gazetteers, he did not merit even a shadow of a mention, and was completely ignored in the official history. In an ironic reversal of the fortunes of fame, while his brothers' much touted achievements are almost unknown today, the name of Wu Yuxiang is celebrated in the world of Taijiquan.

The fates of Wu, Yang, and Chen converged at an herbal medicine store in Yongnian, called Taihetang (The Grand Harmony Hall). The Wu family owned the property rented to Chen Dehu, a native of Chen Village, who operated the shop business, and Yang was a young indentured servant of Chen. Chen Dehu brought Yang back with him to Chen Village in his retirement. Chen Changxing, the patriarch of the Chen Village art, was teaching the clan children at the compound of Chen Dehu's house.[1]

Yang was no ordinary servant. Amid his chores he picked up the Taijiquan lessons. Soon his talent became known to the master who then took him in as a student. After Chen Dehu passed away, Yang's bond papers were burned,[2] and he returned to Yongnian around 1835.[3] Yang's unorthodox kungfu of "softness," dubbed the "cotton fist," came to the attention of Wu Yuxiang, who was more disposed to martial arts than literary studies. So impressed was Wu that the gentry scholar condescended to study under Yang.

In 1852, Wu Yuxiang journeyed to Chen Village to seek out Yang's teacher, Chen Changxin, but on route he happened to stop over at nearby Zhaobao Village. There he was told that Chen was too old and ill to receive anyone (Chen passed away the following year). He was then introduced to Chen Qingping (1795 – 1868), another native of Chen Village, who had married into a Zhaobao family, and was well known locally as a master of the art. Instead of proceeding to his destination, Wu stayed behind at Zhaobao for about a month to learn the "secrets" of the Chen Village art from Chen Qingping.

There is no record of Wu Yuxiang's martial accomplishments in the Wu family archive. This is not surprising as the family tradition was driven to literary, not martial, achievements. Wu Yuxiang's interest in martial arts was clearly not regarded as being of significance, relative to the literary and civil successes of his brothers.

The practice of Taijiquan became popular in Beijing after the fall of the Qing Dynasty (1644 – 1912), and Wu Yuxiang's name would be pushed forward as a pillar of the art. Wu Laixu's biography of his grandfather says that Wu Yuxiang stayed in Zhaobao for 40 days and learned the art from Chen Qingping, but makes no mention of Yang Luchan. Li Yiyu (1832 – 1892), Wu Yuxiang's nephew and student, referred to Yang Luchan simply as "a certain Yang of Nanguan," not meriting a full name. Placing a person of Yang's low station above Wu in the lineage tree would have been an affront to their high social standing. The Wu lineage officially extols Chen Qingping as the progenitor of its art.

Wu Yuxiang's journey to Chen Village that ended in Zhaobao was actually undertaken to visit his eldest brother Wu Chengqing (1800 – 1884). The brother had recently been appointed the magistrate of Wuyang County after he finally obtained the Jinshi degree at the age of 52. Wuyang, in the south, neighbors Wen County, where Chen Village is located.

A remarkable discovery took place at Wuyang. According to Li Yiyu, the magistrate brother found a text of Taijiquan in a salt shop authored by a Wang Zongyue, believed to be of the latter part of 18th century. Wang Zongyue's historicity is tied by a single thread to this text.[4] Given the isolation of author and text, with no links in time or place, the discovery seems a perfect mystery. Notwithstanding, the text would become the orthodox canon of Taijiquan. No Taijiquan discourse takes place without reference to it. From the vantage point of its discovery, one cannot help but be awed by the biblical proportion of its influence in the Taiji world.

Shadowing the mystery of the discovery is the personage of Zhang Sanfeng who was thrust on center stage as the creator of Taijiquan. The source came from the house of Wu Yuxiang. Li Yiyu had compiled a collection of essays on Taijiquan. In a hand-written copy dated 1867, he made an entry in the margin of *Short Preface to Taijiquan*, "Taijiquan began with Zhang Sanfeng of the Song Dynasty (960 – 1279)." For unclear reasons, after the death of his uncle in 1880, he overwrote the entry that the creator of the art was unknown, but the revision was ignored. The world clearly wanted to believe in an itinerant Taoist alchemist, sighted variously in the Song (960 – 1279) through the Yuan (1279 – 1368) to the Ming Dynasty (1368 – 1644), a life spanning at least 300 years.[5] Even though scholarly research works have debunked the Zhang Sanfeng creation story,[6] it still remains in popular circulation today.

The historical citation that relates Zhang Sanfeng to martial arts is found in the epitaph of Wang Zhengnan (1616 – 1669), composed by his student, Huang Zongxi, both fervent Ming patriots who wielded both pen and sword in the underground movement against the foreign Manchu invaders:

> "… Therefore we call Shaolin the External School. The Internal School [Neijia Quan] originated with Zhang Sanfeng of the Song Dynasty. Sanfeng was a Taoist immortality seeker of the Wudang Mountains. [The Song] Emperor Huizong (1101 – 1125) summoned him, but the roads were impassable and he could not proceed. That night in a dream he received a martial art from the God of War and the next morning single-handedly killed more than a hundred bandits."[7]

This is the only record connecting Zhang Sanfeng to martial arts. It was also the first classification of martial arts into "internal school" (neijia) and "external school" (waijia). To sanctify the aura of mystique, it was certainly most befitting to attribute Taijiquan, a neijia art, to the Taoist immortal Zhang Sanfeng.

Li Yiyu's assertion of Zhang Sanfeng as the creator may simply be an attempt to graft the Taoist immortal into the lineage tree to give the art legitimacy, a Chinese cultural practice of attributing discoveries to ancient sages. The Zhang Sanfeng creation story has been repeated, sometimes with embellishment, since the first publications of the art.

Leaving aside the historicity of the figure, the injection of Zhang Sanfeng into martial arts was laced in myth. Historians have noted that both the author (Huang Zongxi) and the subject (Wang Zhengnan) were pragmatists, not given to myths and miracles. It is believed that the epitaph story was a political allegory of Han Chinese resistance (internal) against the foreign Manchu rule (external). This is analyzed in an article by Stanley Henning,[8] and also in Douglas Wile's book.[9] Readers interested in the Zhang Sanfeng story can read a well-researched article, rich with bibliographical references, by Bing Ye Young.[10]

Figure 2.6 Zhang Sanfeng of Wudang Mountains

The oddest thing about the creation story is that it did not come from the Taijiquan predecessors of Wu Yuxiang: Chen Changxin, who transmitted the art to Yang Luchan or Chen Qingping, who taught Wu Yuxiang. Neither Zhang Sanfeng, the purported creator, nor Wang Zongyue, the author of the discovered text, are mentioned in the Chen family records or the archives of Wenxian County (that administers Chen Village). The Chen Family Genealogy traces the masters of the art before Chen Changxin and Chen Qingping, generation by generation, back to Chen Wangting (c. 1600 – 1680) as the progenitor.

Wu (Hao) Taijiquan

Wu Yuxiang made two direct contributions that would have a lasting imprint on Taijiquan. The first is the compilation of the core body of early Taijiquan literature, which was expanded by his nephew, Li Yiyu, and his brothers. Douglas Wile refers to them as the Wu-Li texts.[11] Almost all Taijiquan literature in the 1920s and 1930s flowed from the Wu-Li collection.

Second, Wu Yuxiang is the lineage originator of Wu (Hao) Style Taijiquan. Wu's best known student was his sister's son, Li Yiyu, who like him was a comfortably endowed scholar and shared his passion for the art. It was Li who compiled Wu's collection of articles and added his own work. These are preserved in three hand-copied volumes (1881), known as "the old three volumes" (*lao san ben*).

Li Yiyu's best known student was a fellow Yongnian native, Hao Weizhen (1849 – 1920) who in turn taught his son, Yueru (1877 – 1935). Then Hao Yueru began to teach the art as a profession, which led to the growth of this branch of practice. In the 1930s Hao Yueru traveled south to Shanghai, Nanjing, and other cities to further spread the art with his son, Shaoru (1907 – 1983). Their followers call it Hao Style Taijiquan, but it is acknowledged as of the Wu Yuxiang lineage. So the Wu Yuxiang line of transmission has come to be known as Wu (Hao) Style Taijiquan.

Sun Style Taijiquan

The Wu Yuxiang line also spawned another school of Taijiquan, called *Sun Style Taijiquan*. Hao Weizhen, the third generation of the Wu lineage, was visiting Beijing in 1911 and was taken ill. Sun Lutang (1861 – 1932), an accomplished martial artist, had recently established himself in Beijing. As an expert in Xingyi and Bagua boxing, which share similar "internal boxing" theory with Taijiquan, he had come to know of Hao by reputation. So he went to call on him to pay his respects. Finding him sick, he tended to his recovery. Hao was very grateful and repaid Sun's kindness by teaching and sharing with him his knowledge of Taijiquan. Later Sun incorporated the elements of Xingyi and Bagua into his Taijiquan practice. In 1921 he published *Taijiquan Xue* (A Study of Taijiquan).[12] His followers would later call this Sun Style Taijiquan.

The Wu Yuxiang camp played yet another pivotal role in the development of Taijiquan. Without the Wu Yuxiang connection, Yang Family Taijiquan would not have spread as widely, just as without Yang Luchan, the Chen Village art would have remained undiscovered by the world.

Yang Luchan in Beijing

Yang Luchan's move from Yongnian to Beijing was instrumental in the propagation of Taijiquan. Taijiquan would be propelled from the Beijing base in post-dynastic China. Wu Yuxiang's second brother, Wu Juqing (c. 1802 – 1885) arranged for Yang Luchan to teach martial arts to the Manchu nobility in the capital. Wu Juqing, Yongnian's most famous son, was serving his last stint in Beijing at the Ministry of Justice; he retired in 1859.

When Yang first arrived in Beijing, there was skepticism of his "cotton fist" art. His very ordinary physique did not inspire any martial prowess. People were thus even more amazed when he handily defeated his challengers. He was quickly christened "Yang the Invincible," and was retained in the household of a prince as a martial arts instructor. He later paid a last visit in homage to Chen Village in triumphant Qing official regalia. According to the village elders, he got down from his horse at the gate and walked into the village to pay his gratitude and respect.

Yang Luchan's stay in Beijing was at a time when China was engulfed in internal strife and was helplessly being confronted with foreign aggression and plunder. The calamities of the Yellow River flooding in 1851 and 1855 were read as heavenly forebodings of Qing's decline, and the displaced populace swelled the ranks of revolts. The Taiping Rebellion (1851 – 1864) had carved out a part of south China and proclaimed the Taiping Heavenly Kingdom with its seat of government at Nanking, but it was crushed by a siege that exacted a human toll of about 100,000. The country was also beset with the Nien Rebellion (1851 – 1868) in the southwest, and Muslim revolts in the northwest.

The Qing rule might have succeeded in quelling the rebellions, but the country was ill-prepared and ill-equipped to face the military might of the West. China's vulnerability was exposed when British fire power handily defeated the imperial forces in the First Opium War (1839 – 1842), triggered by China's enforcement to stop opium smuggling by the British traders. The war ended with the Treaty of Nanking, which ceded Hong Kong to the victor with indemnity of war reparations, including reimbursement of the opium destroyed, and opened the major ports to British merchant ships. The treaty was the first of the unequal treaties imposed on China. In the Second Opium War (1856 – 1860) the British-French alliance foisted another of the humiliating unequal treaties on China: Kowloon was ceded to Britain, opium trade was legalized, British ships were given the right to carry indentured Chinese to the Americas, and costly war reparations were exacted.

The two Opium Wars were seen by the Western Powers and Japan as an open season to plunder the Middle Kingdom (as China is called), which ensued in the decades that followed. This was aptly depicted in the French cartoon, showing the powers carving up the *Chine* pie (fig. 2.7).

While the country was being pulled asunder by internal and external forces, surprisingly, Chinese martial arts managed to flourish in the capital. The lives of the nobles and princes, though affected, were not wanting in comfort and luxury. One of their indulgences was the patronage of Chinese martial arts, with the princes collecting martial arts experts like prized thoroughbreds.

Figure 2.7 A French political cartoon in late 1890s, depicting Queen Victoria, German Wilhelm II, Russian Nicholas II, and the Meiji Emperor of Japan carving up the *Chine* pie, while the French Marianne looked on with keenness, and the powerless Qing official protests in horrified exasperation.

Quite a few names in martial arts were made in the mini industry spawned by the patronage. Besides Yang Luchan, the fame of Dong Haichuan (c. 1813 – 1882), the founder of Baguazhang (eight-trigram palm), was also established at this time in Beijing. The Hong Kong TV series (2003), *Tai Chi Master (Taiji Zong Shi)* could not resist featuring a fictitious dual between Yang and Dong fighting to a standstill.[13]

There is also an account of an epic bout between Dong and Guo Yunshen (1829 – 1898), one of the masters of Xingyiquan (five-element boxing system). Sun Lutang, the father of Sun Taijiquan, learned his Xingyiquan from Guo.

The gentle art of Yang Luchan was most welcome by the nobility in Beijing. It did not unduly tax the physical comfort, and at the same time it held out the promise or at least the pretension of martial prowess. After Yang Luchan passed away in 1872, the patronage continued with his sons, Banhou and Jianhou, who were never out of commission for their services.

It is quite remarkable that Taijiquan patronage was uninterrupted even at the period when the capital was seized with the fervor of reform movement to modernize the imperial rule. It was clear that the Middle Kingdom was no longer the majestic dragon that commanded the "Four Seas" but had become a "sick old man," helpless in the world of superior Western military power. The court officials and the intelligentsia were wrenching between conflicting Confucian norms, self-interest, hubris of the past, and the new Western values. The call for reform could not be held back. The reform effort rolled out with the slogan, "Self-Strengthening Movement" (*Ziqiang Yundong*), which exhorted the retention of Chinese culture as it set out to take from the West, the science and technology of firearm manufacturing and ship building. Unfortunately, while the Meiji Restoration under the slogan, "Enrich the nation; strengthen the military" (*Fukoko kyohei*), led Japan to military power, the Chinese reform movement was derailed when Empress Dowager Cixi (1835 – 1908) reasserted her regency power in a palace coup. The empress put her nephew Emperor Guangxu (1871 – 1908) who initiated the reform under house arrest, ending the *One Hundred Days Reform* in 1898. She had been the de facto ruler "behind the curtains" of the previous emperor, her son Emperor Tongzhi (1856 – 1875). She passed away in 1908, only one day after her nephew the emperor died under suspicious circumstances at the age of 37.

Wu (Jianquan) Style and Guangping Yang Style

None of Yang Luchan's students in Beijing left a mark except for his two sons, Banhou and Jianhou. (His student Wu Yuxiang of Yongnian was from the pre-Beijing period.) The most notable student of the Beijing group of this period was a student of Banhou, a Manchu officer of the Imperial Guard Brigade, named Quan You (1834 – 1902).

Figure 2.8 Wu Jianquan (1870 – 1942) in "Single Whip"

Quan You passed the art down to his son Wu[14] Jianquan (1870 – 1942) who standardized the form, and perpetuated it down a line of succession, called Wu Style Taijiquan. The name Wu (吴) shares the same pinyin spelling as the Wu (武) of Wu Yuxiang, but it is written with a different character, which is a source of confusion.

Another student of Master Banhou from this period was Wang Jiaoyu, a stable hand in the household of a Manchu prince who was Banhou's patron. One day Banhou chanced upon someone practicing what he was teaching the prince. That person was Wang who had been secretly siphoning the master's lessons to the prince. Noting his earnestness and that he was Han Chinese, the master agreed to instruct him on condition that he passed a perseverance test. He was given a hundred days to make his body supple enough to bring the chin down to touch his toe without bending at the knee. Wang succeeded and thus was accepted. Later, Wang would subject his would-be disciples to the same chin-to-toe rite. Kuo Lienying was put through the rite when he sought to be a disciple of Wang in 1925. This is the same Kuo who together with Cheng Manching, are the aforementioned "Two Titans" who pioneered the development of Taijiquan in the United States in the mid-1960s. The Wang branch is now known as Guangping Yang Style Taijiquan, which it believes to be the "unwatered-down" version of Yang Banhou's art.

Fig. 2.9 Author inspired by the challenge of the chin-to-toe rite (1972)

Yang Style Taijiquan in the New Generation

By the time the torch of Taijiquan was passed down to Yang Luchan's grandchildren, the Qing Empire was existing only in name. The Eight-Nation Alliance of Western Powers[15] had quashed the Boxer Rebellion (1899 – 1901) and exacted an exorbitant 450 million taels of fine silver as war reparations from China.[16]

On October 10, 1911 officers of the elite New Army in Wuchang mutinied. The city fell in a day, marking the demise of Qing, which is commemorated as the Double-Ten Wuchang Uprising. The last symbolic 6 year-old Emperor Xuantong (Puyi) abdicated on February 12, 1912, officially ending the Qing dynasty of 268 years and ushering in the new Republic of China. Yang Banhou had died in 1892, and his brother, Jianhou was in his twilight years. The Taijiquan baton was passed on to Jianhou's two sons, Yang Shaohou (1862 – 1930) and Yang Chengfu (1883 – 1936).

Figure 2.10 Yang Shaohou (1862 – 1930)

Figure 2.11 Yang Chengfu (1883 – 1936)

Thus Taijiquan rode in the eye of the dynastic storm and entered new China. Shorn of its queue of Manchu patronage, the practice of the art would be popularized. In 1912 a new martial sports center, called the Beijing Research Institute of Physical Education, was established in Beijing to promote martial arts by a group of students, headed by Xu Yusheng (1879 – 1945), a scholar and an ardent lover of Taijiquan. For the first time the teaching of the art was open to the public. The institute's earliest instructors were the third-generation Taijiquan masters, Yang Shaohou, Yang Chengfu, and Wu Jianquan, as well as Sun Lutang.

In those early years, there was only one Taijiquan and differentiation among styles if any, served only to identify and honor one's teachers. However, the demarcation lines began to set among the followers as they grew in enormous numbers across the major cities in the 1920s and 1930s. That period saw the first boom of Taijiquan, when the masters traveled extensively in China to spread the art. In 1926, Yang Chengfu went to Nanjing, Shanghai, Hangzhou, Guangzhou, and Hankou. Two years later, Wu Jianquan moved to Shanghai, at the invitation of Shanghai Wushu Society and Jingwu Sports Society, and in 1935 he founded the Jianquan Taijiquan Association there. Hao Yueru and his son, Shaoru traveled to Shanghai, Nanjing, and other cities to promote their branch of Taijiquan. Also, in 1928, Chen Fa'ke came to Beijing from Chen Village.

By the time of the demise of Yang Shaohou in 1930 and Yang Chengfu in 1936, Taijiquan had permanently assumed the identities of the different styles, taking the names of their respective founders. Yang Family Taijiquan was already the dominant style, and the many disciples of Yang Chengfu made it even more prevalent.

After the defeat of the Chinese Nationalist forces by Mao's Red Army in 1949, many fled the mainland to Taiwan, and Taijiquan followed in the exodus. Most of the Yang Taiji practitioners overseas today can trace their teachers to Yang Chengfu's disciples, notably, Cheng Manching (1902 – 1975), Dong Yinjie (1898 – 1961), Fu Zhongwen (1903 – 1994), and others. Their followers and those of Yang Chengfu's four sons, Yang Zhenming (1911 – 1986), Yang Zhenji (1921 – 2007), Yang Zhenduo (1926 –), and Yang Zhenguo (1928 –), collectively, form the huge base of the large majority of schools currently practicing the Yang Style Taijiquan form, standardized by Yang Chengfu.

Five Classical Canons of Taijiquan

The 1920s saw a burst of publication of Taijiquan texts: Xu Yusheng, *Elucidation of Taijiquan Postures* (1921); Sun Lutang, *A Study of Taijiquan* (1924); Chen Weiming, *The Art of Taijiquan* (1925); and Yang Chengfu, *Taijiquan Practical Applications* (1931), which was edited in 1934 as *Complete Taijiquan and Applications*. The materials of the books were drawn mainly from the collection of papers in the family archives of Wu Yuxiang and Yang Luchan.[17] The writers then were not particular about scholarship or historicity. With no peer review, the citations and the derived texts were not always consistent. For instance, there was a glaring concoction[18] in the book by Yang Chengfu, likely ghost-written by his disciple anxious to sanctify the grandson's lineage status. Douglas Wile provides a thorough analysis of the materials published in this period.[19]

At the core of the early literature are five texts that have come to be known as the *Five Classical Canons of Taijiquan*. These five texts are referenced in almost all Taijiquan books or discourse, though with some textual differences. We take the texts in the book by Chen Weiming (1881 – 1958), an early disciple of Yang Chengfu, which are studied and translated by Barbara Davis.[20] The five canonical texts are:

1. *Taijiquan Treatise (Taijiquan Lun* 太极拳论), attributed to Zhang Sanfeng
2. *Taijiquan Classics (Taijiquan Jing* 太极拳经), attributed to Wang Zongyue
3. *Elucidation of Thirteen Postures (Shisan Shi Xinggong Xinjie* 十三势行功心解), attributed to Wu Yuxiang
4. *Thirteen Posture Song (Shisan Shi Ge* 十三势歌), anonymous
5. *Playing Hand Song (Dashou Ge* 打手歌), anonymous

The Chen Village Taijiquan Texts

The Cultural Revolution (1966 – 1976) ravaged through China, destroying old institutions and Chen Village was not spared. The village temple was razed to the ground and the practice of Taijiquan—vilified as of the old culture—was banned, and Taijiquan texts were destroyed.

But the writings of Chen Xin (1849 – 1929) and his book, *Illustrated Explanations of Chen Family Taijiquan (Chen Shi Taijiquan Tushuo* 陈氏太极拳图说)[21] survived. The book was completed in 1919 but only published posthumously in 1933 with funds raised by Chen Pan-ling (unrelated to the Chens of Chen Village) and other martial arts enthusiasts.[22] Chen Xin, a 16th generation descendant of the Chen clan, was groomed by his father, Chen Zhongshen, to be a scholar. It is said that his Taijiquan did not reach the proficiency of his brother, Chen Yao, but the might of his pen would triumph.

Preceding Chen Xin by two generations, Chen Changxing (the patriarch who taught Yang Luchan) left behind two essays on the practice and application of Taijiquan:[23]

- *Ten Essential Principles of Taijiquan (Taijiquan Shi Da Yao Dian* 太极拳十大要点)
- *Important Words on Taijiquan Applications (Yong Wu Yao Yan* 用武要言).

Preserved also are two poems by Chen Wangting, the creator of the Village art:[24]

- *A Poem of Uneven Verses (Chang Duan Ju* 长短句)
- *Song of Boxing Canon (Quan Jing Zongge* 拳经总歌).

These Chen Village essays do not correspond to the texts of the Five Classical Canons of Taijiquan with the exception of the *Playing Hand*

Song. Chen Village has an almost identical version of this song. The Chen literature will be revisited from time to time.

Taijiquan in Chen Village

In the three generations since Yang Luchan left Chen Village and introduced the art he learned from Chen Changxing to the outside world, Taijiquan had flourished, taking the names of Yang, Wu (Hao), Wu, and Sun. All the while, Taijiquan was by no means languishing in Chen Village. It continued to be practiced, as it had been centuries before.

Figure 2.12 Chen Changxing (1771 – 1853)
14th Generation Patriarch of Taijiquan

The Chen family archive records a roll of notable masters from every generation, going back to Chen Wangting. In the generation after Chen Changxing, there were the trio, Chen Gengyun, Chen Changxin's son, and the twin brothers, Chen Zhongshen and Chen Jishen, nephews of Chen Youben. Chen Youben is famed as the progenitor of what is now known as the Chen Family Small Frame (*Xiao jia*) Taijiquan, as opposed to Chen Changxing's Large Frame form. Chen Youben was also the master of Chen Qingping who taught Wu Yuxiang in Zhaobao. The twin brothers were renowned for their skill in long weapons.

The martial utility of Taijiquan in war was put to a test again during the Taiping Rebellion (1850 – 1864). The local gazetteers describe that in 1853 a force of rebels under the ferocious leader nicknamed Big Ram Head (Da Dou Yang) attacked Chen Village.[25] The village was defended by a militia of local warriors trained in Taijiquan. The rebel leader came charging in on horseback, but Chen Zhongshen fearlessly stood his ground and thrust a long-pole weapon at Da Dou Yang. Da Dou Yang parried the thrust, but Chen Zhongshen pulled the pole back. The pullback action generated a tremendous vibrating force[26] in the flexible three-meter long pole, which struck the rebel leader, sending him to the ground, whereupon the Chen warriors cut off his head. Thus the village was saved. Chen Zhenglei, a present 19th generation master, often regales the class with this inspirational feat whenever he teaches the long-pole weapon.

While the practitioners under Yang Luchan in Beijing were largely of the nobility and gentry, the Chens in the village were farmers who practiced the art for survival against bandits and outlaws. Chen Changxing and his son, Chen Gengyun, earned their living as security escorts protecting merchant convoys traveling through the bandit-infested provinces of Henan and Shandong. Their martial prowess became well known to the bandits in this region, who learned to stay away from caravans carrying flags displaying their insignia.

There is a stone memorial erected by the people of Laizhou Township in Shandong province commemorating Chen Gengyun. It recounts how Gengyun's heroism and martial skills saved the town from bandits led by a notorious Tian Er-wang. This memorial would later lead to the patronage of the Chen Village martial art by the foremost warlord of the time, Yuan Shikai (1859 – 1916).

Yuan Shikai was a colorful general who played his political hand adroitly. He sided with the Empress Dowager against the reformers in the 1898 palace coup. When the Qing imperial rule became hopeless, he joined the Republican cause. Yuan wrested the presidency of the new Republic from Sun Yat-sen (revered as the Father of the Republic of China), after forcing the last Qing emperor, Puyi, to abdicate in 1912. Four years later, Yuan proclaimed himself the emperor of China, believing that heaven favored imperial rule, but his imperial rule was short-lived, lasting less than three months.

Many years earlier, when Yuan Shikai was the governor of Shandong, he had chanced upon the memorial honoring Chen Gengyun during an official tour of the province. He was so enthralled by the tales of the martial prowess of Chen Gengyun that he sought out the hero. Assured that his son, Chen Yanxi, had attained his father's skills, the governor invited him to serve in his household. Yanxi was treated as a prized acquisition as he defeated all the famous martial artists that came his way. However, the art did not take root under Yuan's patronage. In the six years of his stay, Taijiquan was more admired than pursued. With the excuse of needing to care for his ailing mother, Chen Yanxi returned home to Chen Village to practice medicine to the end of his days.

Chen Fa'ke, introduced earlier, was the son of Chen Yanxi. Fa'ke's arrival in Beijing in 1928 was brought about by another change in the political winds within China.

Chen Fa'ke (1887 – 1957) in Beijing

In 1928 Chen Zhaopi (1893 – 1972), an 18th generation Chen Village Taijiquan master, arrived in Beijing, escorting a shipment of medicinal herbs. At that time, Taijiquan was already in vogue in the city. So the head of Tong Ren Tang Pharmacy, Yue Youshen, invited him to give Taijiquan lessons. The news of a Chen Village Taijiquan master and a direct descendant of Chen Changxing who taught the founder of the predominant Yang Style, created a lot of excitement and interest in Zhaopi's visit. Classes were quickly formed at the City Hall of Beijing, as well as at Chaoyang and Yuwen universities. Several associations also invited him to give lessons.[27]

Figure 2.13 Chen Zhaopi (1893 – 1972)

Not long after Chen Zhaopi began teaching, the political winds brought a brief but not inauspicious disruption to the Beijing Taiji classes. The Nationalist government had just moved its capital to Nanking. This ushered in the "golden decade" of Kuomingtang rule, which saw a euphoric burst of cultural activities in the new capital. Riding on this wave, the Nanking Central Martial Arts Institute (*Nanjing Zhong Yang Guoshu Guan*) was founded. Upon learning that an illustrious Chen lineage master was teaching in Beijing, the Nanking mayor immediately dispatched an invitation to recruit him. Chen was truly loath to abandon his students, who had just started to learn the "First Routine Form," but he was even more loath to forsake a prestigious appointment at the newly founded institute at the seat of the new capital, not to mention a cushy salary of a hefty 200 yuan a month, a luxurious sum by Chen Village standards at that time.

His students were naturally most disappointed about his leaving but were quickly assuaged by the master's solution. He told them that he had studied his Taijiquan from his third uncle, Chen Fa'ke, whose kungfu skills were "a hundred times better" than his own. Their disappointment quickly turned to elation on hearing that Chen Fa'ke would take his place in Beijing.

Figure 2.14 Chen Fa'ke (1887 – 1953)

Thus a second Chen master, six years senior to Zhaopi, left Chen Village for Beijing. Suddenly, there were two Chen lineage masters in China's two most important cities. The Chen Village art would quickly soar in recognition and popularity under the tutelage of Chen Fa'ke and Chen Zhaopi. Chen Fa'ke stayed in Beijing for 28 years until his death in 1953. Chen Zhaopi would return to Chen Village in 1958 to train a new generation Chen masters.

Chen Zhaopi took early retirement and returned to Chen Village against the entreaties of his son, who protested the backward mobility from city back to rural. But the father was adamant in his mission to preserve the art of Taijiquan in the village, which he feared was dying out. He had visited the village earlier in spring and was appalled and saddened that Taijiquan had dwindled in its birthplace, while he was trying to promote it outside.[28]

Village life was harsh enough, but the government campaign of the Great Leap Forward (1958 – 1961), which pushed steel production even in the rural hinterlands, impoverished the countryside. The current generation of Chen masters would always tell us that they never understood eating a full meal growing up then. Nevertheless, the youngsters trained hard under the tutelage of Chen Zhaopi. With no other distractions, they would practice daily and in the evening gather at the home of the master.

Emerging from this crop are the world renowned "Four Great Jingangs (Gems)," Chen Xiaowang (1945 –), Chen Zhenglei (1948 –), Wang Xi'an (1944 –), and Zhu Tiancai (1944 –). Chen Zhaopi's dedication brought about the renaissance of Taijiquan in Chen Village.

Besides Chen Zhaopi's efforts, Chen Zhaokui (1928 – 1981), the second son of Chen Fa'ke, also took up the baton, traveling to many cities and bringing up a corps of future masters. He returned to teach in the village on several occasions after Zhaopi passed away. The main Chen Family Taijiquan forms practiced today are those propagated by Chen Zhaopi (the Old Frame Forms), and Chen Zhaokui (the New Frame Forms).

Chen Qingping, who taught Wu Yuxiang briefly in Zhaobao, had two other illustrious students, He Zhaoyun and Li Jingyan, who would spawn two other styles of Taijiquan. The form practiced by the followers of He is called Zhaobao Taijiquan, taking the name of the town. The practice of Li developed a distinctive characteristic of sudden changes in the flow of the movements, likened to "thunder and lightning" (*hulei*), and so is called *Hulei Jia Taijiquan*.

Figure 2.15 Chen Zhaokui (1928 – 1981)

To recapitulate, Taijiquan saw its first burst of major growth around 1930, with Yang Chengfu heading the Yang style in Shanghai; Wu Jianquan, the Wu style also in Shanghai; Hao Yueru, the Wu (Hao) style in Yongnian; Sun Lutang, the Sun style in Beijing; and Chen Fa'ke, the Chen style in Beijing. Virtually, all the modern Taijiquan forms practiced today can be traced to the masters of this period. Comparing their postures in old pictures, there is very little resemblance between Chen Fa'ke's Taijiquan and that of Yang Chengfu or among those of the other leading masters.

Chousi or Chansi

When Chen Zhaopi presented Chen Village Taijiquan in Nanking, this kind of art was no longer a novelty, and those who had studied Taijiquan of the other styles were only too keen to compare notes with the Chen system. As expected, they saw the Chen form as different in character and in flavor—the coiling motion interspersed with explosive actions, the foot-stomping, and jumping kicks. Chen Zhaopi explained that Taijiquan motion is driven by the basic "silk-reeling energy" (*chansi jin*), which gives it the coiling characteristic.

These differences immediately caused a stir among the wushu community. Chen Zhaopi's Taijiquan movements did not seem to conform to the practice principles of "moving energy like drawing silk" (*yun jin ru chousi*) or of "stepping like a cat." The debate raged on between *chousi* on the one hand, which likened motion to drawing silk from a cocoon, and *chansi* on the other hand, which characterized it not just of drawing but of spiraling as well, to incorporate the body's rotational motion.

Chen Zhaopi would diplomatically defuse the contentiousness of the arguments by pronouncing that both methods were right, and neither wrong. The Yang school was not wrong, as they were practicing Taijiquan in accordance with their principle of chousi, and similarly, the Chen school was right, with theirs of chansi.

As to the explosive actions within the form, Chen Zhaopi explained that it was *fajin*—a sudden release of inner strength (neijin). They were able to reconcile with it as the advanced training of Yang also included a secret practice of "fast sets."

Chen Fa'ke was more taciturn about theory, and when pressed and inclined, would explain by demonstration. More often than not, he would deprecatingly invoke his famous response, "Wo buzhong (I am not good)," to evade further discussion, so much so that he was nicknamed, "Chen Buzhong." The echoes of the past debates can still be heard today. Some Taijiquan experts still question whether the explosive movements and the foot stomping of Chen Style are in accord with Taijiquan principles or even good for health.

Chen Zhaokui and Chen Zhaopi of the 18th generation lineage (1965)
Most of the Chen Taijiquan's "large-frame" forms practiced today are taught by
them.

3
Historical & Cultural Perspective of Taijiquan

The very name of Taijiquan augurs something of monumental order. The word Taiji denotes "grand extremes," encompassing all, from the extreme polar end of yin to the other extreme polar end of yang, and signifies totality or completeness, where there is nothing so large or so small that is not within it.

The grandness of Taiji embraces all things in the universe, of Heaven (*Tian* 天), Earth (*Di* 地) and Man (*Ren* 人). Taiji permeates Chinese philosophy, with roots going back to the antiquities of time. The ancient thinkers resorted to Taiji theory to expound everything—it served as a "grand theory of everything."

Taijiquan is a system of martial arts based on the principles of Taiji. Because of the grandness of the theory, Taijiquan is often interpreted as the "Ultimate Boxing System."

Taiji concepts are uniquely Chinese, steeped in culture and a long history, so they do not present well on a Western canvass. That does not mean that one has to be well-versed in Chinese culture or philosophy to appreciate the art. However, a brisk walk through history to review the Taiji concepts of *yin* and *yang*, *bagua* (eight trigrams) and *wuxing* (five elements), and *I-Ching* (*Book of Changes*) will provide a cultural backdrop to set the art in context.

Taiji Theory

Taiji is introduced in the old Chinese texts as:

> Wuji ("Limitless") becomes delimited in the birth of Taiji
> Which manifests two forms (liang yi 两仪): yin and yang.
> The two forms give rise to four symbols (si xiang 四象),
> From which eight trigrams (bagua 八卦) are derived.
> The eight trigrams spawn sixty-four hexagrams.

The theory postulates a primordial state of boundlessness of "non-being" (wuji 无极) from which Taiji is born—the coming into being of things, together with the law of duality that differentiates them as *yin* 阴 or *yang* 阳. The fundamental nature of being lies in the mutual polarities of yin and yang (*yin yang xiang sheng* 阴阳相生).

The idea of polarities is present in all cultures, for example, the opposites of black and white, right and wrong, positive and negative, and so on. The old Greek philosophers used the dichotomy of "true" and "false" to construct the logic of mathematics, which endures as the language of science. The ancient thinkers of China used the duality of yin and yang as the basic building blocks of symbols to decipher all things in the universe. Although it does not have the same rigor of logic, the yin-yang duality also has endured, as the foundation of Chinese metaphysics.

Originally, the character of yang referred to "the sunlit, south side of a mountain," while yin "the shaded, north side." The illumination of the sun in the etymon of yang, connotes the quality of strength, dominance, and control, while yin, the opposite, of weakness, submissiveness, and yielding. Heaven (*tian* 天) is designated yang and earth (*di* 地), yin. Darkness is yin, brightness is yang; male or masculinity is yang, female or femininity yin; active is yang, passive yin; day is yang, night yin; hot is yang, cold yin; hard is yang, soft yin; motion is yang, stillness yin; opening is yang, closing yin; extending is yang, folding yin. The yang designation has a consistent attribute of firmness and control, and yin, of flexibility and yielding.

The defining feature of the duality theory is *change*. The postulate of change breathes dynamics into the yin-yang states, which are governed by the following principles:

1. Yin and yang aid one another (*yin yang xiang ji* 阴阳相济). Although yin and yang are inherently opposite in character, they are not treated as agents of conflict. Rather, in the change, one studies their complementary relationship and how they mutually aid one another.

2. In the state of being, within yang there is yin and within yin, there is yang (*yin zhong shu yang, yang zhong shu yin* 阴中属阳，阳中属阴). So in change, the states cannot become totally yin or totally yang. That is, yin cannot be without yang, and yang cannot be without yin in the change (*yin buli yang, yang buli yin* 阴不离阳阳不离阴). This reinforces the complementary mutuality between yin and yang.

3. Yin, at its peak, marks its decline and the ascendancy of yang, and yang at its peak, marks its decline and the ascendancy of

yin (*yin ji sheng yang, yang ji sheng yin* 阴极生阳阳极生阴).
This also respects the complementary mutuality between yin
and yang. For example, yin of night changes to yang of day,
and yang of day to yin of night, where one ends, the other
begins, in an endless cycle. Moon waxes and wanes, tides rise
and fall, winter solstice marks the height of the yin phase, and
the beginning of new warm yang energy to bring forth spring.
Yang force peaks in midsummer, the summer solstice, to yield
to the phase of cool yin.

4. Regulating the changes is the *principle of harmony or balance*
   between yin and yang. This is a metaphysical balance of neither
   excessive nor deficient in yin or yang. Taiji study centers on
   seeking this balance. But there is no quantitative measure of
   how yin is yin or how yang is yang so balance is more than that
   of a scale balance.

Figure 3.1 Taijitu (Taiji Symbol)

The ubiquitous Taiji symbol or Taijitu[1] (fig. 3.1) encapsulates all the
Taiji principles graphically. Wuji is represented by the circle, which
gives rise to Taiji, depicted by the two halves of black (yin) and white
(yang). The little white eye-dot of yang in the yin black half and the

yin black dot in the yang white half depict that within yin there is yang and within yang there is yin. The dynamics of change are depicted by the shape of inverted fish, each half flowing into the other. The harmony is illustrated by the whole symbol itself in the visual balance between yin and yang, namely, the absence of excess or deficiency of yin or yang.

Yin-Yang Study in Taijiquan

The following verse in *Taijiquan Classics* expresses the yin-yang concepts with respect to Taiji boxing.[2]

Taiji zhe wuji er sheng 太极者无极而生
Yin yang zhi mu ye 阴阳之母也
Dong zhi ze fen 动之则分
Jing zhi ze he 静之则合
Wu guo bu ji 无过不及
Sui qu jiu shen 随曲就伸

Taiji, born of wuji,
Is the mother of yin and yang.
In motion things move apart.
In stillness things combine.
Not overextending and not being short,
(Not to be in excess or to be deficient)
One flows through the twists and turns.

Taijiquan is a study of body motion in the yin-yang model. The proposition is that motion regulated by Taiji principles gives rise to power of the grand Taiji order—the consummate neijin (internal strength) that underlies the magical prowess of Taijiquan kungfu. Thus, the objective is to train the body to move in accord with the yin-yang principles.

However, the magical kungfu feats of neijin, examined closely, are not inconsistent with physics. As esoteric as Taiji theory may seem, there is a scientific rationale to the methodology beneath its yin-yang garb. More importantly, the body relates to the yin-yang logic and concepts in its comprehension of how to train and generate motion for power as well as aesthetics.

The practice of Taijiquan is to understand the dynamics of yin and yang and to decipher the conditions of excessive or deficient yin or yang, namely, of *yin-yang imbalance*. The training forges the body to reduce excessiveness or strengthen deficiency in yin or yang. Thus imbalance is improved without having to pin down balance. The practical concern is not balance but to know imbalance and to resolve it by staying in the middle ground of not being too excessive or deficient in either yin or yang (*wu guo bu ji* 无过不及).

In other words, Taijiquan aims to build the body's comprehension of yin-yang imbalance and to develop the means to resolve the imbalance. The yin-yang model is not a structure of axioms to formulate theories that lend to a reduction to basic principles as in science. But, by the same token, it is because its organic rationalism that no matter how complex things may grow to be, they remain within its scope.

Bagua 八卦 (Eight Trigrams)

The yin and yang of Taiji give rise to a universe of yin-yang representations, like the binary strings of zeroes and ones in the digital world. Graphically, yin and yang are represented by *yao-lines* (*yao* 爻):

> a broken-line dash — — for yin
>
> a solid-line dash —— for yang.

The yao-line representation is symbolically consistent: the solid line of yang conveys firmness or strength and the broken line of yin, yielding or weakness. The representation also captures the principle of change:

joining the broken dash, transforms it to yang, and breaking the solid dash, changes it to yin. According to traditional beliefs, yao-lines are an ancient invention of 2800 B.C.[3]

By placing the two yao-lines, one on top of the other, the composites of yin (earth) and yang (heaven), yield four symbols that correspond to the four seasons and the four cardinal directions. By adding a third yao-line to represent mankind, the three-row yao-lines form eight trigrams, called *bagua*, which capture the essence of the universe with respect to the three natures of "heaven, man and earth."

Table 3.1 Bagua names and symbolic associations of each trigram.[4]

Number	Trigram	Name	Image	Attribute
1	☰	Qian 乾	Heaven (Tian 天)	strong
2	☱	Dui 兑	Lake (Ze 泽)	joyful
3	☲	Li 离	Fire (Huo 火)	light-giving
4	☳	Zhen 震	Thunder (Lei 雷)	movement
5	☴	Xun 巽	Wind (Feng 风)	penetrating
6	☵	Kan 坎	Water (Shui 水)	dangerous
7	☶	Gen 艮	Mountain (Shan 山)	resting
8	☷	Kun 坤	Earth (Di 地)	devoted, yielding

Bagua is a diagram where the trigrams are placed in an octagon. There are two arrangements: *xiantian* pre-heavenly (or pre-birth) and *houtian*, the post-heavenly (or post-birth).[5] Bagua of the post-birth sequence is found in the compass of fengshui (Chinese geomancy), a study of spatial relationships and object placement in a building or landscape to align fortuitously the flow of energies. The pre-birth sequence is commonly seen in bagua mirrors hung outside Chinese homes to ward off ill winds.

Figure 3.2 Pre-birth Arrangement   Figure 3.3 Post-birth Arrangement

Figure 3.4 Bagua Mirror

In Taijiquan, the "eight gates of energies" (peng, lü, ji, an, cai, lie, zhou, kao) correspond to the eight trigrams. (This will be discussed in chapter 9.) Also, the boxing system of Bagua Zhang is based on bagua theory.

Bagua trigrams are the building blocks of the 64 hexagrams of *I-Ching, Book of Changes*. No discussion of Chinese philosophy, however cursory, is complete without referencing it. Indeed it permeates everything Chinese.

I-Ching (Yijing) Book of Changes

The I-Ching is the oldest and foremost of the Five Chinese Classics of traditional Chinese literature.[6] Its genesis was inspired by the discovery of bagua by the legendary sage-ruler, Fuxi (c. 2800 B.C.). Structurally, I-Ching consists of sixty-four hexagrams or *gua* 卦, formed by placing one bagua trigram on top another. A gua is a six-row combination of yao-lines, and stripped of all its imagery, it is just a six-bit sequence of binary numbers. But what makes it most unique and rich contextually are the bagua representations of the concepts.

In the I-Ching cosmogony, the birth of Taiji from Wuji gives rise to the primal energies of yin and yang. The purer and lighter of the yang essence ascends to form heaven (symbolized by Qian hexagram) and the grosser and darker of the yin essence congeals to form earth (Kun hexagram), together with the myriad things that come into being, with the birthmarks of yin and yang. Therefore, the belief is that all phenomena in the universe are represented in the guas and the yao-lines of I-Ching in perpetual change.

Under each hexagram is a body-text, which describes the image and representation of the gua, dense with symbolic meanings, and appended with yao-texts that tell of the gua's six individual yao-lines. The abstruse corpus of I-Ching is held at the top by the hexagram Qian (Heaven), and below, by Kun (Earth).

The hexagram Qian is the "Creative," or the "Initiative," whose primal energy causes the beginning and begetting of all beings, and Kun, of the opposite character, is the "Receptive," or the "Yielding." The perpetual motion of change is driven by the Initiative in Heaven, and the Receptive (Earth) flows in accord.

The core tenet of the I-Ching is the Tao of Change that Heaven rules Earth in the perpetual motion of change. If Earth (Kun) runs counter to the dictates of Heaven (Qian) in violation of Tao, it courts disaster. Therefore, earthly affairs can be understood through the I-Ching window of heavenly bodies and signs. I-Ching provides a map, albeit a cryptic one, to guide the reading of Heaven and to divine the right path on Earth in accord with Tao in order to avoid calamities.

I-Ching has been used as a book of divination since antiquity. Its enduring ingenuity lies in two things: the organic nature of the gua texts that seem to fit the situation at hand under consultation and the change represented by the transformation of the yao-lines. The dynamics of the yao-lines constructs a time flow through the guas, connecting past, present, and future. The following passage says it more eloquently.[7]

> "The Changes is a book
> From which one may not hold aloof.
> Its tao is forever changing -
> Alteration, movement without rest,
> Flowing through the six empty places;
> Rising and sinking without fixed law,
> Firm and yielding transform each other.
> They cannot be confined within a rule;
> It is only change that is at work here."

By historical tradition, the body-texts of the guas were compiled by King Wen (c. 1099 – 1050 B.C.), and the yao-texts were appended by his son, the Duke of Zhou. By that time, the guas had already been formulated and in use for hundreds of years in *Yi (Change) of Xia* and *Yi of Shang.*[8]

In the waning years of the Shang Dynasty (c. 1600 – 1046 B.C.), the stature of the Zhou Clan rivaled the court of Shang King Dixin. The Shang King, under a ruse, held Ji Chang, the lord of the Zhou Clan as a prisoner, but released him after a costly ransom. During his seven-year captivity Ji Chang wrote and compiled the body-texts of the 64 hexagrams, which became I-Ching (*Yi Jing*). Ji Chang also promulgated the Mandate of Heaven that the right to rule is bequeathed by heaven.

After the Zhou lord's death, his son vanquished the Shang King and founded the Zhou Dynasty (c. 1046 – 256 B.C.) as King Wu, claiming the Mandate of Heaven. He crowned his father posthumously as King Wen. King Wu died three years after and his young son ascended the throne as King Cheng. The Duke of Zhou, King Wu's brother, did not succumb to usurping power, but consolidated the Zhou rule as regent. Besides annotating I-Ching with the yao-texts, the duke was also credited with compiling the *Book of Odes (Shijing)*,[9] among other contributions. The upright duke has been held reverentially throughout history to the present day as Zhou Gong 周公.

It would be another five hundred years or so before I-Ching would be expanded significantly. Confucius (*Kongfuzi* c. 551 – 479 B.C.), a historical icon of Chinese philosophy, was totally enthralled by I-Ching. He delved into the mystery of the guas to his old age. It is said that he studied it so much that the leather thongs that held the bamboo strips together as a book had to be replaced three times from wear and tear. In his twilight years, the learned philosopher lamented that he did not have more years to study the book.[10] Confucius's rich annotations, known as the "Ten Wings," gave I-Ching the wings to soar.

"Hundred Schools of Thought"

King Wen's I-Ching and Zhou Gong's *Book of Odes* represent the early blooms of Chinese philosophy. They would burgeon in the latter part of Zhou into the "Hundred Schools of Thought." The Zhou Dynasty comprised two periods: Western Zhou (1046 – 771 B.C.) and Eastern Zhou (771 – 256 B.C.). The central rule of Zhou eroded in 770 B.C. when its capital was sacked and moved eastward to Chengzhou (present-day Luoyang, Henan). Since then, the princes and feudal lords increasingly carved out regional territories for themselves as Eastern Zhou further degenerated over the two sub-periods: Spring and Autumn Period (771 – 481 B.C.) and Warring States Period (475 – 221 B.C.). It was during these times of divisions and contentions as autonomous states were formed that Chinese philosophies flourished with "Hundred Schools of Thought."

Confucius was a product of this era. Lao Tzu (*Laozi)*, the venerable sage who personifies the *Book of Tao (Dao Dejing)* was an older contemporary of Confucius. Sun Tzu (*Sunzi*) won his place in history as a military genius when in 506 B.C. he defeated the Chu army of 200,000 troops with only 30,000 by brilliant maneuvers. The victory elevated the State of Wu to preeminent power. He is better known as the author of the timeless masterpiece, *The Art of War*. Other well-known historical sages are Micius (*Mozi*, c. 470 – 390 B.C.), a strong critic of the Confucian and Taoist schools, and the founder of *Mohism* (which propounds the philosophy of universal or impartial love, *jian ai* 兼爱); Mencius (*Menzi*, c. 372 – 289 B.C.), a foremost exponent of Confucianism; and Chuang Tzu (*Zhuangzi*, c. 369 – 286 B.C.), an iconic sage of Taoist philosophy. In that era, scholars roamed the warring states in search of patronage, fame, and fortune. Many of the lesser known scholars were no doubt significant figures in their own times but are mired in the thicket of history.

Zou Yan (c. 305 – 240 B.C.), from the State of Qi, was highly lauded in his time. He was feted and honored as a learned scholar in every state. It was said that in the State of Yan, King Chao swept the path before him and asked to sit below him among his students. Zou Yan was an erudite scholar whose knowledge of I-Ching and Tao was deep and wide. He had traced the origin of things to the primordial energies of yin and yang, and from the theory, derived the formations of the famous mountains, lakes, and rivers. His theory explained the rise and fall of dynasties going back to the mythical Three Rulers and the Five Emperors,[11] and it applied to statecraft, as well as to relationships between the high and the low. According to the Grand Historian, Sima Qian,[12] he also categorized the animals, the plants, the precious objects, and even the "things hidden from man's eyes, and beyond the Four Seas." However, the historian did not disguise his skepticism of such theoretical schemes of grandeur, noting that though the princes and nobles were impressed and influenced by his teachings at first, they could not put any of them into practice.

Wuxing (Five Elements or Phases)

Associated with yin-yang theory is the concept of *Wuxing* 五行 (Five Elements or Phases), which is a classification under the five elements: Wood, Fire, Earth, Metal, and Water. It developed alongside yin-yang and bagua, and appeared in the ancient *Book of History (Shujing)*.[13]

Hindu Upanishads uses a similar classification scheme but of four elements: Fire, Water, Earth, and Air. The same four elements appeared in pre-Socratic Greek philosophy, which was applied to medicine by Hippocrates (c. 460 – 377 B.C.). Up to the Middle Ages, the health of a person was viewed as a balance of four bodily humors or fluids (with the corresponding element): blood (fire), yellow bile (air), phlegm (water), and black bile (earth).

What sets wuxing apart is that, beyond the classification scheme, the concept embodies two structural relationships between the elements, which define two cyclic orderings.

The first ordering is "engendering or supporting" (*xiangsheng* 相生):

Wood engenders Fire, which engenders Earth, which engenders Metal, which engenders Water, which engenders Wood.

The second ordering is "subjugating or controlling" (*xiangke* 相克):

Wood subjugates Earth, which subjugates Water, which subjugates Fire, which subjugates Metal, which subjugates Wood.

These structural relationships translate to influences between the representations under the elements (fig. 3.4).

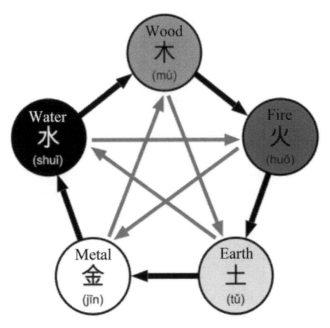

Figure 3.4 The two orders of wuxing

Wuxing is an integral part of Taiji Theory. Collectively, the theories of yin-yang, bagua, and wuxing form the Taiji metaphysics.

Table 3.2 is a partial list of classification by wuxing elements in common usage. The classification applies to the diverse fields of traditional Chinese arts: geomancy (fengshui), astrology, music, painting, medicine, martial arts, and so on. The wuxing influence is present in daily Chinese life. Indeed, the wuxing footprints appear throughout the dynastic history of China.

Table 3.2 A partial list of wuxing classification

	Wood	Fire	Earth	Metal	Water
Direction	east	south	center	west	north
Season	spring	summer	late summer	autumn	winter
Weather	wind	heat	damp	dry	cold
Color	green	red	yellow	white	black
Flavor	sour	bitter	sweet	pungent	salty
Yin Organs	liver	heart	spleen	lungs	kidneys
Yang Organs	gall bladder	small intestines	stomach	large intestines	urinary bladder
Body Parts	tendons	vessels	muscles (flesh)	skin	bones
Body Fluids	tears	sweat	saliva	mucus	urine
Sense Organs	eye	tongue	mouth	nose	ear
Emotion	anger	joy	worry	sadness	fear

A Wuxing Glimpse of Chinese Dynastic History

The fifteen-year span of Qin Dynasty (221 – 206 B.C.) was but an instant of time relative to long periods of the older dynasties of Xia, Shang, and Zhou, which lasted hundreds of years each. The brevity was ironic as the Qin Empire was arguably the mightiest in Chinese history. The fate of Qin had been read as an utter disregard of the cosmic influence of wuxing.

In the 26th year of his rule, the King of the State of Qin conquered the last State of Qi, bringing the seven states[14] under his rule, thus unifying all the lands under Heaven and closing the Warring States Period (c. 475 – 221 B.C.). It was epochal as the country had never been under such total central rule and the unified territory had never been so expansive in its history of two millennia. The king styled himself the First Emperor of China (Qin Shi Huangdi); the name China was derived from Qin (pronounced as Chin).

The Qin Empire saw itself as the successor of Zhou Dynasty, which had reigned under the wuxing auspices of Fire. To align with the wuxing order of Water subjugating Fire, Qin identified its rule with Water, just as Zhou had with Fire when it vanquished Shang, which subscribed to the sign of Metal. It seemed that the Qin rule totally violated the wuxing virtue of Water.

To rule the newly-founded Qin Empire, the Confucians advocated the traditional system of fiefdoms. But the chancellor, Li Si (c. 280 – 208 B.C.), prevailed over them arguing that fiefdoms would become independent and challenge the central rule, a fate that befell the House of Zhou.

He reaffirmed the structure of governance based on the doctrine of the School of Legalism.[15] The empire was divided administratively into thirty-six provinces. Each would be ruled by a governor, an army commander, and an inspector, and official positions would be filled by men of merit.

The Legalist doctrine in governance had been adopted a century earlier in the Qin State in the reign of Duke Xiao (361 – 338 B.C.) under the stewardship of the prime minister, Shang Yang. The radical reforms then established a system that rewarded those who were productive (in compliance with the rule) and punished those who were not. As everyone was "equal under the law" in service to the state, aristocracy was swept aside and replaced with meritocracy. Under Shang Yang's reforms, agriculture grew and military gained might. The state that had long been in the periphery became one of the strongest among the warring states. The doctrine of Legalism that invigorated Qin State turned out to be ruinous in the newly-founded Qin Empire under the aegis of Water.

The Qin emperor embarked on the mega projects of building the Great Wall, the E'fang (An Fang) palace, the extensive infrastructure of roads and canals[16] necessary to serve the far reaches of the new empire, and the mammoth mausoleum (which housed the famous life-size terracotta army[17]) to prepare for his afterlife. These undertakings seemed befitting for the historic empire to last "ten thousand years." But the reward-and-punish system of Legalism was perverted by corrupt officials to generate the increasing labor and resources needed to meet production quotas. Conscripts and convicts were sent to distant work sites never to return. How could heaven countenance such a burden on the populace that had just survived the throes of wars?

The Confucian scholars blamed the blight of the people on the Legalist doctrine, and argued that the governance was failing for lack of the Confucian virtues of humanity, rituals, and proprieties. Li Si, fighting for his life, pointed to the imperial might and right: the might of Qin had no precedence and the emperor's achievements had no peers in history. Li Si turned the tables and blamed the guile of the scholars—flattering and criticizing in turn to confuse the common people—for undermining the morale of the newly-founded empire. He prevailed upon the emperor to decree the burning of books to stamp out the influence of the scholars. In the infamous bonfire of 213 B.C. the accumulated writings of two millennia, the ancient songs and the books of learning of the Hundred Schools of Thought, were put to the flames. But I-Ching was spared, as well as the books on medicine and agriculture. When the Confucian scholars remonstrated, Li Si caused 460 of them to be buried alive, which completely suppressed any further dissent. (For all his political shrewdness, Li Si was later undone and executed by the guileful chief eunuch Zhao Gao.)

Figure 3.5 Qin Shi Huangdi (First Emperor of China) 259 – 210 B.C.

How could such a wholesale, draconian, and cruel suppression of philosophies square with the soft and generative virtues of Water? The corruption of the Legalist system that sent hundreds of thousands of war-wearied people to servitude in the mega projects was clearly a transgression of the wuxing order of Water engendering Wood to nurture. Qin Dynasty, instead of lasting "ten thousand years," collapsed within three years after the death of the First Emperor.

All the same, the legacy of Qin Shi Huangdi is preserved in perpetuity. The achievements that culminated in the reunification of China, the administrative structure of governance, the rule of law, the standardization of measures, money, and of the written Chinese characters, were all crucial to China staying unified over the next two millennia to the present.

Unrolling the scroll of China's dynastic history to the end, one too sees the wuxing imprint in the last dynastic change. In 1636 the Manchurian Jurgen Khan (Hong Taiji) elevated his title to emperor and renamed his new empire the Great Qing, signaling his clear intent to succeed Ming Dynasty (1368 – 1644). Earlier in 1616, he had named his empire the Later Jin Dynasty, after the glory of the first Jurgen Jin (Gold 金) Dynasty (1115 – 1234). But as the new empire grew, the Khan saw that the many princes were still caught up in myopic self-interest, and there was no sign of the infighting abating. He was advised that the element of Metal (Jin), which identified the rule, was not auspicious, and that the empire's name be changed.

The new name, Qing 清 was chosen. It means, "clear, pure" and the left radical of the character is "water." Both the water etymon and meaning signified the Water element of Qing, thus consistent with the wuxing order of Metal engendering Water, namely, Jin giving rise to Qing. More auspiciously, in the wuxing order of Water subjugating Fire, Qing, under the cosmic influence of Water would be poised to vanquish the Fire of Ming. The Ming character 明 was associated with the Fire element by the left radical "sun" 日.

Qing   Ming

清   明

Who could discount the value of the folklore belief of wuxing in the character 清 emblazoned in the banners, fluttering majestically, signifying the new order of Great Qing against the character 明 of the demoralized and decrepit Ming, destined to fall as ordained by the wuxing order? With the Mandate of Heaven withdrawn, the Ming's "ruling qi" was completely sapped. The Qing conquest of China was not even won by a great decisive battle, but hastened by the Ming general guarding the northern frontiers, Wu Sangui, who switched allegiance and opened the gates of Shanhai Pass to let the Qing army into Beijing in 1644. The mighty Qing army merely mopped up the

Chinese rebels led by Li Zicheng, who had earlier taken the capital and established a brief rule. So one could only hear the collective sigh, "This is Tian Yi (Heaven's Will)!" The Qing would rule China until 1912.

Traditional Chinese Medicine

Traditional Chinese Medicine (TCM) views the human body as a microcosm of the universe governed by Taiji theory. TCM physiology posits a non-physical network of twenty major *jingluo* (meridians or channels) interconnecting the internal organs, and a metaphysical life-force energy, called *qi,* that courses through the body. The vital organs (zangfu) are classified under the wuxing scheme (Table 3.2).

TCM relates health to qi flow in the meridian network as regulated by the principles of yin and yang, bagua, and wuxing. A body's health is governed by the store of qi and the holistic balance of the organ functions in conjunction with their wuxing influences. Ill health reflects a discord of yin and yang or stagnating qi flow. In other words, health is a harmony of the music of yin and yang.

Chinese physicians diagnose sickness primarily by reading a patient's pulse to discern yin-yang imbalances of qi relative to the organ system. Treatment consists of a prescription of herbs, acupuncture, or therapies to remedy yin-yang imbalances and to nurture qi. The rejuvenation of qi, in essence, is the TCM panacea for all ills. A good store of qi helps the body to self-heal.

TCM practice is supported by case studies accumulated over the centuries and analyzed in the framework of Taiji metaphysics. However, much work remains to be done to link the theory of qi and the jingluo-meridian system to medical science. Some progress is underway to bridge the gulf at the level of basic science, notably in the research by Dr. Shin Lin, Professor of cell biology, biomedical engineering and integrative medicine at the University of California, Irvine.[18]

Hua Tuo (c. 110 A.D. – 207) is the most recognized name in the roster of famous Chinese physicians. To be hailed a "Second Hua Tuo" is the highest accolade for a physician. A series of acupuncture points along the spine, called the "Hua Tuo Jiaji," are named after him. He devised the qi building exercise called, *Five Animal Frolics* (fig. 3.7). (The drawing of the exercise postures was among the archaeological finds in the Mawangdui excavations between 1972 and 1974.[19]) However, he is remembered most for his singular skills in surgery.

He diagnosed appendicitis and recognized that it could not be cured by herbs or acupuncture, but by surgery. It is recorded that he used a cocktail of "numbing powder" (mafeisan) and warm wine as anesthesia. He cut open the abdomen, removed the diseased part, stitched it back, and applied an ointment. The patient awoke and recovered, nurtured with herbs.

Lamentably, the pioneering practice of surgery failed to survive after his death. Most of his books on medicine were lost. This loss deprived Chinese Medicine not only of development in surgery, but also advancement in medicine that would have been impelled by the science of surgery.

By historical tradition, Chinese Medicine goes far back to the legendary Yellow Emperor (c. 2697 – 2597 B.C.). The oldest book of Chinese medicine is *Yellow Emperor's Classic of Medicine* (*Huangdi Neijing*), which consists of four texts, *Suwen, Lingshu, Taisu,* and *Mingtangjing*. It was written as a dialogue between the Yellow Emperor and his minister-cum-sage-physician, Qibo. A version survives to the present day, and still serves as a basic text in Chinese Medicine.[20]

It should be noted that in the long tradition of Chinese medicine, the culture of practice is rooted in theory and case studies, and not about supernatural healing power. Claims of supernatural cures had been many, but none had been used to successfully treat the "dragon body" (*longti*), as an emperor's body was referred to.

Taoist Practice and Early Qigong (Daoyin and Tu'na)

The West may be familiar with the aphorisms from the *Book of Tao (Dao Dejing)*, but Taoist practices are quite different. Taoism had absorbed the philosophy of Taiji by the time of the Han Dynasty (206 B.C. – 220 A.D.). The School of Yin-Yang (Yin-Yang Jia) and the School of Taoism (Daode Jia) had coexisted as two of the Six Schools of Philosophy[21] during the Warring States Period (475 B.C. – 221B.C.). After Han officially adopted the School of Confucianism, the influence of the other Schools gradually receded and were merged. Since then, the ruling elites were drawn from the literati trained in the Confucian tradition. Although Taoist and Confucian thinking are opposites like yin and yang, they coexist like the front and back of a palm. Scholars adhered to the strictures of Confucian norms in office, but in retirement they found respite in the natural way of Tao.

Taoism is also a religion (Daojiao), a mix of polytheistic, mystical, and folklore beliefs. The practice embraces I-Ching in divination and includes alchemy, astrology, the occult arts, and shamanism. In Taoist temples, one worships a pantheon of gods who inhabit the Heavenly Realm. The Dragon Emperor heads a celestial court of ministers, including a host of immortals.[22] There is an underworld of Hell replete with its own bureaucracy. It depicts a ledger that keeps the merits or demerits of everyone for the day of reckoning. To be sure, the images of torture and suffering portrayed of Hell in the temple are truly hellish and grotesquely scary.

Taoism places no emphasis on religiosity—no regular weekly services or preaching. The practice is less preoccupied with salvation in the afterlife, but more concerned with living in the present life. People go to the temples to pray on special days or as the need arises for divine intervention of their welfare or that of their dear ones. One simply becomes a user-believer by participating, with no initiation rites of conversion. Whether one joins in or not, the vibrancy of the festivities during religious occasions overwhelms the whole community, and one becomes a part of it. Taoism touches everyday Chinese life by the presence of the statues of deities in homes and workplaces, especially those that preside over luck, wealth, and health.

The facet of Taoist practice that has become familiar to the West is qigong, the art of qi energetics. The many qigong practices today are derived from or inspired by the Taoist practice of cultivating longevity.[23] The theory is that by returning to the "infant state" to reset the biological clock one can achieve longevity. This does not mean reversing an aged body, but refers to the state of qi. Taoists propound rendering qi "pure" as qi of the fetal state, thus returning to the infant state.

Taoists draw a distinction between qi of a growing fetus in the womb, called "prenatal qi," and qi after birth, called "postnatal qi." Prenatal qi has the original essence associated with early cell growth. Thus, prenatal qi rejuvenates youth. Postnatal qi is nurtured in the body by the intake of air (also called qi) and food. The Taoist practice of inner alchemy (neidan) is to render postnatal qi to the prenatal state.

The Taoists also explain that prenatal qi, bestowed by the mother, fuels the "flame of life." After birth, it is consumed gradually throughout one's life until it depletes, when life ends. Neidan (inner alchemy) transforms postnatal qi to prenatal qi, thereby replenishing it to prolong life.

The practice of inner alchemy is depicted in old neidan text as distilling qi in the "cauldron of the dantian" to purify it to prenatal qi (fig. 3.6). Complementing neidan is waidan (external alchemy), a protochemistry of preparing elixir pills from herbs or "magical" plants.

Neidan incorporates "fetal breathing" (taixi) in daoyin and tu'na, as early qigong is known. *Daoyin* 导引 means "leading or guiding to induce," and *tu'na* 吐纳 , means "breathing in (the fresh) and breathing out (the stale)." The Taoist sage, Zhuangzi (c. 369 – 286 B.C.), described the meditative practice of exhaling old breath and inhaling new, and the calisthenics of imitating animal movements to guide and induce qi circulation, as secrets to live as long as Peng Zu.[24]

Figure 3.6 Inner alchemy of transforming qi to prenatal qi

There are two broad disciplines of qigong: one, the physical regimen of calisthenics typified by "Five Animal Frolic" (*Wuqinxi*) (fig. 3.7), the "Eight Section Brocade" (*Baduan jin*), or their derivations, and the other, the quiet non-motion practice of meditation, in sitting or standing postures.

Quest for Longevity

It was traditionally believed that immortals resided in Mount Penglai, in the Penglai Islands of Immortals (Penglai Xiandao), and they held the secrets of longevity. It was only to be expected that the First Qin Emperor, after conquering all of the lands under heaven, would turn his attention to the quest of immortality. The emperor commissioned mariner Xu Fu to fetch the elixir of life from the island. Xu Fu returned to report that he had found the guardian-god of the "sacred mushroom," the food of immortality, but he lacked the sacrificial gifts to be received. The emperor readily sent him back with a fleet of ships laden with rich gifts of all kinds and three thousand virgin boys and girls, to win the favor of the gods. Xu Fu never returned from the second voyage. It is believed that he landed in Shingu, Japan, where there is a shrine in his honor.[25]

The emperor also summoned the best alchemists of the land to produce elixir pills, which he took in increasing dosages. It is likely that mercury in the pills hastened his death at the age of 48, a sad, ironic end to an invincible emperor who survived several assassination attempts.

The world conqueror Genghis Khan (c. 1162 – 1227) also sought the Taoist secrets of immortality. After defeating the Khwarezmid Empire (Persia) in 1220, the Khan led part of his army back to the Mongolian steppes, which he longed for. The remaining army was under the command of Jebe and Subutai, who went on to sack the Caucasus and Russia, writing their names into the annals of the greatest generals.

The Khan had heard of the Taoist master, Qiu Chuji (1148 – 1227)[26] and of his magical powers. Responding to the Khan's personal entreaties, the Taoist master traveled west with his retinue to meet the Khan. The journey was chronicled by Li Zhichang, one of Qiu's disciples in *Travels to the West of Changchun* (Qiu's Taoist name). When they met, the wise Taoist master dashed the hopes of the Khan when he quickly dispelled the popular myth that he was 300 years old. The Khan felt enlightened by his teachings, and bestowed honors on him, which greatly helped his Taoist Quanzhen Sect to flourish.

Craze of Qigong Practice

In the late 1970s and through the 1980s, qigong movements, which promised self-fulfillment and power enrichment, swept across China, as if to quench a thirst left in the cultural dearth after the Cultural Revolution (1966 – 1976). Fame and fortune beckoned, and qigong masters claiming all kinds of supernatural abilities appeared everywhere in China. Cults began to form around qigong masters, and the claims became more and more outlandish.

Qigong masters demonstrated paranormal abilities to move objects over space by qi, cure illnesses via qi transmitted to patients in faraway cities, emit qi to change the taste of water, read Chinese characters sealed inside an envelope, light fire with qi, and a host of other incredible feats.[27] Most of the demonstrations seemed like poor magic tricks, and indeed they were. Some of the so-called superhuman feats could be readily explained.[28]

Sima Nan was enamored with the power of qigong. In 1981 he devoted himself to become a master.[29] He quickly became disillusioned when he found out that all of the so-called paranormal abilities involved only practiced skills and trickeries, and even more disillusioned when he realized that the agenda was only money and greed. His journalistic integrity got the better of him, and he went on a one-man crusade to debunk the qigong charlatans, and along the way had many of his bones broken. He posted a reward of one million Chinese yuan for anyone who could demonstrate a paranormal phenomenon that he could not duplicate or expose. No one has successfully taken on the wager. With the press exposing more and more fake qigong, and the government cracking down on cultist qigong, the fervor of qigong subsided as quickly as it rose.

Qigong today is a popular exercise for health but with far less hype of paranormal abilities. Taijiquan is a qigong in that the exercise nourishes qi, but it is more than qigong—it is a training to cultivate inner strength. Taijiquan boasts of extraordinary kungfu based on inner strength, but makes no claims of paranormal abilities.

Taijiquan Is an Experiential Art

Taiji theory may be profound and esoteric, but Taijiquan is an art of practice. One studies the art by embarking on a journey of practice, not by pursuing the Book of Changes (I-Ching). Mastery of Taijiquan is not achieved by intellection of yin and yang, bagua (eight trigrams), and wuxing (five elements), but through many layers of experiential comprehension. Yang Luchan's mastery of the art did not come from reading Taiji theories—he was illiterate. Chen Fa'ke did not engage in Taiji dialectics, nor did he leave behind any copious notes of theories, but he was a walking embodiment of Taiji theory.

The point is that the comprehension of Taijiquan is a body process. Taijiquan is an experiential art. One has to put in the time and effort to temper the body to absorb the principles. That is not to say that the theoretical underpinnings play no role, but that the experiential knowledge is necessary to reinforce the validity or otherwise of the understanding of theory.

Practice

Delve less in stories of origin,
Or in whose lineage is more pure.
Look for the principles of the art.
Differences in forms do not authenticate a theory.
Practice, practice, and practice
To infuse the yin-yang principles in the body.
The magic is in the ease of yin-yang change.
Honor thy master and the lineage
For the teachings and inspiration.
The claim of monopoly of the art
Or glorifying mysticism
Do nothing to develop one's Taijiquan.

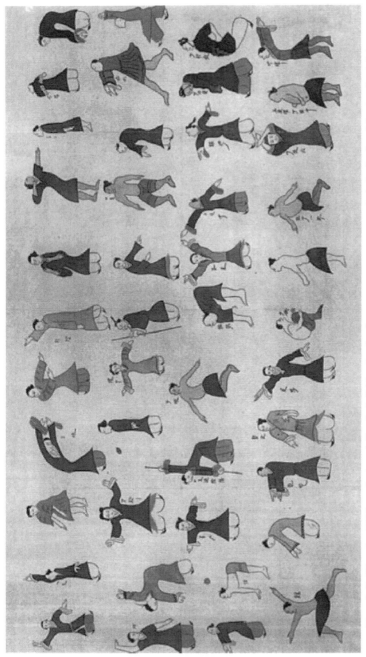

Fig. 3.7 Chart of "Five Animal Frolic" (*Wuqinxi*) qigong postures, each labeled, of limb stretching, breathing and gymnastics, attributed to Hua Tuo (c. 110A.D. - 207)

4
Synthesis of Taijiquan

Cultural Stew of Qigong and Martial Arts

Wushu (Chinese martial arts) was already developed in Spring and Autumn Period (771 – 481 B.C.).[1] An early martial arts personage was Yuenu, a lady of the State of Yue in the reign of King Goujian (496 – 465 B.C.). Goujian's name had long been etched into the Chinese psyche by the story of his travails and determination that forged a most improbable reversal of fortunes.

The protagonists then were the king's two ministers, Fan Li and Wen Zhong. Besieged with a remnant force of five thousand, King Goujian was facing obliteration at the hands of King Fu Chai of the State of Wu. Heeding the advice of Fan Li, Goujian sent Wen Zhong to sue for peace, and supplicated himself as a slave to King Fu Chai, thus averting the annihilation of Yue.

In captivity, Goujian humbled himself lowlier than a slave in serving King Fu Chai. The King, moved to see his former rival so utterly broken and humiliated in submission, granted him clemency to return to Yue, against the vehement opposition of his ministers. Steeled with resolve, Goujian lived spartanly and toiled alongside his people to rebuild Yue, but ever careful not to arouse Fu Chai's suspicion. He continued to sleep on a bed of twigs, and would daily taste a gall bladder hung on his door lest he forgot the bitterness of his captive days.

Fifteen years later, the State of Yue revived and grew so strong that Goujian conquered the unsuspecting Wu, and wrested hegemony from King Fu Chai in a most dramatic turn-around of historical fortunes.[2] The legacy of Goujian is evoked in four characters:

Wo xin chang dan
臥薪嚐膽
Sleeping on twigs and tasting gall

Less notable in the eyes of historians was the contemporaneous martial heroine, Yuenu, but her legendary swordsmanship still pierces through the thicket of two and a half millennia to the present with undiminished brilliance in the world of Chinese martial arts. The celebration of a martial heroine was an early recognition that combat was an art not just of strength. Yuenu had grasped the essence of internal martial arts. She expounded to King Goujian that her methods incorporated "breathing and consciousness; harmony of the internal and the external."[3] This says that Chinese martial arts and daoyin and tu'na (qi energetics) were already intertwined then.

Wushu has long been regarded as a discipline of self-cultivation. This evolved with the development of the solo practice of form routines, called *taolu*. A taolu is a choreographed series of martially inspired movements, which can be long and demanding. With taolu practice, the mastering of martial arts becomes a self-cultivation of the mind and body, akin to the practice of qi energetics.

Wushu's development is also influenced by the tradition of *wenwu,* the pursuit of the literary (*wen* 文) and the martial (*wu* 武). Wenwu took root in the Confucian ideal of a well-rounded scholar, one cultivated in the six arts, two of which, archery and charioteering, were military pursuits; the other four were calligraphy, music, rites, and mathematics. Wushu's cultural heritage is entrenched in the wenwu tradition.

Wushu was mixed early on in a cultural stew pot with the tradition of daoyin-tu'na. Stirred in with wenwu and the Taiji theory of yin and yang, it would only be a matter of time that a spark of human ingenuity would produce a synthesis of a wondrous art in the confluence of the right circumstances. One such set of conditions came together at the onset of the new foreign Manchu rule when loyalty to the old Ming still lingered, and that spark was kindled by Chen Wangting (c. 1600 – 1680), a descendant of the martial-scholar tradition, in his retirement, at a nondescript place called Chenjiagou (Chen Village).

The Founding Patriarch of Chen Village

The blue blood of martial tradition ran in Chen Wangting; it had coursed through the veins of the previous nine generations of the Chen family. His ancestor was Chen Bu, who migrated in 1372 to the place that would be known as Chen Village. It was then a part of Huaiqing Prefecture in Henan Province.

Huaiqing witnessed an upheaval of heaven and earth in the dynastic fall of the Mongolian Yuan Dynasty (1271 – 1368). Huaiqing was one of the last holdouts against the conquering Ming. Led by Tie Mu'er, an able Mongolian general, Huaiqing put up a valiant defense, killing a great number of Ming forces, before falling. This defiance of "Heaven's will" so incensed the Ming leader that upon ascending the throne the new emperor ordered the "Three Cleansings of Huaiqing," to rid the place of bad seeds. The scorching campaigns laid the eight counties of Huaiqing so completely to waste that not a rooster's crow or a dog's bark could be heard for miles.

Five years later, the Ming government instituted a migration policy to resettle the war-torn regions. Chen Bu and his family were originally from Zezhou County (Jincheng today), Shanxi Province. They had fled northwest from famine to Hongdong County, and were thus caught up in the wave of migration with tens of thousands of other families in the central plains of China. Because the families were gathered under a huge old tree, called "Big Scholar Tree" (*Da Huai Shu*),[4] their descendants would later say that their forebears came from the Da Huai Shu.

In the trek to the new land, Chen Bu was soon acknowledged as the group's leader by his resourcefulness and deeds of caring and selflessness. Arriving at Huaiqing, the migrants built a new village in the south eastern part, and named it Chenbuzhuang (Chen Bu Hamlet),[5] in recognition of Chen Bu's leadership. But the land turned out inhospitable—it flooded easily and the soil was saline. After two years, they decided to resettle in the known fertile grounds of Chang Yang Village, five kilometers away.

Though Chang Yang was better situated, the village was plagued with pillage and terror by bandits who infested the nearby hills of Qing Feng Ling. Chen Bu, who came from a martial tradition, was not deterred on that count. He trained and organized the villagers, who not only beat back the bandits, but wiped out the menace in their lair. After that, the village flourished. Soon, because of the dominance of the Chen families in the village, people began to call it Chenjiagou (Chen family *gou*), as a creek or ditch (*gou*) ran north-south through the village. Chen Bu instituted the training of martial arts, marking the beginning of the Chen family martial arts in the village, in the reign of the first Ming Emperor Hongwu (1368 – 1398). Martial arts developed alongside farming for two and three-quarter centuries to the last Ming emperor, when the Chen family martial tradition would be reborn as a new art that would be known as Taijiquan. This would be ushered in by Chen Wangting.

Chen Wangting (c. 1600 – 1680)

Chen Wangting, a ninth generation descendant of Chen Bu, was born in the reign of Wanli Emperor (1572 - 1620), at a time when the Ming Empire was beginning to decline. The emperor who was enthroned at nine, had become disillusioned and retreated into the inner sanctum of the palace. As more and more matters of state were handled by the eunuch gatekeepers, the latter's power rose, which culminated in the unbridled dominance of the eunuch, Wei Zhongxian, which continued into the court of the next ruler, Tianqi Emperor (1620 – 1627).

By the time of the last Chongzhen Emperor (1627 – 1644), the Ming rule was teetering on collapse. The government was facing a peasant uprising led by Li Zicheng (1606 – 1645) and more ominously, the foreign threat of the Manchus from the north. The Manchus had been held back steadfastly by Yuan Chonghuan, one of Ming's ablest generals, who was guarding the northern frontier. In 1630 Yuan was promoted to field marshal, which proved to be his undoing. The new prominence alarmed his enemies in the imperial court, who in age-old palace intrigue framed him as colluding with the Manchus. His execution would later open up a fatal crack in the northern defense.

Chen Wangting was a natural talent in wushu and was also diligent in literary (wen) studies. He grew up mastering the family arts, and was particularly good in archery and the long weapon, called "Spring Autumn halberd." According to his biography, Chen Wangting was feared by brigands and bandits in Shandong Province as he had killed many of them while escorting merchant caravans through the region.

In 1632, Chen Wangting passed the county-level examination as a martial scholar (*wu xiangsheng*), and was given a junior post as commander (*xiang bin shou bei*) of the garrison of Wen County.[6] Even as he aspired for higher office, his ambition was tempered by the social and political iniquities of the times, which grew from the corrupt influence of the eunuchs controlling the imperial court. The only career path open to him was to strive for a higher official position through a provincial-level degree (*wuju*). In a twist of fate, while participating in the higher-level military wuju examination at Kaifeng, an unfortunate incident forced him to flee for his life.

In the test of archery, the candidate was to shoot three arrows at the target while galloping on horseback. Chen Wangting's first arrow hit the bull's eye, and in quick succession, the second and third arrows followed, each hitting and splitting the previous arrow in the target. It happened so fast that the score-keeper, dumb-founded, rolled the drum only once, signifying one hit. Chen Wangting rode up to the drummer. But the score-keeper sneered at the archer to cover his own error. Chen Wangting, whose temper was already flaring, drew his sword and slew him in on the spot.

A junior officer reported to his superior that the candidate, Chen Wangting had killed a *bei*, a term referring to a lowly soldier. The superior gave Chen a knowing glance, and shrugged, "Oh, only a bei was killed." The term bei literally means a "tortoise." Chen Wangting, catching the cue, immediately galloped off without looking back, as the junior officer clarified that he was talking of a soldier, not an animal. By the time the superior ordered a pursuit, Chen Wangting was already out of reach.

Chen Wangting rode west to Dengfeng, and found refuge in the local peasant uprising led by Li Jiyu in Yudai Mountains. Li Jiyu (unconnected to Li Zicheng who was leading a larger peasant rebellion) was a Robin Hood-style rebel, robbing from the rich to care for the poor, and so was revered more as a hero than feared as a villain in the local communities. It was not clear if Chen Wangting shared in the cause of Li Jiyu, as he had already left the mountains when the Ming government forces mounted a concerted attack and routed the rebels. Li Jiyu was captured and beheaded, his head impaled on a pole for display in the capital. His heroic deeds, however, are preserved in ballads still sung to this day in Dengfeng.

Chen Wangting, no longer pursued by the authorities, returned to Chen Village. While taking refuge in Yudai Mountains, he came to know a Jiang Fa, whose martial skills had enthralled him. Jiang Fa had escaped from the Ming attack and found his way to Chen Village. Chen Wangting took him in under the guise of an itinerant worker, and he stayed on as Wangting's lifelong companion. The Chen Village lore has many tales of Chen Wangting and Jiang Fa. Village folks still point to the location of Jiang Fa's grave, and recount the story of Jiang Fa frightening away the ghosts that used to haunt the place. The old portrait drawing (fig. 4.1) shows Chen Wangting and Jiang Fa.[7]

Chen Wangting still had not found his cause when the last Ming emperor ignominiously hung himself in a tree in the palace garden after the rebel forces of Li Zicheng stormed into the Forbidden City. But Li Zicheng was not in the heavenly stars to occupy the dragon throne. The new Ming custodian of the northern frontiers, General Wu Sangui (1612 – 1678), weighing the option between the inevitable rising tide of the Manchu devils he knew and the Li rebels he did not trust,[8] decided to throw in his lot with the Manchus and opened the gate at the crucial Shanhai Pass. The combined forces entered the capital and routed the peasant rebels, ushering in the new Qing rule in the eventful year of 1644. Li Zicheng fled but was captured and killed, ending his brief imperial moment in history.

While not lamenting the fall of a corrupt and bankrupt government, Chen Wangting was nevertheless saddened to witness the collapse of the 276-year Ming dynastic rule. As much as he aspired to be a hero in the new era, he could not bring himself to serve in the new foreign

Manchu regime. He saw no point in the county-level literary degree (wen xiangsheng) he had just earned. Depleted of higher calling and sapped of ambition, Chen Wangting retired to Chen Village. That might just have been the end of the Chen Wangting story, one of unfulfilled promise. But as Chen Wangting tilled the land and tended the soil, unbeknownst to him, the seed of Taijiquan was being germinated within.

Figure 4.1 Chen Wangting and Jiang Fa holding the Spring-Autumn halberd

Awakening and the Creation of Taijiquan

Practicing daoyin and tu'na, reflecting on I-Ching and Tao, and contemplating life, Chen Wangting had an awakening of Zhuangzi's discourse on Tao. He saw the wantonness of lawless killings and the vagaries of officialdom. Honor, heroism, fame, fortune, and the many things he strove for, suddenly rang hollow. He felt a release from the fetters of human follies. Savoring the waters and the mountains, he soaked in the tranquility and grasped the bliss enjoyed by the immortals.

With heart serene, Chen Wangting's insight of martial arts heightened in practice. He had an epiphany of the principle of *wan fa gui yi* 万发归一. He saw the "ten thousand" skills and techniques of martial arts tracing to the source—the nucleus of motion at the dantian. He experienced wuji, the state of undifferentiated non-motion and the unfolding of Taiji yin and yang in motion. He discerned that jin 劲 (internal strength) arose from the integrity of the form structure in the myriad changes in motion, and he perceived the duality of jin—the "softness" in agility and the "hardness" in strength.

More significantly, in the awakening, he discovered that *chanrao* 缠绕 (coiling) was inherent in body motion. The insight crystallized: the jin of chanrao motion was at the core of martial arts—the leverage of chanrao (coiling) motion was the source of the art's wondrous power. Martial arts historians, Tang Hao (1897 – 1959) and Gu Liuxin (1908 – 1991) would hail this discovery as seminal in martial arts. The chanrao discovery was memorialized in the line of Chen Wangting's *Song of Boxing Canon (Quan Jing Zong Ge)*:[9]

Zhu kao chanrao wo jie yi
诸靠缠绕我皆依
I fully rely on coiling as the basis of all my combat techniques

The beauty of Taiji unfolded and manifested in his body. Inspired, Chen Wangting created a radically new "soft" training methodology of wushu, drawn from the cultural stew pot of daoyin and tu'na, Chinese Medicine, and Taiji. The creation ushered in a new epoch of the Chen family martial arts—the birth of Taijiquan.

Chen Wangting also devised an ingenious "soft sparring" called "Push Hands" (*Tui Shou*) to train and test the relative skills of partners. The push-hand practice also minimizes the bloody noses and broken bones that commonly attend combat sparring. He also introduced the method of "sticky spear" for spear training.

Chen Wangting had finally found his calling. His musing is expressed in the poem of "long and short" verses, *Changduan Ju.*[10]

Uneven Verses
by Chen Wangting

Ah, of those years
Clad in armor with resolute valor
Countless brigands and bandits I had slain,
And many a times faced death in the eye!

The honor and glories bestowed
All now seem so hollow and vain!
In feeble old age I can only sigh
And find refuge in my volume of Huangting[11]
Which I keep close as a constant companion.

In idle times, I forge new methods of quan (boxing)
In busy times, I tend the fields.
Whenever there is leisure
I teach my offspring and students quan
To be "dragons and tigers" as they wish.

I pay my grain taxes early
And never leave debts uncleared.
I have no use for pride and flattery,

T'is easy to yield and tolerate.
People call me silly
Or think me crazy
The words only cleanse my ears.

I pay no heed to officialdom.
Lo! The high officials in noble regalia
Always worried and fearful
Not to wrong their superiors.

How can it compare
With the peace and comfort in my heart.
I covet neither fame nor fortune.
Of worldly affairs,
I've seen the ploys and intrigues.

I imbibe the mountains and streams
Happy and carefree as a fish in water,
Worry not of rise in fortune
Nor of fall in misfortune,
But only of peace and health.

I live a plain and simple life
Envying not and resenting none.
I avoid the vagaries of ups and downs
And care not who wins or loses.
If this is not how immortals live
Then what is an immortal?

Chen Family Taijiquan

The tradition of Chen Family martial arts as reinvented by the ninth generation patriarch Chen Wangting has passed down from generation to generation without break to the present. One can read fascinating stories of the martial feats of each generation's masters in the Chen Family Genealogy.[12]

The old training routines consisted of seven sets: "Five Sets of Boxing" (Wu Tao Chui), "Long Fist" (Changquan), and "Cannon Fist" (Paochui), as well as weapon sets, including straight sword, broadsword, spear, staff, halberd (guandao), and others. By the time of Chen Changxing (1771 – 1853), the seven sets had been consolidated into two routines, the First Routine (Yilu) and the Second Routine (Erlu) (also called Cannon Fist), together with the various weapon series. These sets and routines are still practiced today.

Chen Youben, Chen Changxing's cousin, was also practicing the consolidated routines, but with variations, which later came to be known as the Small Frame Routines (*Xiaojia*), to distinguish it from Changxing's Old Frame (*Laojia*). Chen Qingping who briefly taught Wu Yuxiang, the founder of Wu (Hao) Style Taijiquan, was a nephew Chen Youben.

The art had been closely kept within the Chen clan, until Chen Changxing took in Yang Luchan as a student. Yang went on to found Yang Style Taijiquan, which in turn spawned the many Taijiquan schools of today. (This is recounted in chapter 2.)

Chen Wangting was probably not the only person to have synthesized martial arts with Taiji theory. The cultural stew of wushu and qigong (daoyin-tu'na) is always there for anyone to nourish kungfu mastery. Indeed, all Chinese kungfu systems include some qigong practice. The martial arts of Xingyi Quan, based on wuxing (five elements) and Bagua Zhang, based on bagua (eight trigrams), emphasize the development of internal energy.

Neither can it be said that Chen Wangting's synthesis was without influence from other martial arts. Tang Hao and Gu Liuxin pointed out that some of the postures in the Chen form routines are similar in name and form to those found in the authoritative *Boxing Classic* compiled by Qi Jiguan (1528 – 1587), a Ming general. Also, the first movement of the Chen form, "Buddha's Warrior Pounding Mortar

Board" (Jingang Daodui) closely resembles that of the movement, "Cannon Striking Fist" (Ji Shou Pao) of Taizu Changquan, a Shaolin boxing routine.[13]

The oft-repeated critique disputing Chen Wangting as the creator, argues that an art based on such esoteric Taiji theory, is simply too profound to be created by a "lowly garrison commander" in a backwater "hick town." This echoes an early writer's opinion that "whoever invented this subtle and profound martial art must have been an ancient Taoist possessed of the highest wisdom and could not possibly have been a common man."[14] The argument is spurious. Great things have been achieved by people who have come from just such small places and of common origins. Although predominantly agrarian, Chen Village was not without literary talents. It could count one jinshi—the highest literary degree holder—among its illustrious sons, Chen Buchan (of the 12th generation). Moreover, Chen Village lies south of the Yellow River, in the swath of the cradle of ancient Chinese civilization. The Shaolin Monastery in Mount Song, home of Shaolin Boxing, is only a hundred kilometers or so to the south.

The critique confuses the complexities of I-Ching and Taiji with the art of Taijiquan. The wonders of Taijiquan come from the practice of the art, which is about training, not the profundities of the theory. The creation of the art was an insightful application of the metaphysics of yin and yang to the mechanics of body motion, not a consequence of an intellectual pursuit of the recondite theory. As remarked before, the greatness of Yang Luchan's Taijiquan flowed from his body not his intellection of theory.

That Chen Wangting's creation was able to develop, grow, and transmit down the generations, was due in large part to the foundation of the Chen family martial tradition, which had begun centuries earlier with Chen Bu, the first ancestor. This provided the fertile ground for the art's growth, without which it might have languished and disappeared.

Tang Hao (1897 – 1959) Martial Arts Historian

Chen Wangting's place in the ancestral pantheon has long been established in the Chen Family Genealogy, but his place in Taijiquan, as the creator, would be affirmed by Tang Hao, a martial arts historian. Since his youth, Tang Hao had always loved wushu. He became a school teacher, the usual upward mobility for one who was poor but talented at literary studies. Though not his profession, he was always in pursuit of wushu. He spent all his meager savings collecting wushu books of historical interest.

In 1927 he went to Japan to study political science and law, but he also continued his martial training in judo and kenjutsu. From outside, he became more keenly aware of the blight of social iniquities and the technological backwardness in his own country, in contrast to Japan's ascendant military might. China seemed diseased, unable to adapt to change. The malady also afflicted Chinese martial arts, keeping it stuck in its past. Cloaked in the guise of traditions that indulged in fanciful legends and myths, Chinese martial arts was stymied—transmission was veiled in secrecy. Looking at it from abroad, Tang Hao was more acutely aware of the detrimental effects of the malady on the future of Chinese martial arts that he loved.

After he returned from Japan, Tang Hao worked as a lawyer, but his love of wushu would be more consuming. He joined the Central Martial Arts Academy (Zhongyang Guoshu Guan) and would go on to pioneer the study and become the Sima Qian[15] of the history of Chinese martial arts.

In 1930 and 1931, Tang Hao went to Chen Village to conduct field research on Taijiquan and uncovered Chen Wangting's creation and contribution in quan (boxing) in the archives, which marked the great watershed of the Chen Family martial arts tradition.

Whatever the varied accounts of Taijiquan's origins, there is no dispute that all the major schools, Yang, Wu (Hao), Wu, and Sun, descended from Yang Luchan and Wu Yuxiang; there is no dispute that Wu Yuxiang studied under Yang Luchan and Chen Qingping; and there is no dispute that Yang Luchan received his transmission from Chen Changxin. Therefore, all the major schools of Taijiquan came from the Chen Family tree.

There is no mention of Zhang Sanfeng in the historical archives of Wenxian or the family records of Chen Village. Whatever the claims of his historicity, there is nothing to connect him to Chen Changxin or the Chen Family martial tradition. The only thing certain that can be said of Zhang Sanfeng creating "internal boxing" is a story wrapped in myth (discussed in *Discovery at a Salt Shop in Wuyang*, Chapter 2).

Tang Hao also researched the history of Shaolin Boxing. His book, *Authenticity of Shaolin Secrets*, brought out many gross inaccuracies in the original book, *Shaolin Secrets*, which had long been held as an authoritative resource of Shaolin boxing. Tang Hao's research findings brewed up a ferocious storm of protest. [16]

Military historian, Stanley Henning, created a similar storm in the Taijiquan community with his article (1994), *Ignorance, Legend and Taijiquan*, which chronicled the myth of Zhang Sanfeng. [17] The sentiments of the mindset that cling on to the myth are echoed in Henning's rebuttal essay (1995), *On Politically Correct Treatment of Myths in the Chinese Martial arts*, which concludes with the paragraph: [18]

> "The bottom line is, polite deference to the myths surrounding the Chinese martial arts is not only unwarranted but also unworthy of serious scholarship. It is high time that self-styled American martial arts "scholars" took a big step forward out of the 1920's and up to the threshold of the 21st century."

Chen Wangting was no doubt larger than life, but his story was only too human. There was no anecdote of him receiving divine revelation of boxing secrets nor even inspiration from "a crane fighting a snake."

Chen Wangting's martial prowess was legendary but not supernatural. His poem, *Song of Boxing Canon (Quan Jing Zong Ge* 拳经总歌), describes only an ingenious art.

Song of Boxing Canon
by Chen Wangting

Charging, retreating, back and forth, all can plainly see,
I fully rely on coiling as the basis of all my combat techniques.

To strike and push you have to step in.
Grappling and locking joints are more subtle;
Wrestling and throwing are easier to understand.
How many know to dodge or yield?

Retreat to feign loss may seem defeat;
T'is to lure in and counterattack to achieve victory.
Stick and adhere to follow is a wondrous skill,
From which, an offense launched flies out like a sling shot.

I block as I advance,
But hidden is my elbow strike to the heart.
Quick as the wind, I follow pounding with cannon fists.

My legs can sweep low,
Or raise high to strike the face.
Or I can kick to the side, left or right.

With front covered and back protected,
My defense cannot be breached.
Distract in the east to strike in the west, one must know.
Upper and lower body must be coordinated in mutual support,
One must not be late in advance to attack or retreat to dodge.

Covering to protect the head and face is common.

Piercing into the heart and internally within the ribs, that is rare.

A teacher who does not know this theory

How can he discuss the merits of the skills?

Taijiquan Diaspora

Taijiquan followed the exodus to Taiwan in 1949 upon the fall of the Nationalist Government in China, beginning its diaspora, and would spread to Hong Kong, Southeast Asia and the rest of the world. The art reached the shores of America in the mid-1960s with the arrival of Kuo Lienying in San Francisco and Cheng Manching in New York.

The practice of Taijiquan then was predominantly of the Yang Style, with a few of the other schools represented. Notably absent outside of China was the Taijiquan of the Chen Family tradition. A few practitioners of the Chen Style did make it to Taiwan, however. Among them were Pan Wing-chow (1905 – 1996), a student of Chen Fa'ke in Beijing, and Du Yuze (1896 – 1990), who had studied with Chen Yanxi, the father of Chen Fa'ke.

The "bamboo curtain" had kept Communist China closed to the rest of the world. Suddenly, in the spring of 1971, the West got a glimpse of Red China through the eyes of the U.S. Table Tennis Team. While on a tour in Japan, the team received a surprise invitation to visit China—an overture of the "ping pong diplomacy."

Then on February 21, 1972, the world awoke with the bombshell news that President Richard Nixon had arrived in Beijing for a historic visit, and the West feasted on the real-life footage of Mao's China. Two months later, on the anniversary of the U.S. Ping Pong Team's visit to China, the Chinese Ping Pong Team came to the United States. Their visit to the Berkeley campus is still fresh in my mind. The ping pong exhibition matches were simply electrifying; the gymnasium was brimming with excitement of the historic rapprochement.

In the fall of 1972 the culture of Chinese kungfu, hitherto confined in the West to the Chinatowns, was thrust into the American living rooms with the launch of the television series, *Kungfu*, which ran through 1975. It was about a Shaolin monk (David Carradine), roaming the Wild West in search of his half-brother. The theme centered on the ever cool sojourner extricating himself unscathed from the lawless gunslingers and sluggers with fascinating kungfu moves, which were always more graceful than violent. In the meanwhile, Bruce Lee came along and burst into the international scene with the movie, *Enter the Dragon* (1973). The song *Kungfu Fighting* by Carl Douglas (1974) filled the airwaves. The culture of kungfu was being etched into the Western mindset and with it, a resurgence of interest in Taijiquan.

Although Nixon's visit had begun the thaw in the Sino-U.S. relationship, and interest in China was surging in the United States, the door to China remained closed. China was having her own problems then. The excesses of the Red Guards, which had turned the country upside down during the Cultural Revolution (1966 – 1976), were being reined in. Zhou Enlai, the premier, whose statesmanship always served as a counterpoise to the revolutionary zeal of Mao Zedong, was falling ill with cancer. In 1974 Zhou was able to reinstate Deng Xiaoping, his protégé, who had been purged at the outset of the Cultural Revolution. But Deng was purged again, engineered by the "Gang of Four," headed by Jiang Qing, Mao's wife, a few months after his mentor-protector Zhou passed away in January 1976. Then that same year, on September 9, Mao Zedong too succumbed to age, and barely a month after, the Gang of Four precipitously fell from grace. Deng's political fortunes bounced back, and he was again reinstated. This time, nothing could dim his shining star, and by 1978 he had ascended to paramount leadership. His vision and pragmatism set the nation on the course to the unimaginable economic growth of present-day China. Deng Xiaoping's calligraphy, "Taijiquan is magnificent," ushered in the modern era of Taijiquan.

"Taijiquan is Magnificent" (Taijiquan Hao)

As the Cultural Revolution subsided, came a revival of martial arts in China, which trickled out into the world. Taijiquan and kungfu enthusiasts the world over were full of excitement to share in the arts as practiced in the motherland. Taijiquan practitioners in particular were anxious to discover Chen Family Taijiquan that they had only heard of.

At the very first opportunity, Miura Hideo led a group of Taijiquan practitioners from Japan to visit China in 1978, and was granted an audience with Vice-Premier Deng Xiaoping. Deng was touched by the Japanese devotion and love of Chinese culture, capped by the group's impromptu performance of Taijiquan for him. He applauded enthusiastically, "Taijiquan hao! (Taijiquan is magnificent!)." Hideo earnestly requested that the Chinese leader preserve the words in calligraphy to commemorate the historic occasion, which Deng graciously complied.

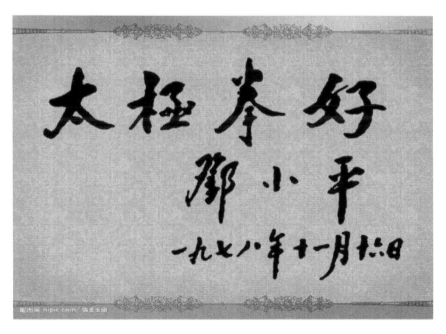

Fig. 4.2 "Taijiquan is magnificent." Calligraphy by Deng Xiaoping Nov 16, 1978

It would take Mr. Hideo three attempts, fighting and navigating through the Chinese bureaucracies, to get permission to travel in the hinterlands to Chen Village. In the third attempt he bypassed the foreign office, and went straight to the Henan provincial authorities with the help of the Tourist Department. Chen Village was hardly prepared to welcome any foreign visitors, but ready or not, in March 1981 Miura Hideo and his group of thirty descended on the village, with as many if not more officials and media people from both Japan and China. The televised broadcast of the event by NHK, Japan's premier TV station, literally dragged the village into the new century, and hoisted Chen Family Taijiquan onto the world stage. The world was captivated by the power-packed explosive fajin actions that interspersed the slow-motion demonstration, and more so by the wondrous kungfu skills of Taijiquan.

The visit spurred a deluge of more foreign visitors. In that year, over ten delegations from Japan alone followed. Visitors came from Singapore, Malaysia, Canada, Europe, and the United States, to see and learn Chen Family Taijiquan. Because four of the more accomplished Chen Village practitioners were always featured, they quickly came to be dubbed by the press as the *Si Da Jingang* (Four Great Gems). These are the current nineteenth generation masters, Chen Xiaowang, Chen Zhenglei, Wang Xi'an, and Zhu Tiancai.

In 1983, Chen Family Taijiquan went abroad for the first time to Japan. Chen Zhenglei and Wang Xi'an were part of the first delegation of the exhibition and goodwill tour, arranged by Miura Hideo. So great was the appreciation of the original tradition of Taijiquan that the Chen Village masters were honored with an audience by the emperor's brother at the Imperial Palace. Also, in the same year, the Singapore Wushu Association requested specifically for a Taijiquan instructor from Chen Village, and Zhu Tiancai was sent. Zhu and his sons continue to spearhead the promotion of Chen Taijiquan in Singapore and Malaysia.

Chen Xiaowang   Chen Zhenglei

Zhu Tiancai   Wang Xi'an

Si Da Jingangs (The Four Great Gems) of Chen Taijiquan:
The 19th generation grandmasters from Chen Village.

In 1985, Chen Xiaowang also visited Japan with Chen Zhenglei and Chen Guizhen, a female practitioner. Chen Zhenglei remembers the last conversation he had with Miura Hideo. Hideo expressed gratefulness and joy that he had finally fulfilled his dream of bringing Japanese practitioners to Chenjiagou and Chen Family Taijiquan to Japan. In June 8, 1986, Miura Hideo, who put heart and soul into the promotion of Chen Family Taijiquan, passed away. He paved the way for the propagation of the Chen Village art to the world.

The Four Great Jingangs (Gems) Come to the United States

It would be two more years before a Chen Village Taijiquan master made it to the United States. Chen Xiaowang came in 1988, accompanied by provincial officials on a goodwill tour, which took them to Tulsa, St. Louis, and San Francisco. He appeared as a special guest at the "Taste of China" Friendship Demonstrations that summer in Winchester, Virginia, and gave an electrifying performance:[19]

> Take yourself back to that year [1988], when taiji practice was almost all Yang school and the Chen style was relatively unknown. In the highlight Masters' Demonstrations, Chen Xiaowang's beginning slow movements appeared solid and expected. The first suggestion of things to come was the foot-stomp of the "Warrior Pounding Mortar" movement that resounded on the basketball court. Although the movements were mainly done with the familiar slowness, the postures were decidedly more martial in character. Then he let fly a punch with a fearsome grunt. It rang out like the crack of a whip, his silk uniform snapping on his body. The audience gasped as if struck by the "fajin." The power was self-evident. By this time, everyone was mesmerized, hanging on his every move. Quickened paces and a few more "fajin" interspersed with the slow movements. Coming to the end, he launched into a succession of explosive movements. Sparks seemed to be flying out. Finally, the rubber sole squealed sharply as he spun around to face the audience as he started. Thus he

concluded the demonstration to thunderous applause. This debut opened the floodgates of enthusiasm for the art that continues to reverberate to this day.

However, Taijiquan enthusiasts had to wait until the summer of 1996 before Chen Xiaowang returned to New York. Then the other Chen Village masters came too, with Chen Zhenglei arriving a month later that same year, in Washington D.C.; Zhu Tiancai followed in 1998 in Los Angeles; and Wang Xi'an in May 2000 in Houston. Since then, they have come almost yearly to conduct Taijiquan workshops around the country. Other well-known Chen masters also came to the United States, such as Chen Qingzhou, Zhang Zhijun, Ma Hong, and Feng Zhiqiang, as well as many from the younger generation. In addition, the masters of the other schools of Taijiquan too came from China, including the sons of Yang Chengfu, Yang Zhenji and Yang Zhenduo.

This marks a new chapter in the propagation of Taijiquan. Never before has there been such access to so many grandmasters and to such an abundance of resources of their teachings in videos and books. The "Four Great Jingangs," as well as the other great masters, travel the world over to spread and promote the art tirelessly, and students often journey in pilgrimage to China to see their masters.

During this period, I have come to know Chen Zhenglei, Chen Xiaowang, and Zhu Tiancai well, as a student and as a friend. I have helped organize their workshops in the United States every year. Working with these masters is both a privilege and a blessing. The bulk of the material in this book is drawn from the many hours spent with each of them over a decade.

Pushing hands with Chen Zhenglei

Chen Xiaowang adjusting a broadsword posture

Qinna push-hands with Zhu Tiancai

Figures 4.3 Author learning with three of the Four Jingangs (Grandmasters)

Praying at Longmen Grottoes, Luoyang, Henan.

At the entrance of the White Horse Taoist Temple

At the entrance of the Shaolin Temple
In a tour of Henan with Zhu Tiancai in 1999

Holding Lord Guanyu's
Spring & Autumn halberd

Jin Taiyang, Wang Xi'an, Zhu Tiancai, and author

Jin Taiyang (Kris Brenner), a very dedicated Chinese Martial artist, was residing in Chen Village when I visited with Zhu Tiancai in 1999. She is an indoor disciple of Wang Xi'an.

Practicing on the grounds of Chen Zhaopi Memorial in Chen Village.

5
Neijin Phenomenon

The Martial Art of Neijin

What is the particular fascination with Taijiquan given that one can develop fighting skills from any of the kungfu systems? There is a wondrous grace in the kungfu of Taijiquan—one hardly sees the exertion of physical strength, almost as if the laws of physics are being cheated. The power of the kungfu is "soft," unlike the crushing blow of a knock-out punch or a roundhouse kick. Taijiquan's kungfu is *neijin* 内劲 (internal strength).

Taijiquan is not modest about its kungfu prowess. A verse in *Taijiquan Classics* proclaims that it is superior to the other martial arts systems.[1]

Si zhi pang men shen duo 斯枝旁门甚多

Sui shi you qu bie 雖勢有區別

Gai bu wai hu zhuang qi rou 概不外乎壯欺弱

Man rang kuai er 慢讓快耳

You li da wu li 有力打无力

Shou man rang shou kuai 手慢讓手快

Shi jie xian tian zi ran zhi neng 是皆先天自然之能

Fei guan xue li er you wei ye 非關学力而有为也

Cha si liang bo jian jin zhi ju 察四两拨千斤之句

Xian fei li sheng 显非力勝

Guan mao die neng yu zhong zhi xing 观耄耋能御衆之形

Kuai he neng wei 快何能为

The systems of martial arts are many
Though they vary in techniques,
Most are of the stronger subduing the weaker,
Or of the faster beating the slower.
The strong overcoming the weak,
Or the slow hand losing to the fast,
Are in the order of natural abilities
Not necessarily related to kungfu training.
Examine the martial skill of Taijiquan,
"Four ounces overcoming a thousand pounds."
Clearly superior strength does not always prevail.
And an old master defeating a bunch of hooligans,
Shows that neither does the faster always win.

Witness the physique of a Taijiquan master—it is remarkable for its ordinariness, unlike the hulk of a professional wrestler. The gentle and slow kungfu training of Taijiquan does not appear formidable or intimidating. It seems that anyone can train to achieve the martial skills of Taijiquan. How can one not be intrigued or beguiled by such prospects? Best of all, one does not have to succumb to old age in Taijiquan—the practice matures gracefully with age.

So it is as portrayed in Ang Lee's movie, *Pushing Hands* (1992), showing grandpa Chu doing his Taijiquan exercises in the morning. Transplanted from Beijing to a New York suburb, it is clear at the outset that the chemistry between him and his non-Chinese-speaking American daughter-in-law, a stay-at-home writer, is all wrong, sharing the house, her with her chips, and him with his dumplings. Despite his son's best efforts and Confucian filial insistence, grandpa Chu leaves the house one day without telling anyone but only a note asking that they not look for him. He lands a job in a Chinese restaurant as a dishwasher. The dishes are piling up faster than he can get them out, causing a dish-jam, with the cooks standing over the woks waiting for clean plates to dish out the food. The hard-nosed boss decides to fire him on the spot and he pleads for another chance. Completely unsympathetic, the boss goes on a self-righteous tirade and insults him as a useless parasitic worker of the Chinese communist welfare system, ignorant of real hard work in the glorious capitalistic way of America.

The berating stings him so badly that he decides to quit, but not without putting up a stand for his old country and his dignity sullied by the insults. He curses at the capitalist-exploiter of human labor and challenges the boss to physically move him from the spot where he stands. Enraged the boss charges at him and punches him, but ends up hurting himself, without budging old Chu a bit. He orders his staff to throw the old man out, and with reluctance they try. But Chu stands immovable from his spot as the cooks and busboys heave and shove at him. His face reddening and body shaking with rage, the boss threatens to fire the whole crew if they fail to throw the old man out. In a show of solidarity with grandpa Chu, the entire kitchen staff take off their aprons and walk out. The boss then calls in the hooligans to deal with the old man still standing on the same spot. The thugs descend on him all at once, but each one is repelled effortlessly, falling off like flies, by some invisible adroitness of the old man's Taijiquan skills. That is the *miao* (magical wonder) of Taijiquan kungfu, the stuff of neijin, not of mere physical strength.

This depiction is not a hyperbolic exaggeration of Taijiquan's martial prowess. An old clip posted in YouTube shows Cheng Manching, one of the early masters who popularized Taijiquan in the United States, repelling his students like kids, sending them flying off, and also shows him withstanding the push of several without being moved.[2]

Chen Xiaowang stood on one leg, taking a drink of water at leisure, as he was pushed without being budged, which was captured on Taiwan national TV.[3] To stay a concerted push of twenty persons is impressive, but the drama obscures the kungfu skill of "immovable as a mountain." Chen Xiaowang's kungfu was severely tested by Longwu, the two-time strongman champion of China and hailed the "Asian Hercules" by the press. The strongman could lift and nudge a car into a parallel parking space between two cars and move an 18-wheeler freight truck. Xiaowang was 67, but Longwu, half his age and twice his weight, failed to move him in an open challenge of three one-minute rounds.[4]

We have moved and shoved at furniture that weighs a lot more than an average Taiji master. Surely then to push someone standing still over would not be a great challenge. The Taijiquan master, of course, is not a piece of furniture. He does not react to the push by fighting back, but adjusts his body structure internally to redirect the force to the ground. The internal dynamics keeps the master's posture in accord with Taiji principles—at ease in balance.

Nevertheless, skepticism lingers. Taijiquan cannot be more benign and further from the speed and power of combat. The training does not drill the combinations of punch, kick, and block, or the techniques of wrestling, grappling, and take-downs. This incongruence is not about an Occidental mindset meeting the abstruse Orient. The enigma is equally bewildering to an inquiring Chinese native.

Taijiquan is not without vigor or strength. It may not have the fast tempo of aerobics or kick-boxing, but the exercise carries the same physical loads. Whether moving slowly or quickly, the practitioner is bearing the same weight of the body's entire frame. Slowness in motion does not lessen the force of gravity. In fact slowing down a weight-bearing task requires more control, and thus more effort. Try to do push-ups in slow motion, and you will see the extra effort needed. An obvious advantage of slow motion is that it allows you to pace the action to the body's capacity to sustain the workout longer. You can burn off fat in Taijiquan without being consumed in exhaustion.

To peel a little off the mystery, think of the unorthodox soft training method as a process to condition the mind and body to a desired state, just as the tempering of steel does for its tensile strength. The objective is not to master how slowly to execute a movement, but to instill the body with Taiji principles to cultivate *neijin* (internal strength). In so doing, the body gains comprehension of the range of factors governing motion and strength.

The "Hidden Power" of Neijin

Taijiquan kungfu is characterized by an absence of strenuous physical strength and a flair of incredible power—the "hidden power" of neijin. If you saw a burly guy suddenly grapple and armlock a smaller person from behind, subduing him in pain, you would think of it only as bullying. If instead, the big bully was thrown to the ground, you would applaud the wrestling skill of the smaller guy. Such an incident occurred in Chen Village in 1953, but the outcome was far more dramatic—it exemplified the "hidden power" of neijin.

In his early forties, Chen Zhaoxu, while in the shadow of his legendary father, Chen Fa'ke, was already acknowledged as a Taijiquan expert in his own right. Chen Lizhi, his contemporary of the same age, addressed him as "little ninth uncle" as Lizhi was of a generation younger. Lizhi was a great deal bigger and taller than his 130-pound uncle. He had only heard of his uncle's martial skill but had never seen him in action. Lizhi was also a skilled Taijiquan practitioner.

As it happened, both were attending a ceremony to welcome guests who had come to pay homage to their ancestral home in Chen Village. The bigger Chen Lizhi was trailing a step behind the smaller Chen Zhaoxu. Unable to resist his penchant for mischief, Lizhi suddenly grabbed Zhaoxu's arm from behind, twisting it in an armlock, and teased, "Little ninth uncle, if someone from behind ..." Before he could finish, Lizhi was seen propelled flying 10 feet up, hitting the ceiling beam. As he came crashing head down, Zhaoxu caught him in time to save him from injuries, and chided, "Are you looking to be killed?" While the visitors were nonplussed by the drama, the local folks were totally delighted to be treated to a display of such wondrous neijin. Soon, the whole village was talking about Chen Zhaoxu's "hidden jin" just as we would of spectacular sports plays. The incident is cherished in Chen Village by the byline, "If not for Chen Lizhi's prank on his little ninth uncle, Chen Zhaoxu's hidden miao (wondrous) jin might not have been revealed."[5] It left an indelible impression on his son, Chen Xiaowang, and marked a turning point for the lad of eight then, inspiring him to realize his father's Taiji heritage.[6]

Johnny Coulon's Strength

The amazing feats of human strength are not confined to Chinese martial arts. Johnny Coulon was reported to have "superhuman" strength. Mr. Coulon was a bantamweight boxing champion from 1910 to 1914. After retiring from the ring in 1920, he appeared in vaudevilles, billing himself as the man who no one could lift, a challenge that was made more tantalizing by his midget frame, standing at 5 feet and weighing only 118 pounds. He became a cause celebre in Paris when the Parisian strongman of the day, Yves le Boulanger, who just a few weeks earlier had been hailed for his Herculean strength, failed to lift him. The New York Times on Dec 21, 1920, headlined this incredible feat,[7]

PARIS PUTS COULON SECOND TO NEWTON
Scientists Acclaim Him as a Discoverer of New Physiological Phenomena.

While the scientists were nonplussed, Coulon made no claims of any paranormal powers and only confessed that he discovered his skill by accident. Meanwhile, Johnny was happy with his star billing, earning him more than enough to open his famous gym in Chicago.

From the perspective of Taiji theory, Coulon had been able to break the participant's lifting force. His right-hand finger pressed against the side of the lifter's neck and his left hand controlled the lifter's wrist to dislocate the latter's center, and at the same time, his body adjusted to maintain balance, much as Taiji masters would do.

Fig. 5.1 Wrestler Afflis trying to lift Johnny Coulson.
LIFE photo by Francis Miller.[8]

Posture and Strength

We associate muscle size with strength. Strength comes from muscles, but muscle bulk does not determine body strength. The force of any physical task, simple or demanding, is produced by body muscles working together, which relates to posture.

The incident of my economist friend, Harry V., changing tires for the first time, illustrates strength in posture. With wrench in hand, he instinctively bent forward to reach for the bolt, and proceeded to undo it, his arm extended along the bar of the wrench. Since only the component of the force perpendicular to the handle counted toward torque, a large part of Harry's muscular force was unproductive. More debilitating was the awkward posture—head and chest leaned forward, almost falling over—unwittingly assumed for a convenient reach. As he applied force, the body had to expend muscle energy to keep the posture from falling. Much of the work of Harry's muscles went to keep his balance and to produce sweat, and only a small part to the task at hand, to generate the torque to undo the bolt.

So though by no means a weakling, Harry failed to move the nut in the initial attempt. Inexperienced and inept as he might be with things mechanical, he quickly realized that he was not doing it right. Just as he instinctively went for a convenient reach by stooping forward, with the same instinct he adjusted his body, moving closer to the rim. Changing his body alignment and the angle of grip, he found a better leverage. By the time he came to the third bolt, he had become proficient. He had found the right posture, the right alignment, and the right grip. He could utilize his leg muscles, thus more of his body mass, to power his action. By trial and error, he got the muscle groups to work together better through proper posture and alignment.

Time is not a critical factor in mundane tasks, permitting repeated trials and errors to get the action right. Sports or martial arts do not afford such luxury. A fastball zips into home plate in less than half a second. Pitched even at lesser speeds, bunting a baseball would be scary for a novice. To hit a home run, the bat must be swung hard enough to hit the ball at about 70 mph with precision, at the right spot and proper angle, all within a split second. When a punch comes straight at the face, there is no time to think, let alone try different modes of intercepting.

In sports, martial arts, or any performance arts, training disciplines the body to move in balanced postures, so that muscles can work in concert to produce the power and speed needed. Stellar performances are an exhibition of cultured strength and power of the different parts of the body working together as a whole body. The grace and poise of Midori's triple axel jump is a discipline of the whole body.

Tiger Woods' Long Drive

We think of Tiger Woods' 400-yard drives as spectacular because we struggle with drives at half the range, but not as magical. Actually, at the speed the golf ball takes off at the tee—180 mph of Tiger's drive—a projectile can attain a maximum range of 726 yards, launched at a 45-degree angle. A range of 400 yards would be short! That, of course, is only a calculation on paper. The much reduced range is due to air resistance and wind, and the effects of turbulence immediate to the ball in flight. Dr. Raymond Penner finds that to achieve maximal long-range drives under atmospheric conditions, the launch angle should be less than 15 degrees.[9]

There are three distinct phases of the golf drive. The first is the speed of the clubhead at impact; the second, the collision between the clubface and the golf ball; and the third, the flight of the ball. The player's control is only in phase one, to generate the highest speed possible at the club's downswing and to strike the ball accurately for a correct angle of launch. Right at the instant of impact, physics takes over. The take-off speed of the ball is determined by collision science, and the range of the drive by aerodynamics of projectiles, subject to wind and atmospheric conditions.

So knowing the physics is the easiest part of the game. The hard part is to generate the speed of the clubhead and to strike the ball accurately. For a 400-yard range the clubhead must strike the ball at about 125 mph. The arms' muscles alone are not enough to generate the horsepower necessary to produce a club swing at lesser speeds. The power must be recruited from muscles of the upper and lower body working together in the proper order.

Tiger Woods describes how the whole body works in his power swing, "I try to swing the club back with everything—hips, shoulders, arms and hands—working together. When I turn my shoulders fully, they accommodate the swinging of my arms to create a strong, unified package at the top of the backswing."[10] He underscores the point that he does not use his arms alone, characterizing the swing as a "soft arm" shot: "in each case the key for me is matching my arm and body speed to control distance and spin. I call it my *'soft arm'* shot because the feeling is that *my arms are connected to my lower body* as it turns through the shot. In other words, I don't try to power the shot with my arms and wrists alone." (Italics added.)

Therein lies the difficulty, to get the hips, shoulders, arms and hands to work together in the swing. The body is stubborn and acts with convenience of habits: it tends to recruit muscles immediate to the action, namely, the muscles of the arms and shoulders to do the work, not incorporating those of the other parts of the body and not coordinating between the left and the right.

To improve the power of one's golf swing, the key is to first break the habitual pattern of muscle recruitment. This may not be addressed by the standard modes of power-training, such as lifting weights or swinging against a resistance belt.

The unorthodox slow-motion methodology of Taijiquan functions to restrain the body from its habitual action, then trains to engage muscles of the whole body, from legs to waist, up back to shoulders, arms, and hands, to work in proper coordination. This Taiji methodology can be applied to complement the training in golf or any other sports in generating power.

Golf may not be as dramatic as breaking bricks, but the force produced in Tiger's long drives is about 2,250 lbs! The force arises in the collision between the clubhead and the golf ball. Viewing it from the clubface at impact, you see the ball squished almost flat and then regains shape to fly off. This occurs in less than half a millisecond. The 2,250 lb force is created in the brief moment of collision. Unfortunately, this enormous force cannot be harnessed for one's personal use, like lifting furniture.

Breaking Concrete Blocks

A karate expert breaking 10 slabs of concrete in one blow is certainly an impressive feat. When we accidentally run into a wall, unwittingly inviting a confrontation with concrete, we seldom escape unscathed. So we applaud the triumph of the human body over concrete when we see the concrete slabs smacked to pieces by bare hands.

The drama is in the staging. When we see a sledgehammer being wielded to land on a performer's head, we cringe in fear for the poor bloke. But the hammer strikes and breaks the stack of bricks placed on the head with no harm to the performer. [11] Another frightful demonstration is a performer lying sandwiched between two beds of nails, and a huge cement block is laid on top to further compress the body between the nails. [12] Then several assistants hammer away at the huge cement block and break it with no harm to the performer. Some claim the feats as paranormal, while skeptics dismiss them as tricks. As it turns out, there is no trickery, nor is there supernatural ability, only trained skills with the help of physics, rather than in spite of it. [13]

Fig. 5.2 Physicist David Willey sandwiched between two beds of nails

Contrary to common experience, bone is stronger than concrete. Bone can withstand 40 times more force than concrete. Imagine a concrete cylinder comparable in size to a bone under compression, and you can get a sense of its weakness relative to bone. Indeed, the femur of an adult can withstand a compressive force of about 23,000 lbs. [14] This is very comforting scientific knowledge, of course, if you want to break concrete blocks. In a collision between the bones in your hand and concrete, at the force where one of them will break, it is no longer just faith, but scientific fact that the concrete is the one that will give way. Nevertheless, you can get hurt unless you are trained.

Ronald E. McNair had a 5th degree black belt in karate and also a Ph.D. in physics. Sadly, he perished with six other astronauts in the Space Shuttle Challenger that tragically exploded in flight on Jan 28, 1986. As a karate expert, he knew how to break concrete slabs and as a physicist, he knew that breaking bricks was just a collision between the hand and the bricks.

He studied the speed and energy, and the elastic properties of the materials in breaking.[15] Using strobe lights, he found that beginning students could swing karate chops at about 6 m/s (20 ft/s) and black belts like McNair himself, at 14 m/s (46 ft/s). He also calculated from the elastic properties of materials that for an average fist mass of 0.7 kg (1.54 lbs), the impact speed needed to break a concrete block was only 5 m/s, and for a pine board, 4.2 m/s.

These are ordinary speeds, which anyone with little or no practice can easily attain. For example, if you let your fist free-fall from a height of 3 ft, it will reach the speed of 4.2 m/s. So from the physics standpoint, breaking boards should be an enterprise that anyone can do with little instruction. To convince her Physics 101 class of the collision principle, Dr. Juliet Brosing had her students parade up one by one to break pine boards.[16] You could hear the chuckles and see the smile on their faces, a mix of satisfaction and surprise at their own strength, as just about everyone succeeded in breaking the boards in the first attempt.

Highly trained experts are setting amazing records breaking all kinds of materials with bare hands. One of the most prolific breakers is Norwegian Narve Leret, a Kyokushin karate master who holds 14 Guinness World Records. He burst into the world breaking scene on December 5, 2006, breaking a record 90 concrete blocks, each 3.5 inch thick, in 18 seconds. It was an exhibition of super but human strength, a highly trained skill of using the whole body.[17] Narve was relaxed and focused; the muscle groups of his entire body worked in coordination as he brought his hand down to bear on the concrete, shattering the blocks arranged in stacks placed in a row. There was no drama save that of the crashing concrete, stack by stack, in rhythmic timing, as he moved down the row. Amazingly, he topped the record on November 16, 2008, breaking 700 in 26 seconds. The concrete blocks were stacked up in two rows, wide enough for him to walk in between, and just below the height of his waist. In the action, he hopped along between the stacks, pounding away more efficiently than a stamping machine, with both his fists crashing into the concrete slabs at each hop, in a clever use of the whole body mass.[18] Narve talked of his dedication to training, which incorporated meditation and slow-motion practice to cultivate focus to use the whole body in action.

Momentum

The force that we commonly experience results from a change in motion, more precisely, a change in momentum. (The momentum of an object is the product of its mass and velocity.) We have a good sense of the factors of mass and speed in force. We fear being hit a car because of its mass compared to that of a bicycle. We also know that the higher the speed the more devastating the car crashes.

Force is related to change in momentum by Newton's Second Law of Motion, which is expressed mathematically as:

Average Force = Change in momentum/Time Duration.

The equation confirms what we experience: the larger the change in momentum (mass and speed), the greater the force generated. The inverse relationship of the time duration says that the shorter the time it takes for the change to occur, the greater the force. We experience the factor of time duration often enough when we apply brakes to bring a car to a halt (bringing its momentum to zero). The huge surge of force generated when we slam on the brakes is the short time duration in which the car's momentum is brought to zero.

However, we sometimes misinterpret what we experience. For instance, we think that the punching machine in a carnival measures the force of one's punch, and we think of a knock-out punch as of tremendous force. In fact, it is misleading to talk of the force of a punch per se. The same punch does not generate the same force.

There are two distinct forces involved in a punch action. The first is the force of the muscles generating the motion of the fist. The second is the force of impact of the fist striking its target. This impact force depends on what is struck, a pine board, a brick, or a pillow. So the same punch can generate different magnitudes of force.

The force in the memorable 1965 knock-out punch in round one by young Muḥammad Ali, was the impulse force of Ali's right fist catching the head of Sonny Liston squarely. Ali did not generate the force, only the motion to deliver the swift punch, and the corresponding momentum. Liston contributed as much by being caught in the solid impact. If Liston had turned his head just a bit, it would not have been as devastating.

Whether it be boxing, karate, kungfu, tennis, or golf, the key to greater force is to build up the momentum in the strike, kick, throw, or swing. This can be done either with more speed or more mass, the two factors of momentum. A trained fighter can throw a punch about three times faster than a novice, thus increasing threefold the momentum in advantage. There is, of course, also the obvious advantage of speed to reach the target before it moves away. The other is to increase the mass in the action.

Using the Whole Body

One cannot do much to increase the mass of a fist even if one puts on more weight. More weight would also mean more body mass to move around, affecting speed and agility. However, much can be done to increase the mass factor by involving more of the body mass in the power action. This is the idea of using the whole body.

We have seen the clever use of the whole body by Narve Leret in breaking concrete blocks. The whole-body mass is employed when a defensive linebacker crashes into a running back. Hurling one's whole body at a target comes at a great price, the loss of control, which accounts for the many injuries in football. This whole body maneuver may seem easy, but it takes courage, and its applications are limited.

The sport that takes a most notable advantage of body mass is sumo wrestling. The advantage of weight works in sumo wrestling because the ring is small, about 15 feet in diameter, and the rules are simple. You win if you can force your opponent outside the ring or cause him to fall, that is, any part of his body except the sole, to touch the ground. In the tight ring space, a behemoth wrestler can bulldoze his opponent out of the ring with sheer mass. The 6' 8" Akebono (Hawaiian Chad Rowan) used his 501 lbs to the fullest advantage to thrust, slam, or slap many of his opponents off the ring, which gained him induction into the highest rank of yokozuna (grand champion) in January 1993, a historic first for a foreigner. Another outsider, a Samoan giant, Musashimaru (Fiamalu Penitani), weighing slightly heavier at 520 lbs, but shorter at 6' 3" also gained the coveted title of yokozuna in 1999.

Massive weight is necessary by the nature of sumo. Sumo wrestlers consume great quantities of chankonabe, a stew rich with proteins of fish, chicken, tofu, beef, and vegetables. Though of dubious culinary distinction, the special diet without fail fattens the sumo wrestlers to the right bulk. But they keep agile and flexible—they do the split—as they put on weight. They know that sheer size is no substitute for skills in techniques.

By the start of the 2002 season, the phase of dominance by the huge Pacific Islanders had come to a close; they were being replaced by Mongolian wrestlers. At the pinnacle in 2006 was a 22-year old Mongolian, Asashoryu Akinori (Dolgorsuren Dagvadorj), standing at 6 ft, and weighing a light 321 lbs. Promoted to yokozuna in March 2003, he had garnered along the way, quite an impressive number of sumo records under his mawashi loin belt. On 11/28/2005 Asahi Shimbun, the leading Japanese daily proclaimed:

"Yokozuna Asashoryu, sumo's most dominant wrestler ever, won yet again Sunday to close the Kyushu Grand Sumo Tournament with a 14-1 record and an unprecedented seventh straight title (Emperor's Cup)."

To celebrate the occasion, Japan's prime minister, Junichiro Koizumi was on hand to personally award him the coveted Emperor's Cup at the record-breaking consecutive seventh win.

There are six Grand Tournaments a year, and at each tournament every rikishi (wrestler), including the yokozuna, faces 15 opponents. The champion of the tournament is the one with the highest number of wins. At each tournament, a yokozuna has to fight 15 opponents, each intent on toppling him, as beating a yokozuna offers the quickest ascent in the hierarchy. The display of sheer power in a sumo match is exciting enough, but Asashoryu propels the sport to new levels by the virtuosity of his incredible skills that rely on the body's waist power and rotational motions.

The Magic of Rotational Momentum

If there is a secret in martial arts it is the magic of the body's rotational motions. The body can harness more of its mass to increase momentum in action by coordinating its rotational motions, from the feet, ankles, knees to hips, continuing up the spine to shoulders, elbows, wrists, and finally to the hands. This of course presumes the body's perceptivity and discipline of the different parts of the body.

However, our body is often not accustomed to rotational motions. We get disoriented if we are spun around. Our body is more familiar and comfortable with linear motion. That is why we react instinctively to a push by aggressively pushing back. But in a linear dimension, the one with more muscle mass wins. If one is not as fast or as strong, one has to resort to rotational motions in strategy. By negotiating in arcs, one can avoid a direct-line encounter of force against force.

Corresponding to momentum and inertia of linear motion are angular momentum and moment of inertia of rotational motion. But training the body to comprehend and experience the concepts is more important than knowing the physics. The execution of waist power that underlies all power-actions requires the body's fluency of rotational motion. Taijiquan methodically builds this body comprehension through the training of coiling motion called "silk-reeling" (chansi), which is discussed in chapter 8.

Taijiquan's Neijin (Internal Strength)

Neijin 内 劲 translates as "internal jin." The character *nei* 内 means "inner, interior, and internal." The operative word is *jin* 劲, defined as "vigor, power, or energy." [19] Its meaning is more revealing etymologically: the left radical 巠 (internal river) qualifies the right radical 力 *li* (strength). That is, jin is strength that is trained and refined. In Taijiquan, the terms jin and neijin are synonymous, with the latter used to emphasize its internal or hidden character.

Though both jin and li refer to strength, they are differentiated in martial arts, with li often denigrated as brute force associated with sheer muscles. The strength of jin does not appear to come from the musculature. The power of jin, when issued, shows no signs of physical loads. The player remains relaxed and calm, in contrast to the huffing and puffing in exerting physical strength.

Taijiquan training is about building neijin as the body's core strength, but it does not show physically like the sculpted body of a body-builder. However, invigorated with jin, the body exudes the beauty of Taijiquan mastery:

Wai han jian mei 外含见美
Nei han jian gongfu 内含见功夫

Externally, one enjoys the aesthetics,
Internally, one discerns the mastery.

The presence of jin is unmistakable in good Taijiquan. The softness of Taijiquan is not one of weakness, like the burdened motion of a sickly person or the droopiness of a wilting plant. Rather the opposite, the form, powered by jin from within, is spirited and full of vibrancy, like a fireman's hose charged with the energy of gushing water. In short, jin is everywhere in good Taijiquan, its power ever ready for kungfu.

The aesthetics of Taijiquan draws from the fluidity and power of jin—a composite of softness and hardness. The motion flows as a river, but the base is solid as a mountain. Agile, lively, and spirited, the body changes with natural ease. The magic of jin lies in the balance of *rou* (softness) and *gang* (hardness).

Jin has Gang (Hard) and Rou (Soft)

Think of jin as a vocabulary of the art that refers to strength, power, or energy arising from the motion of Taijiquan. The jin terminology in application—neutralizing jin, listening jin, sticking jin, following jin, and so on—indicates the kungfu versatility of jin. More specifically, jin is categorized as *peng, lü, ji, an, cai, lie, zhou, kao,* which correspond to the eight trigrams of bagua. This will be discussed in chapter 9.

The fundamental concept of jin is its dual character: *rou* 柔 (softness) and *gang* 刚 (hardness), which manifest the yin and yang of jin respectively. We can review the yin-yang principles of Taiji in the context of jin duality. *Gang* and *rou* are complementary and mutually reinforcing (*gang rou xiang ji*); within *gang* jin there is *rou*, and within *rou*, there is *gang* (*gang zhong you rou, rou zhong you gang*); the *rou* and *gang* of jin are not static, and their dynamics breathes spirit and liveliness in the form. The ideal jin is both *gang* and *rou,* not lacking in either, namely, the yin-yang balance of jin. The *rou* of jin instills fluidity and the *gang* of jin imparts power.

Taijiquan training tempers hard jin to be soft, and soft jin to be hard so that when expressed, *gang* jin has the agility and liveliness of *rou,* and *rou* jin has the power of *gang.* The wondrous marvel of Taijiquan kungfu springs from the yin-yang balance of jin, like the industrial marvel of steel with its hardness of strength and softness of malleability.

Taijiquan kungfu, in essence, is the "use of softness to overcome hardness" (*yi rou ke gang*). However, its efficacy lies in the *rou-gang* balance of jin. Indeed, the *rou-gang* balance underpins the skills that epitomize Taijiquan kungfu:

Yin jin luo kong 引劲落空
Lead attacking force to emptiness

Si liang bo qian jin 四两拨千斤
Four ounces repels a thousand pounds

Jie li da ren 借力打人
Use opponent's force to strike back

Demonstration of a Spectrum of Jin

Taijiquan art form is like Chinese calligraphy—the strength of jin is like the strength of brush strokes. The form expression is an individual's body comprehension of Taiji principles, so the artistic flavors of jin vary between experts.

Taiji enthusiasts in our area were most fortunate to be treated to an unforgettable performance that displayed a spectrum of jin by three of the *Four Great Jingangs* (Gems) of Chen Family Taijiquan. In the summer of 2000, a confluence of unplanned events brought together Chen Xiaowang, Chen Zhenglei, and Zhu Tiancai at the beautiful home of Anne and Bill Charrier in Potomac, Maryland. This was a rare occasion as the masters had not been together in an intimate setting for some 20 years since they left Chen Village and went their separate ways. It was particularly special for me, as it was the ceremony of my induction (bai shi) as Chen Zhenglei's disciple. Following the feast of Maryland's "silver queen" corns and Bill's BBQ chicken, the grandmasters celebrated with a most memorable demonstration.[20]

Rou Jin Full of Gang Power

Zhu Tiancai performed a section of *New Frame Routine One*, from the first "Buddha Pounding Mortar Board" (Jingang Daodui) to the third Jingang Daodui. The *rou* soft motion flow—silky and effortless—was vibrant with *gang* power from within. Energy coiled through body and limbs, arriving at the extremities precisely like a wave lapping on the shores. The subtle and small circular movements of the hands were clearly integrated with the core of the body's internal energy. When he settled into "Single Whip" (Danbian), the entire body's motion stilled at the dantian center in the commanding posture. With arms spanning left to right, the bow-stance, arched like a bridge, rooted solidly as an oak tree. It was a picture-perfect exemplification of strength and "relaxed expansiveness" (*shu zhan da fang*)—an embodiment of jin. The short performance brought out the shades of *rou jin* that betrayed no lack of *gang* power.

Gang Jin Full of Rou

It is always a treat to see Chen Xiaowang's signature fajin, an explosive release of jin. But in the intimate confines of a living room packed with thirty-some students and friends, the experience of Chen Xiaowang's fajin power that evening was especially electrifying.

Chen Xiaowang began by dispelling the misconception that Taijiquan was only about slow motion. Jovially, he recounted what someone had described to him that Taijiquan looked like slicing a water melon, offering one half to the left (he gestured with his left hand sliding forward under the right) and then the other half to the right (he reversed the gesture to the right). He explained that the soft training was to temper the body and calm the mind to develop jin. Then one could issue jin at will with the fist, elbow, or any part of the body. As he completed the sentence, the front of his shoulder exploded in a strike. His body quaked and the shirt snapped as he let out a fearsome grunt. The audience was awestruck by the fajin power in the intimacy of the living room. He then followed with a few movements in slow motion to expound that jin power came from softness. To get the point across, he suddenly changed pace, and let out one fajin after another, in a medley of elbows, fists, hands, shoulders, and chest. Sparks seemed to be flashing from his body like a July 4 fireworks, each fajin equally as stunning and frightful to the last. Any ghosts or spirits present would have been scared away! The audience thundered in appreciation of such a virtuoso *gang jin*—an exemplary display of *gang jin* full of *rou*.

Gang in Rou and Rou in Gang

Chen Zhenglei is of smaller build of the three masters, but the power of the coiling energy projected in his performance was in no way diminished. The energy released by the foot stamping seemed measured to test the floor's firmness. Interspersed between the qi-energized soft movements, he freely let out fajins from the *Cannon Fist* routine. The fajins worked to a crescendo as he jumped into the air, spun completely around, and landed with the solid boom of a crashing boulder. In the "Fan Hua Wu Siu" movement, he did not spare the floor. The chandelier creaked out an awkward chime and the piano shook, but fortunately no antique pieces fell. The audience again thundered with applause at the range of jin demonstrated.

Qinna Manifestation of Rou Jin

We see the *gang* of neijin by its explosive power and its potential to inflict damage. On the other hand, the *rou* of neijin is not evident, but rou jin's potential to harm is no less formidable. Rou jin is used in *qinna* 擒拿, the art of capturing body joints, which incorporates seizing tendons, pinching nerves, and pressuring acupuncture points (*zhua jin na mai* 抓筋拿脈) to immobilize an opponent, and also the art of escape from same.

Author reading pledge of discipleship to Chen Zhenglei

Bowing to Chen Zhenglei

Bowing to Chen Xiaowang

Bowing to Zhu Tiancai

Ren Guangyi, Lu Xiaolin, Chen Xiaowang   Lu Lili , Anthony Goh, Chen Zhenglei

Author was inducted as the first American disciple of Chen Zhenglei in July 26, 2000, witnessed by Chen Xiaowang and Zhu Tiancai. He was also inducted as a disciple of Chen Xiaowang in 2006 in a Chen Village ceremony.

Qinna is an essential part of Taijiquan's kungfu repertoire. Used in close-quarter combat, qinna forces the opponent to submit in pain. The reason one cannot maneuver to escape a qinna capture is because the body stiffens up in pain. However, if one can relax and follow the qinna pressure, one can escape from being locked. The skill to sense the vulnerability of joints and nerves, to capture or to escape, comes from the softness principle of rou jin.

Steve C. is a longtime student of martial arts in Florida. He wears a pony tail like Steven Segal, and has the height and physique of a bouncer, which he once was. He is proficient with armlocks, which he had used professionally without fail to subdue many a rowdy client who had a drink too many. Steve had heard that many kungfu masters had tried but failed to armlock Chen Xiaowang. Piqued with curiosity, he had wanted badly to try it himself to believe it. His chance came in the late summer of 2001 at the master's workshop in Jacksonville, Florida, when during a break he asked if he could test his armlock on Master Chen, who obliged.

Steve was given free rein to ply his armlocking skill. While he worked all the angles, the master showed no sign of resistance or struggle. Tried as hard as he could, the bouncer's armlock had not the slightest effect on Chen. The students watching urged Steve on with more effort, and it was evident from the sweat beading on Steve's head that he was not sparing the brawn of his frame. At the instant of Steve nodding that he was completely satisfied with the armlock that no one had escaped from before, Chen had amazingly freed himself with nary a wiggle, felling the exhausted Steve to the ground like a child.

Then turning the table, Chen proceeded to do a simple qinna on Steve who screamed in pain when it seemed that Chen had not even applied the qinna. The class roared in belly full of laughter.

Qinna on an Index Finger

That same day at lunch, Kam Lee, my friend and the local kungfu master who sponsored the workshop, asked Chen Xiaowang with a tinge of mischief what if someone tried to do qinna on just an index finger, which seemed so vulnerable. Still fresh with the fun we had at the workshop, Master Chen nonchalantly offered Kam his index finger, "Ni na ba" (Go ahead). Kam was gentle at first, but then quickly realized that his caution was unwarranted, and so proceeded to bend and twist in every direction at the phalanges with all his might to no effect. Chen Xiaowang betrayed no sign of struggle; with rou jin his finger yielded to Kam's efforts like a rubber stub. Moments later, changing the play, the master did a counter-qinna on Kam, causing him to fall off the chair in pain, creating a little consternation in the restaurant.

When I try to qinna the masters, it seems like there are no joints to capture. Their rou jin allows them to follow and divert the pressure against the joints. They use the same rou jin to decipher the vulnerability and nerves of the joints to control them, so that with little effort, one writhes in pain in their qinna.

While the basis of qinna skills is rou jin, the jin response cannot be deficient in *gang*. If the rou jin in qinna lacks *gang*, the jin cannot maintain control in the change. The ease of change between *gang* and *rou* lies in the yin-yang balance of jin. It is the mastery of the *rou-gang* of jin that Chen Xiaowang saved the Henan official tourism and trade promotion tour in Singapore in April 1987.

Chen Xiaowang's Jin Saves the Promotional Tour

The promoters knew well the two cultural products native to Henan Province that would appeal most to the overseas Chinese in Singapore— Shaolin kungfu and Taijiquan. So, Shaolin monk, Shi Yongshou, representing Shaolin Quan, and Chen Xiaowang representing Taijiquan, were made a part of the delegation of 28 that included artists, acrobats, and Henan government officials. The local media played up the news of the two kungfu stars in flesh and blood, plucked from Shaolin Temple and Chen Village, hitherto seen only in movies or wuxia fiction. Posters of the two masters in formidable poses were plastered all over the city.

Lin Jinping, a judo instructor in the Singapore army and an avid martial artist, saw an impressive performance on TV of the fast and dramatic Shaolin, balanced by the soft and graceful Taijiquan. What piqued his interest most was what occurred during the interview of Chen Xiaowang after the performance. Mr. Tan, the interviewer, asked Chen if it was true that he could free himself from any qinna hold as he had read. It was clear from the query that he was not expecting a verbal explanation, so Chen gestured to him to try. Tan proceeded to do what he believed was an impossible-to-escape armlock on him. Chen Xiaowang effortlessly wriggled his arm and freed himself. The 226-pound Singapore master, well known locally as a champion and veteran of several free sparring contests in Taiwan and Hong Kong, and a qinna expert, was amazed at how easily Chen Xiaowang undid his armlock. To be sure, he tried it four times, and each time the escape was as easy as the first. Warming up, Chen Xiaowang then beckoned three of the stage hands to come forward to help. The four armlocked Chen's arms, two on each side. They grabbed his fingers, wrists, elbows, and upper arms. Chen did not resist and allowed each person to get the best possible hold. It seemed that Chen was totally immobilized and that it would need Houdini's magic to escape from the human chain of grappling locks on his arms. But with a short burst of jin, which appeared like an easy jerk, Chen Xiaowang was free and all the handlers were seen falling off from him, as in Ang Lee's movie. The promoters were all delighted with the impromptu demonstration of such remarkable kungfu skills of Taijiquan, which created more talk and more publicity. Mr. Lin, the judo master watching it live on TV was fascinated but at the same time could not help but wonder that it might be fixed. He thought surely he could judo throw him.

An Intrusion that Further Boosted the Promotion

A couple of days later to cap off the official welcoming, a banquet was held to honor the Chinese masters and entourage. Among the guests were government officials, dignitaries from Singapore's sports organizations, local martial arts masters, and aficionados, as well as visiting VIP's from Hong Kong. The dinner went smoothly with the usual long toasts and hard liquor pouring freely. Mr. Lin, the judo master, came with a kungfu companion. They had hoped that there would be a demonstration of sorts. But none was forthcoming. Just at the close of the dinner, he and his friend approached the table of honored guests and openly asked if what they saw of Taijiquan's martial skills on TV was for real and challenged to test it. Chen Xiaowang, having eaten and drunk heartily, was not in the least inclined to oblige but did not know how to decline. How could a kungfu master invoke a well-lined belly as an excuse? So he beckoned them to proceed. The two did the armlocks on the master. Without drama, Chen Xiaowang freed his arms. Feeling somewhat anticlimactic and unsure of being contented, the two nevertheless bowed to salute and thank the master, which seemed to end the intrusion of an otherwise uneventful banquet. As Chen Xiaowang turned to return to his table, the athletic Mr. Lin without warning grabbed Chen Xiaowang from behind to execute a judo throw on him. Dignitaries and guests alike were aghast. With jaws dropped open, they gestured in unison, eyes glued on the scene of impending disaster. The admonishment from the Chinese delegation seemed stuck in the throats, but croaked out in the hushed silence, "Bu hao le!" (Oh, that's bad!) In a flash, to the great relief of everyone, the attacker was seen flying and falling several feet away from Chen Xiaowang. The anxiety that built up to a pitch broke out in a thunderous applause of appreciation to witness such a real-life kungfu feat.

Chen Xiaowang, well-drunk and well-fed, felt a sharp force tugging to lift him. But his center was not perturbed—his dantian energy remained intact. The force of the attack was spontaneously neutralized by Chen's *rou jin*, which at the same time unsettled the attacker. With the opening, Chen Xiaowang instantly issued a short burst of fajin with his shoulder, sending the intruder reeling to the floor. Had Chen Xiaowang's *rou jin* been lacking in *gang* power, he would have been thrown by the judo expert. The news of a local judo instructor throwing the much ballyhooed Taijiquan master would certainly have been disastrous for the Henan promotion. The organizers were doubly grateful to Chen Xiaowang for saving the tour and for generating even more media stories. Gratified and humbled, Mr. Lin bowed most deeply to apologize for the unmannerly intrusion, acknowledging the master's far superior kungfu.

The Four Ounces of "Si Liang Bo Qian Jin"

The forces applied in overcoming the opponent in the anecdotes described above certainly seemed more than *si liang* (four ounces) in the Taijiquan kungfu of si liang bo qian jin (four ounces repelling a thousand pounds).

The skill of si liang bo qian jin expresses the principle of leverage in kungfu. Nevertheless, the practitioner must have sufficient core strength (gongli) of jin to execute the skill efficaciously. No matter how great a technique, without gongli, its use is limited. Chen Yu stresses in his lessons that one needs to build a requisite store of jin to fight.[21] It is only with sufficient gongli supporting the action that the additional small effort of "four ounces" can repel a "thousand-pound" attack. The si liang by itself cannot do much without the leverage engineered by neijin. What can the si liang of a little kid do?

There is no short-cut in the Taijiquan way. One must put in the time and effort (gongfu) to develop the core strength of jin, both *gang* and *rou*, not deficient in either. Then only can one use the proverbial small amount of si liang to break an adversary's strong force.

The basis of this skill is not the leverage of a simple lever, but the principle of "coiling leverage," derived from the body's rotational motion. This is examined in chansi (silk-reeling) motion in chapter 8.

Martial Arts and Sports

Tang Hao, the martial arts historian, lamented that Chinese martial arts was suffering a malady that kept it stuck in the past. Advances in sports provide a stark contrast that dramatizes the predicament of kungfu development.

Martial arts and sports both showcase superiority in strength. Both require trained coordination of muscles, not just muscle sizes. Sports look to science and technology for improvement. Chinese martial arts are mired in secrecy and myth, and shun open exchange. Since the revival of the Olympic Games in 1896 in Athens, sports have made tremendous strides. The long-jump record at the first modern Olympics was 1.81 m. It is now 2.39 m set in the 1996 Atlanta Games by Charles Austin. The high jump underwent a revolutionary change when Dick Fosbury jumped to a gold in the 1968 Mexico City Games, by clearing 2.24 meters with his back arched over the bar, creating the new jumping technique named after him, "the Fosbury flop." The 100 meter dash champion in the first modern Olympics was clocked at 11.80 seconds, and in the 2008 Beijing Olympics, Usain Bolt of Jamaica blazed ahead of the trailing pack to set the new world record of 9.69 seconds.

In contrast, the growth of Chinese martial arts seems stunted in a culture of mysticism and secrecy. The greatest kungfu skills are spoken of only in the past. Masters often speak glowingly of their masters' kungfu, and do not believe that their own skills are comparable to the high-level kungfu of old. Also real skills are often blurred in kungfu fiction (wuxia), which feeds the incredible gravity-defying feats of leaping to roof-tops, running on water, and exchanging blows in midair.

Of course, these spectacular kungfus have not been replicated except in movies.

At the time of the revival of modern Olympics, Taijiquan had become established in Beijing by the Yang family and the torch was being passed on to the third generation successors. The kungfus of Yang Luchan and of his sons were already legendary and believed to be out of reach. On the other hand, sports strive to break records, and have advanced by leaps and bounds since the revival of Olympics. But the level of Chinese martial arts is presumed by traditional beliefs to be declining in each succeeding generation. Even as Chen Xiaowang tells me that this is not true, that kungfus go up and down like waves over the generations, he does not believe that he can get close to his grandfather's kungfu in his own lifetime.

Can science not shed light in Taijiquan kungfu? The almost effortless kungfu prowess of neijin may seem to defy the laws of physics, but neijin does not introduce new science. Whatever neijin is, its manifestation is in the medium of the human body. Thus, the study of neijin can be illuminated by examining the neijin phenomenon in the musculo-skeletal framework. While it is argued that qi and neijin are too esoteric to be susceptible to the instruments of science, without the musculo-skeletal structure, the whole concept of neijin is vacuous. Without muscle structure there would be no motion, rendering any talk of jin meaningless.

In the ensuing chapters, we study neijin in the musculo-skeletal structure, but superimposed with of yin-yang metaphysics so that we do not have lose the "soul" of the art. For example, the rou-gang of jin can be seen as the body's comprehension of force as a vector of magnitude and direction. The approach aims to give a rationale of qi and yin-yang balance in practice so that one can find a training path to reach the higher levels of the art, rather than being held at the mercy of the nebulous it-takes-a-lifetime-to-master mindset.

Chen Xiaowang's welcoming toast of Maotai at his Zhengzhou home.   His son, Pengfei

Pengfei would get no break in training whenever his father was home.

Visiting Grandmasters Zhu Tiancai, Chen Xiaowang and Chen Zhenglei in Zhengzhou in 1999

Chen Xiaowang dishes out kabocha squash soup, his favorite food. Mahla looks on.

With Pengfei, Chen Xiaowang, and Mingwei   Master adjusting my posture

6
Force of Neijin

The kungfu of neijin are extraordinary but they are not paranormal. Neijin does not empower one with super strength. Yet, as seen in chapter 5, Chen Xiaowang, rooted to the ground by neijin, could not be budged an inch by the herculean strength of Longwu, the two-time strongman champion of China.

Neijin is not easy to formulate as its characteristics are internal, and expert opinions differ. Yet it is neijin that distinguishes Taijiquan kungfu from the "hard" martial arts. Yang Chengfu, grandson of Yang Taijiquan founder, Yang Luchan, writes of its internal ethos:[1]

> "When those who practice external systems are using strength it is apparent ... It is obvious that their strength is an external, superficial kind of energy. The strength of practitioners of external systems is very easily manipulated and not worthy of praise."

The force of neijin is differentiated from *li* 力 ("physical force"), which is considered external and associated with muscles. Taijiquan theory avoids the mention of muscles and disdains relating muscles to neijin. In fact, the use of muscles is eschewed in Taijiquan training by the dictate:

Yong yi bu yong li
用意不用力
Use mind-intent not physical force.

The use of external force (*li* 力) may be decried in Taijiquan, but motion is powered by muscles. Neijin may not appear to be associated with musculature, but musculature is essential to neijin. Departing from traditional exposition, this book investigates neijin in the framework of musculo-skeletal structure and physics, and study force generated in Taijiquan motion with reference to posture, balance, muscles, momentum, and rotational motions of the body.

It is true that the claims of *ling kong jin* 灵空劲 or "empty-space" force—force projected without physical contact over space—defy physics.[2] This book does not pursue the validity or otherwise of these claims, except to note that none has withstood scientific scrutiny.[3] The demonstrations posted on YouTube may seem convincing, but they do not show empty-space force moving an inanimate object.[4] No masters of *ling kong jin* have ventured outside of their YouTube postings, say in sports or an open arena, to stake their claims to fame and money. The kungfu skills of Yang Luchan and his sons, and those of the generations of Chen Village masters, as well as those described in the classical literature of Taijiquan, do not relate to *ling kong jin*.

Neijin and Force

When speaking of body force, it is easy to be confused between the muscle force that powers the motion of a punch and the force of the punch that inflicts damage. The body experiences muscle force indirectly through the motion it generates; it experiences force of the punch directly on impact, the consequence of a change in motion (more precisely, momentum).

We do not have to understand the calculus of force in Newton's Second Law of Motion, just to know of the force intrinsic in motion. The force depends on how well the multitudes of muscles work in concert to maintain the integrity of the human bipedal structure— balance—in motion.

We can think of the musculo-skeletal system as a power plant of muscles whose product is motion. The motion-product that we admire is a resultant sum of the movements of the body's numerous parts as presented in athletics, dance aesthetics, or martial arts.

The ideal motion in Taijiquan is one in consonance with Taiji yin-yang principles. It is from this ideal motion that neijin is born, and the force arising is consummate. Taijiquan training is about generating this ideal motion.

> *This book puts forth the thesis that the force arising from the change in Taijiquan motion (motion in accord with Taiji principles) is that of jin or neijin.*

This does seem rather anti-climactic, equating neijin to the force of motion without reference to qi, in light of it having been exalted as some wonder. Indeed, it would be viewed as an affront to the art's philosophy of "not using muscle force." However, the thesis is not about the bulk of muscles but regulating body motion by Taiji principles.

The metaphysics of Taiji may be alien to science, but the body relates to the yin-yang principles with regard to bipedal structure in balance. The body learns to be conversant with the yin-yang principles in their representations—an internal development of refining consciousness.

By virtue of the universality of Taiji theory, Taijiquan reigns supreme. It encompasses all aspects of the body, from holistic health to motion and posture, and from generating strength and power to the strategic states of body structure in combat. The force engendered in the ideal Taijiquan motion—neijin—taps the full potential of the body and enjoys all the yin-yang attributes, which in applications translate to force vector, torque, and leverage. And it bears the hallmark of linghuo (lively) yin-yang dynamics, as manifested in the ease of transformation between rou (soft) and gang (hard) of jin, which makes the force of jin indefensible and unstoppable.

The agenda then is to build the body's comprehension of yin and yang, qi, and jin in the musculo-skeletal framework. First, we take a detour to review quickly and highlight certain features of the physiology of muscles that help in the exposition.

Muscle Movements

The body's skeletal bones are held together by hundreds of muscles. A muscle is a bundle of muscle fibers (muscle cells) which can do only one thing when innervated, which is to contract. The hundreds of bones of the skeletal frame form an amazing engineering complex of lever systems at the joints that function by the contractile actions of the muscles to produce body motion.

At the basic level of a muscle is a motor unit, the smallest contractile system, consisting of a varying number of muscle fibers. Attached to the unit is a nerve (neuron axon), through which signal travels to activate it. Corresponding to each skeletal muscle is a pool of motor neurons in the spinal cord that controls the assembly of motor units making up the muscle. The fewer the number of muscle fibers that make up a motor unit the finer and more delicate the movement it controls. A motor unit in a muscle that controls delicate movements like that of the eye, has less than ten muscle fibers, while those in the thighs, contain more than a thousand fibers.[5]

The energy that powers muscle contraction comes from biochemical reactions. Indeed, the life process of biology, reduced at the molecular level, is a chemistry of forming and breaking bonds. The energy needs in a cell are handled by "battery-molecules" called adenosine triphosphate or ATP. ATP energy is stored in the chemical bonds of the phosphates, which is released for use when a phosphate bond is cleaved. The molecular battery is re-charged by energy mostly from oxidation of glucose and fatty acids stored in the body. There is an ample supply of ATP batteries maintained in the mitochondria in each cell to take care of its energy needs.

Muscle movements are powered by arrays of ATPs in the muscle cells. That is, the basic energy that fuels body motion is derived from the electromagnetic force of the biochemical bonds, which is one of the Four Fundamental Forces of Nature.[6]

"Control" of Muscle Movements

Cultivation of neijin is a discipline of motion. What makes it challenging is that we have no direct control of specific muscles powering motion. We only have limited cognition of the skeletal muscles that we presumably control. When we flex our arms, we are not aware of the biceps and triceps contracting in antagonistic pairs to provide the smoothness of motion, let alone of the motor units in the muscles. We can point to the ball-and-socket joint at the shoulder, the hinge joint at the elbow, or the finger joints of the hand, but we are not conscious of the muscles working them. Amazingly, without us knowing the lever systems of the bones and joints and the muscles powering them, we function incredibly well as a bipedal creature.

What muscles are to be recruited, slow-twitch or fast-twitch,[7] or the strength of muscle forces to be generated in an action, are decisions that we do not have to make, but are programmed within the lower hierarchy of the body's motor system. The control we have is the command of action, which triggers signals to the neuron pools to recruit muscles, so that the muscle movements add up to the intended action as the output.

The command of an action does not recruit the same muscles. Drives are not the same even though the command to swing the golf club is the same. Certainly among individuals, the command produces very different results. We may have the sufficient muscle horse-power in the body to produce a good long drive, but the command may not translate to engaging the right muscles in coordination to produce the motion we want.

Between command at the top hierarchy and muscle recruitment at the bottom hierarchy of the body's motor system is a complex of neural mechanisms of the brain, central nervous system, and other body senses. In a simplification for our purposes, the neural mechanisms can be viewed as a *program-template* that corresponds to an action.

"Practice Makes Perfect"

Practice builds and refines the program-template to recruit the right muscles for a better play, which of course is the adage of "practice makes perfect." However, as many golfers know, practice can be frustrating—it stagnates.

The corrective adjustments that we make in practice are not like the settings of a dial, so many degrees up or down, or so many degrees left or right. Practice can only feed errors perceived into the motor system, to refine and modify the program-template, and hopefully, the golf drive improves accordingly. However, other factors feed into the program-template—one's own motor skills previously developed, which can be positive or negative, as well as other sensory inputs.

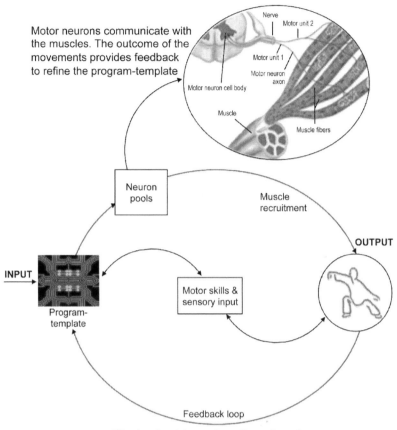

Motor neurons communicate with the muscles. The outcome of the movements provides feedback to refine the program-template

Nerve
Motor unit 2
Motor unit 1
Motor neuron cell body
Motor neuron axon
Muscle
Muscle fibers

Neuron pools

Muscle recruitment

OUTPUT

INPUT

Program-template

Motor skills & sensory input

Feedback loop

The feedback loop of practice refines the signals to the motor neurons to recruit muscles for a better performance of body motion

Fig. 6.1. A schematic chain of muscle activation

These factors vary widely and account for the huge differences in performance skills between individuals. The complexities of these factors limit perfection. Practice can improve the skill at best, but cannot make perfect. Players in National Basketball Association (NBA) score an average of 75% in free throws, and those who make over 90% are very few—between 2 and 6 in each of the eight seasons from 2004 to 2012.[8]

A main obstacle to improvement in practice is the body's habitual mode of generating motion. One cannot improve the golf swing much unless one breaks the habit of the arm and shoulder muscles from dominating the action, and learns to use the waist to coordinate the muscles between the left and right and the upper and lower parts of the body. Between what one tells the body to do—the command—and what the body does—the motion-product—is a huge gap of neural mechanisms that is opaque. Practice is at the mercy of this black box of mechanisms, which include bad habits.

Nevertheless, practice builds cognition of the factors of errors and maintains the objective to improve or hone skills—the mind aspect of training. Taijiquan exploits the mind (yi 意) part by developing an internal dynamics of qi to bridge this gap. Taijiquan cultivates qi and uses it as a medium to transmit yi-command to motion.

Yi (Mind-Intent), Qi, and Motion

The use of qi to discipline motion is nurtured by the practice rule:

Yi yi dao qi, yi qi yun shen
以意导气，以气运身
Use mind-intent to activate qi; use qi to direct motion.

Taijiquan tempers the body to develop qi and builds awareness for the body to move in response to qi dynamics. Qi must be sufficiently developed in Taijiquan training for the yi-qi-motion paradigm to function. Then the body can move as directed by yi and qi, as metaphorically expressed in *Song of Thirteen Postures*:[9]

Yi qi jun lai gu rou chen
意气君来骨肉臣
Yi and qi are the sovereign, bones and muscles follow as subjects.

The yi-qi-motion model parallels the body's motor system: yi as the commander at the top hierarchy, qi as the signal flag (program-template) that directs motion. Once the body is trained to connect qi dynamics to motion, one can discipline motion via yi-qi-motion, which serves as a link of communication through the black box of neural mechanisms. In the verse of *Elucidation of Thirteen Postures,* yi-qi-motion is likened to a battalion drill: qi signals and limbs move following the waist like soldiers filing behind a banner:[10]

Xin wei ling 心为令
Qi wei qi 气为旗
Yao wei dao 腰为纛

Mind as the commander
Qi as the signal flag
Waist as the banner.

However, couched in Taiji principles, the training seems to be in the realm of metaphysics, not physical exercise. Moreover, most of the movements in Taijiquan training do not seem to simulate an action of purpose. Abstruse as it may be, the unorthodox training turns out to be very practical—by following the methodology the body acculturates to yi-qi-motion and gains fluency of the yin-yang language.

"Use Mind-Intent Not Physical Force"

From the beginning and through the years of Taijiquan training, the constant guiding admonition is the practice mantra:

Yong yi bu yong li
用意不用力
Use mind-intent, not physical force.

The first part, *yong yi* (using mind-intent), to command motion may seem obvious, but we have no cognition of muscles. The second part, *bu yong li* (not using li) is generally explained as "not using muscle force," which does not make sense as motion is powered by muscles. The mantra reads like a riddle, but the body relates to it functionally.

The body is habituated to move in response to an external driver, for example, to kick a ball or to strike a target. Directed externally, the muscles immediate to the action dominate, which thwart other parts of the body from supporting the action. We see this in learning new movements as well—one is directed by the external form. Because of the preoccupation to imitate the form, one either puts too much effort, exaggerating the movement, thus "going over" (*guo* 过), or not enough, falling short and "not arriving" (*bu ji* 不及). One leans or shifts weight too much to the left or right. The arms are too extended or droopy; the legs bend too much or not enough; or the chest is held up too tight or is saggy. As a consequence, the posture is stiff here or lax there, and the motion is burdened. We may see the flaws in the external form and make corrections, but there is no cognition of muscle habits. Therein lies the conundrum of practice: how to correct for errors in one's habitual way of generating motion that one is not aware of? The ingenuity of Taijiquan is that the methodology brings corrections simply by adhering to the cryptic drumbeat of yong yi bu yong li. Whatever its meaning, invoking the mantra gives pause to the body from its habitual way of generating motion. It serves to restrain the muscles immediate to the action from dominating, and in so doing, it pares down excessiveness in muscle actions, thus reducing tenseness. This elicits a relaxation and induces a sensation of qi energy.

The mantra not to use force (li) does not mean not to use muscles. It means not to be excessive to curb overexertion of force in action, thus avoiding "clumsy strength" (*zhuo li* 拙力). This renders the motion soft and the body relaxing, and engenders a new experience which gives the practitioner a rejuvenating lift.

The mantra of using mind-intent (yi), coupled with the deliberative slow motion, nurtures awareness of the body. The mere attentiveness forms the rudiments of perceptive skills, which constitute the mind part of the exercise. Without having to decipher the mantra but simply by following it as an article of faith, the induced attentiveness kindles the germination of the vital seeds of the practice—body awareness and relaxation. Tended by the soft training, they grow as the skills of perceptivity, which are basic in the internal training to cultivate neijin.

Taijiquan starts out as any exercise, driven externally by form, but it goes beyond resolving the errors of physical postures. The practice mantra initiates a process for the practitioner to nurture the roles of yi and qi in motion. As practice advances, awareness heightens and the insight of yong yi bu yong li unfolds—one experiences motion responding to yi and qi without reference to an external driver. With this comprehension, one enters the internal phase of the training that forges the yi-qi-motion paradigm. This leads to the harmony of motion and qi dynamics, without one having to delve into the profundities of Taiji theory. Along the journey one reaps the health benefits from the nurturing of qi, even at the early stages of training.

We weave back to the musculo-skeletal frame and study its internal structure to see more of yi and qi in body dynamics.

Body-Frame

From Taiji perspective, the musculo-skeletal frame—the skeleton of bones linked at the joints and held together by ligaments, tendons, and muscles—gives only the physical aspect. The framework does not provide for qi dynamics, which is central to Taijiquan. The term, *body-frame,* is introduced to refer to the skeletal frame with the full dress of skin and flesh, internal organs, and the circulatory systems, as well as qi and the network of meridians, that is, the whole physiologic works of Traditional Chinese Medicine. Also, *segment or segmental part* is used to refer generically to parts attached at the joints of the body-frame, namely, the hands, forearms, upper arms, shoulders, spine, thighs, legs, feet, and so on. Thus, body motion is a composition of movements of segmental parts powered by the multitudes of muscles supporting them, and within breathes the dynamics of qi.

Segmental parts enjoy a certain degree of autonomy in motion. This independence spawns the prolific art forms of motion, but it also breeds stubbornness that frustrates unity of purpose in motion. And segments are not equally endowed.

The hand complex enjoys the highest degree of autonomy and dominates in initiating motion, so much so that it can be said that our mobility culture is oriented by the action of the hands. In just about everything we do, for pleasure or vocation, our hands take the lead in action. The architecture of the hand attests to its rightful dominance. The hand has 27 bones (8 carpals in the wrist, 5 metacarpals in the palm, and the four fingers have 3 phalanges each, while the thumb has 2), and as many joints. To power the fine movements of the hand, there are 34 muscles in the fingers and thumb, 17 in the palm, and 18 in the forearm.[11] Not surprising then, our hands reign supreme in dexterity and precision. But the hand, by habit, reaches out first in action, which can deprive other parts of the body from supporting the action, and thus compromises power output.

Hard-Frame and Soft-Frame Structures

The body-frame of linked segments is dual in character. Viewed as a whole, the structure is a frame, called a *hard-frame*, and viewed as segments forming the frame, the structure is called a *soft-frame*. Implicit in the frame structures are the underlying muscle actions supporting them.

Let us review some familiar actions in the context of frame structures. We see the application of the hard-frame when a defense player in football hurls himself at a quarterback to knock him down. With body mass unified as a solid frame, the hard-frame projects maximal force at impact, but the maneuver comes at the expense of control.

The fists and feet are used most readily in combat. However, if an opponent is too close, there may not be enough room for the limbs to extend in a punch or kick. With cognition of the soft-frame, one can simulate "free ends" with the elbow or the knee. Closer still, the body can summon the shoulder, chest, or hip to strike. Close-quarter combat—wrestling, grappling, submission techniques, and so on—relies on the dynamics of the soft-frame.

A novice golfer attempts a long drive by mustering all the force he can in swinging the club. The player cannot coordinate between left and right or employ the muscles of the lower body to support the swing. As a result, the swing gets no help from the base, and often the front shoulder ends up getting more power than the shoulder behind, causing the swing to drag.

Golf clinics teach a "broomstick exercise" to improve golf swing. This is the exercise of holding a stick against the back, locked between the elbows, and turning at the waist. It trains the torso to turn as a unit at the waist, and balances the left and right sides of the body, both essential in executing waist power. It also conditions the back muscles to augment the power of the swing.

The golf ball sees only the momentum of the clubhead coming at it. The momentum is built up by the rotational motion of the body. The more body mass is involved in the motion, the larger the momentum, and the greater the impact force to send the ball off the tee. Thus in the waist-power action, the key is to coordinate the arms, shoulders, and torso to tap fully the body's mass in rotational motion. Achieving a long drive is not about hitting the ball hard, but the body knowing the frame structure in generating motion. Externally one sees the swing, but the power of the swing is governed by the internal dynamics of the soft-frame.

However, the body is easily forgetful of its frame structure. In fright, the breath is stuck in the chest, and the muscles freeze up in a rigid frame like a statue. One is helpless—the fright blanks out the cognition of the frame structure.

When under pressure or in pain, the body forgets its structure, tenses up, and becomes trapped in the hard-frame. A fighter, captured in an armlock, submits in pain because, forgetting the soft-frame, he is unable to maneuver in the hard-frame.

Even in common tasks the body can be forgetful of its frame structure. For example, in picking up a box, the hands reach out first, causing the body to bend forward. Forgetful of its soft-frame, the body stubbornly keeps the bad forward-leaning posture as it lifts the box, and sprains the back. With awareness of the soft structure, the body can bend at the knees for a better posture and at the elbows for a better leverage to lift the box.

In the hard-frame, the segments are harnessed fully in body mass for advantage in momentum. But this creates the problem of the body becoming stiff, which undermines flexibility of change and control, and is antithetical to the aesthetics of the fluidity of motion. The antidote to stiffness inherent in the hard-frame is the internal dynamics of soft-frame, which breathes liveliness in the body-frame.

The theory of the dual frame structures is about instilling the body with cognition and fluency of the structures. Then the body is mindful of its soft structure while projecting force with the hard-frame. And the body does not lose the integrity of its hard structure when engaging in the soft-frame for agility and control. For the body to know and apply the soft or hard structures at will is at the heart of mastery.

However, one is unclear of the frame structure because the body is muddled about its underlying muscle actions. Taijiquan disciplines muscles through seeking clarity of the frame structures in the yin-yang representation.

Summary of frame structures

Structure	Character	Properties
Hard-frame	External	Unified body mass, power
Soft-frame	Internal	Agility, precision, and control

Yin-Yang Duality of the Body-Frame

The yin-yang garb of Taiji theory is tailor-fit to the body-frame, *with the hard-frame manifesting yang, and the soft-frame, yin.* With this representation the underlying muscles supporting the frame structures literally give meat to the yin-yang framework, which opens up the wealth of Taiji theory to body mechanics.

Regulating body motion by yin-yang principles can then be deciphered in terms of muscle actions underlying the frame structures. However, the christening of the body-frame with yin and yang alone does not embody it with the spirit of Taiji. The body must be tempered to assimilate the yin-yang postulates.

Undergirding the hard-frame is the yin structure of the segments, and overarching the soft-frame is the yang integrity of the frame—one is present in the other. Although of opposite character, the dual frames are complementary and mutually supportive. The frame structure is not static even in stationary postures because of the internal dynamics of the soft structure. Each frame structure has its strengths and weaknesses, and the lack of one in the other renders a weakness.

The liveliness of change (*linghuo* 灵活), a yin virtue, is born of the soft-frame, but a lack of hard-frame integrity (yang) causes body motion to be disconnected, scattered, and confused (*sanluan* 散乱). The unity of body mass in motion, a yang virtue, is induced by the hard-frame, but a lack of soft-frame (yin) flexibility and agility causes the body to be stiff as a woodblock.

The ideal body-frame does not lack yin in the hard-frame, nor yang in the soft-frame, which is the principle of yin-yang balance. The soft-frame enjoys the strength of the hard-frame, and the hard-frame maintains the liveliness of the soft-frame. The body gains the strengths but sheds the weaknesses inherent in the frame structures. Then the body's response is both defensive and offensive—defensive in the liveliness of change of the soft-frame and offensive in the strength and power of the hard-frame.

Biomechanics of Jin

The biomechanics of the *rou* (soft) and *gang* (hard) of jin becomes apparent in frame structures. The power of *gang jin* in offense is derived from the integrity of the yang hard-frame that harnesses full body mass in momentum. The liveliness of *rou jin* that accords ease of change and maneuverability flows from the internal dynamics of the yin soft-frame.

The yin-yang theory thus unifies both the dualities of jin and frame structures: *rou jin* with the soft-frame (yin) and *gang jin* with the hard-frame (yang).

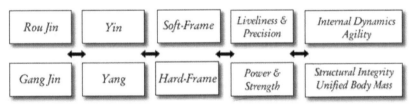

Fig. 6.2 Jin Duality and Frame Structures

Deciphering Muscle Actions

Although we have no cognition of muscles, the body can learn to relate to the effects of muscle actions underlying frame structures or jin with regard to yin-yang imbalance. One can then determine the yin-yang quality of frame structure or jin from the effects, thus indirectly decipher the muscle actions. First, we examine this from the viewpoint of frame structure, and then of jin in the section after.

Let us conduct an experiment of holding an arm in balance. Extend the right arm to the side, almost horizontally but slightly bent, and hold it in position, such as in the posture of "Lazy Tying Coat" in the cover picture. The arm is in physical balance between its weight and the muscles supporting it.

To simulate an effect of muscle actions in the hard-frame, extend and tense the arm. One feels the discomfort of tenseness—muscles are working in excess. The tenseness in Chinese is *jiang* 僵. For an effect of the soft-frame, let the arm droop like a wilting plant. One feels a loss of vigor—muscles are weak in the balance of the arm. The loss of internal firmness or strength is described as *diu* 丢 (lose). In either case, though the arm is in balance, there is internal imbalance of muscle actions, namely, yin-yang imbalance.

The simulation of tensing and letting go trains the body to discern its frame structure and the effects of the underlying muscle actions. But the body cannot resolve the internal imbalance directly as one has no consciousness of specific muscles. However, muscle adjustments can be induced. Upon becoming aware of the discomfort of tenseness, the body learns to relax by "letting go" (*fangsong* 放松), which lessens the muscle actions and brings some relief.

This relief of jiang tenseness can also be simulated by bending the arm slightly and letting the elbow drop (*chen jian zhui zhou* "sinking the shoulder and dropping the elbow"), which lessens excessive muscle actions. That is, the practice rule of *chen jian zhui zhou* induces fangsong relaxation of the muscle actions of the arm. It also nurtures awareness of the shoulder, elbow, and hand.

Another way to see the underlying muscle actions is to enlist a friend. Have the friend hold the tip of a finger, and let the arm fall freely like a cable suspended between the finger and shoulder. This lessens the muscle actions of the shoulder and arm, and induces fangsong relaxation.

By fangsong, the body gains awareness of the arm and its weight, and senses the flow of energy (qi). In this way, fangsong relaxation softens stiffness (*jiang*) and remedies the yin deficiency of the arm structure, and nurtures qi.

In the case of the droopy arm lacking strength, a deficiency in yang hardness, the remedy is trickier. Exerting force to strengthen the arm causes it to tense up, and goes against the dictate of not to use li (force). The Taiji method is first to check the external form and then stretch the arm internally. This internal stretching is *shen jin ba gu* (stretching the tendons and the bones). *Shen jin ba gu* induces awareness of the arm structure and remedies the diu (loss) of "connectedness" of the arm. It strengthens the arm without tensing it, promotes the flow of energy (qi), and cures the deficiency in yang of the soft structure.

One may think that the arm is relaxed, but hold it in position for ten minutes. The soreness that sets in indicates that the muscles are working too much in some parts while too little at others. This reveals yin-yang imbalance at a deeper level, which is again deciphered as *jiang*—the effect of excessive muscle actions—and as *diu*—of deficient muscle actions. The imbalance can be resolved accordingly at a higher level of consciousness.

Although the experiment addresses only the arm, the lesson applies to the structure of the whole body. This approach introduces one to balance from a developmental perspective in the context of fangsong, qi and body structure, which leads to Taiji balance in the next chapter.

Discerning Imbalance as Jin Errors

Next we examine muscle actions underlying motion. Take the first movement of Taijiquan—raise both arms are to shoulder level. The motion may be simple, but it serves to illustrate the effects of the underlying muscle actions as any motion. If the muscles of the arms and shoulders dominate, it obscures the awareness of the wrist and elbow, and the motion is stiff and tight. The same term *jiang* 僵 (stiff, tense, tight) is used to describe this condition of excessive muscle actions of the arms and shoulders.

Excessive muscle actions in motion are more readily recognized when two persons tussle in a pushing contest. Not wanting to be pushed over, both sides push hard at one another. This exertion of force butting against one another results in a display of excessive muscle actions, described as *ding* 頂 (pushing against the top). Hence, the error of excessive muscle actions in generating motion is discerned as *ding jin* 頂 勁 as well as *jiang jin* 僵勁. This "sickness" of jin—a condition of yang deficient in yin—renders the motion stiff and dull.

If the muscles powering an action are weak, the motion is lax like a hose with no water pressure. The motion suffers from a loss of connectedness between the different parts of the body. The same Chinese character *diu* 丢 (lose) describes this disconnectedness in motion. The error of deficient muscle actions in generating motion is discerned as *diu jin* 丢勁. The sickness of diu jin—the form appears scattered, weak, or limp—is yin deficient in yang.

Thus, yin-yang imbalances are deciphered as *jin errors*: jiang jin (or ding jin), an effect of excessive muscle actions, or diu jin, a result of deficient muscle actions. To strive for the ideal motion is to seek a support structure of "neither diu nor ding" (*bu diu bu ding* 不丢不頂), that is, neither lax nor resisting. (*Bu* 不 means negation.) The resolution of yin-yang imbalance then becomes a pragmatic process of reducing jin errors—the lesser the jin errors the stronger the jin.

Since imbalance in the frame structure is also deciphered by the same factors of the underlying muscle actions, we conveniently refer to the errors of muscle actions also as jin errors. In practice then, from either viewpoint of jin or frame structure, muscle actions are disciplined through the resolution of jin errors. The error of jiang jin is remedied by fangsong relaxation and the error of diu jin by internal stretching (shen jin ba gu).

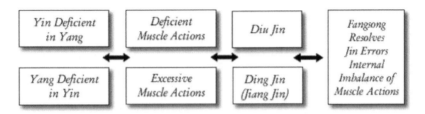

Fig. 6.3 Schematic illustration of Yin-Yang Imbalance

Tool of Fangsong

One can think of *fangsong* 放松 as a tool to chip away the jin errors, but the tool has to be developed by the practitioner through practice. At the initial phases of training, the error of jiang jin is identified as a discomfort of tenseness or stiffness. The natural response to the discomfort is to fangsong, an ordinary Chinese expression, "to let go and relax." This simple mechanism—to relax once jiang jin is realized—is the rudimentary tool of fangsong. The tricky part is when things become subtle as the practice advances.

The action of fangsong to resolve jiang jin is not active in the sense that one is directing a reallocation of muscles—so much here and so much there—which one cannot do. In the fangsong relaxation, the muscles settle into another level of support. This induces a reset of the muscles with less tenseness, thus reducing jiang jin—a passive action. In a manner of speaking, fangsong reduces jiang jin "without doing it," a manifestation of the Taoist art of "action without action" (*wei wu wei* 为无为).

On the other hand, the remedy for diu jin by internal stretching is active. The attentiveness in stretching "the tendons and bones" induces connectedness between the segments of the body-frame, and thus builds up cohesiveness and strength in the motion and posture.

For convenience in exposition, we use the term *fangsong* to incorporate the dual functions of relaxation to soften jiang jin and internal stretching to invigorate diu jin. In practice, fangsong tempers "relaxation" with "stretching," and "stretching" with "relaxation." By alternately relaxing and stretching one reduces the range of jin errors, thereby sharpening cognition of the frame structure and the fangsong process itself.

Fangsong settles one in the middle ground between jiang (or ding) on the one hand, and diu on the other, and in so doing, disciplines muscle actions "not to be over or not to be short" (*wu guo bu ji* 无过不及).[12] Too much, the structure is tight (jiang), or too little it is lax (diu). It is like loosening or tightening the screws of a swivel desk lamp: too tight, the arm of the lamp cannot swivel, or too loose, it collapses.

A master often rebukes a student's form in practice as *guo le* (having gone past) to point to a movement or posture that is overextended, or as *bu dao wei* (not having reached) to point to one that is short. The admonishment nudges the practice to stay in the middle ground. The rule of bu diu bu ding (not lax and not resisting) is also to stay in the middle ground. And as the range of errors becomes smaller, one eventually achieves yin-yang balance.

Qi and Fangsong

We take qi as given in Traditional Chinese Medicine (TCM). The common usage of *qi* 气 is "breath or air" among other meanings, but in TCM, qi is the metaphysical energy that gives life to the body. Qi resides in the blood, organs, bones, and body tissues. Although an integral part of TCM, qi does not have an equivalent in physiology.

Science has yet to define or measure qi, but a Taijiquan (or any qigong) practitioner experiences qi in practice.

We can think of qi as a composite of bioenergies associated with the biological functions of the body's organs. If the organs are not in holistic balance, as when one is sick, then the bioenergies are discordant, and qi is weakened. Conversely, a healthy functioning of the organs gives coherence to the bioenergies, and qi is fortified.

By Taijiquan theory, the fangsong process of reducing jin errors—the resolution of internal imbalances of muscle actions—builds qi. The tempering of muscles by fangsong eases the flow of bioenergies in the flesh and organs, and thus the flow of qi. At the beginning, the experience of qi sensation is intermittent, appearing and disappearing, usually in the hands first. Over time, it becomes steadier with practice. Then gradually one sees the errors of muscle actions in terms of qi dynamics and learns to use qi as a medium to resolve jin errors, which, in turn develops more qi. The resolution of jin errors then melds with the development of qi, and the practice becomes internal—the body responds in qi to regulate motion, instilling and reinforcing the yi-qi-motion paradigm.

The enduring legacy of Taijiquan is that qi grows by the practice methodology, as a plant by tending and watering. Along the way, the qi nurtured in daily practice alleviates stress-related illnesses. In the longer term, the qi buildup invigorates and strengthens the body's constitution, and serves as a natural preventive medicine that shields against chronic ailments. The alluring promise is that the store of qi preserves the "spring of life" in old age, as espoused in the verse of *Song of Thirteen Postures*.[13]

> *Yi shou yan nian bu lao chun* 益寿延年不老春.
> One gains longevity and prolongs the spring of life in old age.

Most practitioners are quite content with the health benefits of qi. Indeed, the qi nourishing formula is the mainspring of the art's propagation. However, qi cultivation is only a means to an end in Taijiquan. Taijiquan uses qi in the yi-qi-motion paradigm to regulate motion to cultivate neijin. But to advance in the internal development, the fangsong skills must be refined continually.

Refinement of Fangsong Skills

As fangsong works to resolve imbalances, it does not tell how close or far one is from the center of balance. To progress, fangsong must ensure that the errors of imbalance get smaller in the process. That is, the fangsong tools must be sharp or the practice stalls. This is particularly the case at the higher levels of training where yin-yang imbalance becomes subtle and elusive.

Chen Xiaowang declares that there are always errors of imbalance (*wucha* 误差) in one's practice, including his own, except of course that we cannot see his errors. He once drew a cone diagram (fig. 6.4) on a napkin to explain. At the beginning, the wucha errors are huge, as depicted by the wide base of the cone. The narrower top portion represents the smaller range of errors at the advanced levels of practice.

Fig. 6.4 Cone of convergence depicting margin of errors

But the path in real practice is not as ideally represented in the cone. Indeed, it can be very wayward. One can stray off rather wildly, as "missing by a hair's breadth can set one off course by a thousand miles." It requires the guidance of a good teacher and one's dedication to cultivate the perceptivity to stay within the cone of convergence in one's training.

The presumption is that the iterative process of detecting and correcting jin errors will eventually lead to yin-yang balance. This depends critically on one's fangsong skills. If the perceptive skills are limited, then the finer imbalances cannot be resolved, like a blur in a low-resolution microscope. If the fangsong tool is not sharp, it cannot reach the more difficult strains of errors. Progress is stymied, and the practice hits a wall.

The practice can veer outside of the cone of convergence unless there is strong mindfulness to stay focused with the right efforts. To advance, one has to reduce the margin of errors, not just the errors themselves. This moves into the internal development of meditation to refine consciousness. Only by sharpening the fangsong tool continually through meditation can the subtlest strains of jin errors be eradicated to nurture the prized bloom of yin-yang balance. (The meditation of Taijiquan is discussed in chapter 10.)

The Way the Body Sees It

Physics tells us about force, but does not teach the body how to produce it. We can calculate the impact force needed to break a jawbone, but we cannot set a dial of parameters for the body to deliver a knockout punch. While the differential equations of forces are necessary in the engineering of a robotic arm, the body's control of its motion is learned. The hands become adept at the use of chopsticks by practice, not by analyzing the forces of the fingers.

The theory of neijin explains force and strength the way the body sees it. The body relates to the *rou* (soft) and *gang* (hard) of jin, not the magnitude and direction of force. The body's fluency of the rou-gang of jin enables the Taijiquan master to maneuver force as a vector and to apply the principle of leverage to advantage.

The kungfu of "leading force to emptiness" (yin jin luo kong) uses both the *rou* and *gang* of jin. The *rou* absorbs, neutralizes, and leads the attacking force away to the side, causing the attacker to falter, while *gang* jin shores up the balance. The internal dynamics of the soft-frame changes the angle of impact, while the integrity of the hard-frame maintains the posture.

The skill of "borrowing opponent's force to strike back" (jie li da ren) takes advantage of the opponent's faltering momentum. The skill of "four ounces repelling a thousand pounds" (si liang bo qian jin) is an application of leverage. By relying on the ease of yin-yang change in the frame structures and the rou-gang of jin, a Taijiquan expert (*gao shou* 高手) disposes of his opponents with seemingly little effort.

In summary, physics gives us the mathematical equations to solve the dynamics of force. Taiji gives us the formula to imbue the body with yin-yang principles. Physics explains the power of neijin; yin-yang metaphysics delivers the power of neijin. The magic of Taijiquan kungfu lies in the spontaneous ease of change between the *rou* and *gang* of jin—the body's fluency of rou-gang duality—derived from the internal dynamics of the muscles operating the complex of lever systems of the body-frame.

Additional Remarks

On a philosophical note, the injection of physics and physiology in the exposition above is not intended to supplant yin-yang theory in Taijiquan. Neither is it intended to argue that science has all the answers nor that science represents complete knowledge. To explain the expanding cosmos, science theorizes that what is not visible—dark matter and dark energy—constitutes a whopping 96 percent of the universe.[14] The window of current science through which we see the universe is very small indeed.

It is easy to be seduced by this gap in science to argue that the neijin phenomenon may have fallen between the cracks of physics. But small as the "visible" universe may be, it is that thin slice of the universe that we reside in. The manifestation of neijin lies in the interactions of the visible universe, and more specifically, it falls within the scope of the forces of gravitation and electromagnetism, which are two of the Four Fundamental Forces of Nature.

The Four Fundamental Forces account for what science knows of the forces that hold matter together, from the scale of subatomic particles of quarks and leptons, to the stars and galaxies of the cosmos. The other two fundamental forces are nuclear forces. The Strong Nuclear Force operates within the range of atomic nuclei, and the Weak force in the subatomic range. The nuclear forces bind neutrons and protons together to form stable nuclei of atoms. Though nuclear technology holds humankind's destiny, nuclear forces have no functional relevance to neijin.

In conclusion, the phenomena of Taijiquan's neijin do not fall outside of the known forces of physics. More specifically, what is attributable to neijin is consistent with body motion in accord with Taiji principles. Taijiquan does not subscribe to any gravity-defying phenomenon such as levitation. Rather, Taijiquan embraces gravity in its training and applications.

Touring the Grand Canyons with Dr. Shin Lin, Lu Lili and Chen Zhenglei in Nov 2005.

Subdued in pain by Chen Zhenglei's qinna hold.

Touring California in 2007 with Chen Zhenglei, his daughter Chen Yuanyuan, and his wife Lu Lili

Pictures taken by Dr. Shin Lin.

7
Taiji Balance

Jin is highlighted at the outset as the core strength of Taijiquan in *Ten Essential Principles of Taijiquan* by Chen Changxin (1771-1853), the 14th-generation Chen Family Taijiquan patriarch.[1]

Qian bian wan hua 千变万化
Wu wang fei jin 无往非劲
Shi sui bu mou 势虽不侔
Er jin gui yu yi 而劲归于一

In the myriad modes of motion
Nowhere is jin not present.
The postures though are not alike,
But underlying is the basis of jin.

In the previous chapter, the quest of jin is reduced to the pragmatics of detecting and reducing jin errors—the fangsong process of resolving yin-yang imbalance of muscle actions supporting the frame structure or motion. This gets at the heart of Taijiquan practice—the cultivation of Taiji balance. We approach Taiji balance from the perspective of the human bipedal structure.

Balance of the Human Bipedal Structure

We know from experience that an object with a wide or heavy base is stable. For example, a cone sitting on its base is stable, but inverted on its vertex, it falls readily. An object sitting on a small support base is unstable because it is easy for its center of gravity (CG) to fall outside the base when perturbed. So the wider the support base, the more stable the balance. Likewise, one deduces that a body with a low CG is more stable.

A human body standing freely does not inspire confidence of stability like a structure with a wide support base. In fact, the body-frame standing on two legs is inherently unstable, which is why we do not have two-legged stools. In a normal standing position, the body's center of gravity is in the lower abdominal region, and the base of support is the narrow space between the two feet. It does not take much for the CG to fall outside the narrow support base if the body is rocked front and back. Yet, not only do we move about with ease, we function very well with a remarkable range of mobility—a testament to the ingenious engineering of the musculo-skeletal structure. We do so because our muscles are constantly working to keep the body in balance.

Balance is a very delicate matter. We have no trouble walking on a "balance beam" traced out on the floor, but quite another on the real thing. We can balance reasonably well on one leg, but wobble if we close our eyes. Whenever we move, our balance is affected. But we are mostly unaware of the compensating adjustments, unless we are trying to recover from a lost balance.

Our balance is monitored by the mechanisms of the inner ear, vision, and proprioception, the body's spatial and motion sense, and is maintained by muscle adjustments, particularly of the legs and feet. The foot has 26 bones and some 33 joints to rival the hand not just in number but also in engineering design that helps define our upright mobility.

Our bipedal functionality is learned and programmed since our toddling years. So we take balance for granted. Nonetheless, it does not take much for us to lose balance. We trip easily even over small obstacles. We become aware of balance only after it is already lost.

Internal Balance

A posture in physical balance may not have the same balance. Consider two standing postures: Posture one is at ease and in posture two, the breath is held and the chest is braced up. The center of gravity relative to the base of support is the same in both postures, but posture two can be pushed over more easily than posture one. Holding the breath and bracing the chest up stiffen the structure and make the body top-heavy and less responsive. On the other hand, the posture at ease is supported by muscle actions that are less tense; its frame structure is softer, so it is more responsive, and can withstand the push better. There is a functional difference in the balance of the two postures. It illustrates "internal imbalance" of the muscle actions underlying the frame structure as in the case of the arm in physical balance, discussed in the last chapter.

We say that there is *internal imbalance at a joint* if there is an excess or deficiency of muscle actions in the support or articulation at the joint. A body is said to be in *internal balance* if the internal imbalances at all the joints of the body-frame are resolved. Internal balance thus defines a totality and comprehensiveness of body balance, which is at the core of bipedal mobility.

Resolving internal imbalance is about tempering muscle actions, but it entails a degree of precision at the joints and, thus, presumes the body's perceptivity. It requires the rudimentary requisites of discerning and resolving errors of muscle actions with regard to jin or frame structure discussed in chapter 6. However, the basic factors of errors in the underlying muscle actions—excessive or deficient—are no different. For convenience, we refer to the errors of muscle actions of internal imbalance also as *jin errors*.

The different approaches—internal balance, balance of soft-frame and hard-frame, and balance of *rou* jin and *gang* jin—meld and unify as one's practice progresses. The concepts are differentiated only from the viewpoint of development, but are equivalent representations of Taiji balance.

Taiji Balance

Taiji balance is the balance of yin and yang. This metaphysical balance is the central principle of yin-yang theory that governs the universe of "heaven, man and earth" (*tian ren di* 天人地). Taijiquan practice does not delve in the cosmic dimension of the concept, but is primarily concerned with the yin and yang of the mind and body. More specifically, Taijiquan's approach to Taiji balance is guided by the yin-yang representations in frame structures and jin (chapter 6).

The yin-yang representations are primarily physical in character, and at the beginning, the fangsong process of resolving jin errors is also physical. But as qi develops and the practice progresses, the body relies more and more on qi to decipher and resolve the yin-yang imbalances. Then the practice elevates to the internal phase, where qi takes on the role of driving motion in the yi-qi-motion paradigm. At the higher levels of practice, the precision required in the fangsong process is nurtured more and more by the discipline of meditation. That is to say, although the representation may be physical initially, the body experiences the more profound levels of Taiji balance as the practice advances.

Thus, the emphasis here is on the pragmatics of infusing the body with the yin-yang principles, at the heart which is the principle of Taiji balance. Taijiquan methodology cultivates Taiji balance and builds a core strength of neijin as a matter of course in practice—the fangsong process of resolving yin-yang imbalances.

From the viewpoint of the body-frame, the resolution of muscle imbalance at the joints eases the flow of qi and motion, thus the internal dynamics within the frame structure. This accords the liveliness of change between the *rou* and *gang* of jin, the basis of the power and agility of neijin in kungfu applications.

Imbued with Taiji balance, the body moves, acts and responds in balance and in mutual support between the upper and lower body, the left and right, and the front and back. More importantly, the liveliness of yin-yang balance enables the body to respond spontaneously to maintain balance. For example, the body responds to keep balance even in unexpected situations (which is more elaborated in *Self-regulating Balance* below). Not surprising then that Taijiquan has been found to be a most effective regimen for balance—most invaluable in old age—in numerous studies.[2]

From another perspective of health, Taiji balance in the development of qi extends to qi flow in the network of meridians interconnecting the organs, and thus, nurtures a holistic balance of the organs. By the theory of Traditional Chinese Medicine, this translates to a healthy constitution. Therefore, the immediate and clearest benefits of Taijiquan practice are balance in preventing falls, and health, which accrue to an old age. Indeed, Taijiquan practice is an investment of incalculable returns!

The practicalities of internal balance call for weighing the conditions of balance at each of "the hundred joints" of the body, which clearly is impractical. Ironically, by turning to the traditional concepts of *dantian* 丹田 (translated as "field of elixir") and qi, we find a practical solution. Dantian is described as the point of the body in the lower abdominal region, three fingers below the navel, and about a third of the way inside.

Dantian Center

When we move heavy objects, we instinctively play with the object's weight to find and use its center of gravity (CG). But when we maneuver our body we cannot tell our own CG. We sense our CG when we lose balance. We may infer the flaws in our balance from the uneven wear and tear of our walking shoes. But these are *a posteriori* knowledge. The challenge is to develop the body's awareness of its CG so that one can capture the loss of balance as it occurs, not after the fact when it is too late to prevent injury or defeat.

Part of the problem in trying to locate the body's CG is that it is not at a fixed location as in a statue. Its position depends on the placement of the limbs, i.e., distribution of body mass.[3] It can be outside the body, as when arched backward in the "Fosbury flop" of high jump or in an acrobatic contortion. To cultivate comprehension of one's CG, Taijiquan disciplines the body to move in postures so that the CG remains functionally at the same location.

The location in question is the dantian. In a regular upright stance, the body's CG is close to the dantian. Taijiquan training focuses on the dantian as a center of reference for the body's placement of segments. This instills a culture of the dantian's centrality, and notionally treats the dantian as the CG with regard to balance.

Paramount Status of the Kua (Hip Joints)

The hips (*kua* 胯) are preeminent among the joints of the human bipedal structure. Taijiquan treats the kua junction as the place where the motion between the upper and lower body divides. The role of the kua in generating waist power relies on this division.[4]

Chen Xin says, "The waist [kua] is the junction between the upper and lower body and is the hub of the body's rotational motion. It must not be loose or stiff, but be flexible to bend or fold." (*Yao wei shang xia ti shu niu zhuan guan chu, bu ke ruan yi bu ke ying zhe qi zhong fang de* 腰为上下体枢纽转关处，不可软以不可硬折其中方得.)[5]

A recurring theme in the canonical texts of Taijiquan talks of the waist directing the body's motion. The phrase, "waist as a banner" (*yao wei dao* 腰为纛), in *Elucidation of Thirteen Postures* evokes the image of the limbs following the waist in motion as soldiers filing under a banner. The second stanza of the *Song of Thirteen Postures* describes motion as originating from the waist.

> *Ming yi yuan tou zai yao ji* 命意源头在腰际
> Command from the mind, move from the waist.

The paramount status of the kua is dictated by the integrated structure of the body-frame. The integrity of the structure means that the movements of the upper body affect those of the lower body and vice versa; the movements of the left affect the right, and those of the right affect the left. The imbalances of the lower body obscure the balance of the upper body. Improving on balances of the left can cause imbalances of the right. In short, in a freestanding body, the balances at the joints are integrated in the support of the frame structure. So adjusting the balance at one joint requires a recalibration of the other joints each time—clearly an impossible undertaking in practice. Taijiquan cuts through the complexity by establishing the kua as the base of reference to resolve imbalances of the joints towards Taiji balance.

The practice begins by making sure that the hips are level in supporting the torso. Applying the fangsong process to the waist and groin region brings an initial order of balance at the kua support. This sets the kua as the base to work on the other joints. The practice chips away the jin errors at the shoulders, elbows, hands, knees, feet, and other joints relative to the kua as the junction of reference. Imbalances are thus resolved repeatedly by fangsong, back and forth, between the kua and the joints. In so doing, the practice is also instilling cognition of the connectivity between the joints and the kua, thus of the soft-frame.

Each time fangsong improves internal balance at the kua, the connectivity between the hub and the joints consolidates and cognition of the frame structure sharpens. In the fangsong process, qi is nurtured and fills the body. The focus at the kua induces the qi to flow to the lower abdominal region, forming a girdle of qi around the waist. The more internal imbalances are resolved, the more fully qi collects in the lower abdomen, and the more Taiji balance develops.

The qi building at the waist-groin region is described in another verse from the *Song of Thirteen Postures*,

> Ke ke liu xin zai yao jian 刻刻留心在腰间
> Fu nei song jing qi teng ran 腹内松净气腾然
> Weilu zhong zhen shen guan ding 尾闾中正神贯顶
> Man shen qing li ding tou xuan 满身轻利顶头悬

> Constantly be attentive to the waist and groin.
> Let the abdomen relax completely, and qi will soar.
> As the tailbone settles, the spirit ascends to the top.
> Suspend the head, and the body is light.

Dantian and Internal Balance at the Kua

The resolution of internal imbalance at the kua is elusive as it is integrated with balance at the other joints—it is proverbially the Gordian knot of Greek legend. Generally, the body has no clarity of the muscle actions at the kua and cannot distinguish between those supporting the body above the waist and those below. In anatomy, we see bundles of muscles binding the pelvis and thighs at the hips, not to mention the complex of nerves, blood vessels, and lymph nodes in the inguinal fold. Complicating the muscle functions are an individual's habits wired into the muscles.

The structure of the inguinal fold accords upright support and bipedal mobility for walking, running, squatting, sitting, kicking, jumping, turning, and so on. However, bound as they are by the bundles of muscles to support the ground-mobility functions of the legs, the motion seems constricted in the range of the ball-and-socket joints at the hips. The legs may not have the same versatility of motion as the arms at the shoulders, but the ball-and-socket joints of the hips are critical to bipedal mobility. Whether stationary or in motion, muscle actions are constantly adjusting within the structure at the hip joints to keep balance. This is the internal motion of the ball-and-socket joints of the kua.

Taijiquan works on the internal motion of the joints to facilitate the kua's versatility. The ease of rotational motion of the waist and the dynamic solidity of the base support in Taijiquan rely on this internal motion. The primary objective of fangsong play at the kua is to enliven the internal motion at the hip-joints, and in this, the dantian's role is central.

The dantian is midway between the kua joints. By referencing to the dantian, fangsong can work on the internal motion of the left and right kua. The dantian thus becomes the central station to direct the resolution of imbalances. The fangsong relaxation and internal stretching at the kua are simulated by "opening the kua" (*kai kua* 开

胯) and "closing inward the crotch" (*kou dang* 扣裆), which keep the "crotch round" (*yuan dang* 圆裆) so that the support is agile and solid at the same time. The liveliness of *yuan dang* is the internal motion of the hip-joints being enlivened.

The focus at the dantian in fangsong induces the qi collecting in the lower abdomen to concentrate at the dantian. *Taijiquan Classics* describes this as "qi sinking to the dantian" (*qi chen dantian* 气沉丹田).

More importantly, the attentiveness in practice instills the connectivity between the dantian and the joints in the qi medium. As qi grows and fills the body more fully, it builds a web of qi communication centered at the dantian. The body learns to use dantian qi as a bubble-level to check for yin-yang imbalances and to direct the resolution of internal imbalances at the hundred joints towards Taiji balance.

However, the practitioner is not expected to see the operation of qi right away. In the initial phase, the fangsong is primarily an external process of tempering and softening the physical form to cultivate qi. In the intermediate phase, the body is more perceptive of qi and begins to comprehend the fangsong mechanics of nurturing qi and using qi to resolve imbalances. In the advanced phase, with qi more fully developed, the practitioner uses qi to drive motion internally to set the physical form (*yi nei qi cui wai xing* 以内气催外形), and the body becomes fluent in yi-qi-motion. The more advanced the practice, the fuller is the body's qi to consolidate the role of qi driving motion. And "motion originating at the waist" (*yuan tou zai yao ji* 源头在腰际) is actualized by the qi in the abdomen initiating motion.

The fullness of qi in the body is reflected in the concentration of qi in the dantian. This qi concentration is referred to as "fullness of dantian qi." In this jargon, the fuller the dantian qi, the more developed Taiji balance is.

Full Dantian Qi (Dantian Qi Baoman)

The crowning achievement of Taijiquan training is the maturing "fullness of dantian qi" (*dantian qi baoman* 丹田气饱满). Full dantian qi represents the formation of the central status of the dantian—the breakthrough of the Gordian knot. It manifests the attainment of Taiji balance and the mastery of the art.

However, dantian qi is often misunderstood as referring only to the local conditions at the abdomen. One can easily be lulled into a euphoria of breakthrough by some qi sensation in the abdomen. The maturing fullness means that qi fills the whole body, breaks through all the joints (*jie jie guan chuan*), penetrates every nook and cranny, and extends to all the extremities:

Yi qi guan tong 一气贯通

Qi extends unimpeded throughout the whole body as one.

There is also an inner aspect, which refers to the fullness of qi in the blood, muscles, tendons, bones, and internal organs. This is discussed later in *Principle of Four Extremities*.

The passage of qi, twisting and winding through the myriad joints to the minutest and distal parts of the body, is likened to threading through "the pearl of nine turns," a poetic lexicon for a most intricate task, as in the verse of *Elucidation of Thirteen Postures*,

Xing qi ru jiu qu zhu 行气如九曲珠

Wu wei bu dao 无微不到

Moving qi is like threading through "the pearl of nine turns,"

No minutest part of the body is not reached.

To sum up, the maturing fullness of qi establishes a qi connectivity throughout the body centered at the dantian. The role of the dantian at the center initiating body motion is actualized by yi-qi-motion: yi-command activates qi in the dantian, and dantian qi drives the motion. The assertion of dantian centrality unifies qi dynamics and motion, giving rise to jin connectivity of the body centered at the dantian.

Chen Xiaowang calls this development, "the formation of the central status of the dantian" (*dantian hexin de xing cheng* 丹田核心的形成).[6] However, it cannot be overemphasized that the central status of the dantian is not bestowed but must be earned through the kungfu training process of "unifying the internal and the external" (*nei wai jie he* 内外结合).

Chen Xiaowang's Principle of Motion

Chen Xiaowang condenses the theory of Taijiquan training to a principle which articulates the central status of the dantian. He calls it *Principle of Motion* (*Yundong Guilu* 运动规律). In his workshops, he often lightheartedly refers to the dantian achieving the status of centrality as "dantian happy."

Chen Xiaowang once told me about his quest that led him to formulate the theory. In his thirties, he was fast coming into his own as an accomplished master, highly praised as being deserving of his illustrious lineage. He had won his share of gold medals in provincial and national competitions. He had great confidence of his own kungfu achievement, having tested the proficiency of his fighting skills.[7]

Great though his acclaims were, he felt unfulfilled in his quest. The essence of the art was still eluding him. He was thinking of what it meant to scale the rarefied heights of mastery, where his father and grandfather had been. The burden of legacy weighed heavily on his shoulders.

He had heard of the famous students taught by his grandfather, Chen Fa'ke, in Beijing. In 1978, scraping up his meager savings, he embarked on a journey to seek them out, full of enthusiasm that he would be led to new terrains of the art. However, his hopes were dashed. To his disappointment, he found that they had not gone beyond where he was himself in the art. He returned home, saddened but awakened that what he was seeking had to come from within himself—a lonely quest.

For the next three years, mindful of his grandfather's own struggle and dedication of practicing "a hundred reps a day," he immersed himself wholeheartedly in practice. One day, he realized body comprehension of the dantian center directing the myriad parts of the body in the qi medium. It dawned on him with clarity that his kungfu skills derived from jin initiated at the dantian control center (*zhuzai* 主宰). He had found the fundamental principle underlying the "ten thousand techniques" of kungfu (*wan fa gui yi*). Chen Xiaowang has gained the insight of the "central status of the dantian" (*dantian wei hexin* 丹田 为核心).

So enraptured was he with the spiritual ascendancy of the art that he dashed about looking for his cousin, shouting, "Lei, Lei!" in the factory where they were working. When he finally found Chen Zhenglei to share his breakthrough, he declared the depth of his joy and contentment that nothing could faze his spirit, not even the assignment to clean outhouses.

The theory of Chen Xiaowang's teachings is encapsulated in:

Principle of Motion

Yi dantian wei hexin 以丹田为核心
Yi dong quan shen bi dong 一动全身必动
Jie jie guan chuan 节节贯穿
Yi qi guan tong 一气贯通

Establish the central status of the dantian.
One part moves, the whole body moves,

Qi energy threading through every joint,
And fills the body unobstructed as one.

Chen Xiaowang explains that the litany of exhortations in Taijiquan training:

- point the crown of the head up with no tension (*xu ling ding jin*),
- keep the body straight, centered, and not leaning (*li shen zhong zhen bu pian bu yi*),
- sink the shoulder and drop the elbow (*chen jian zhui zhou*),
- contain the chest and settle the waist (*han xiong ta yao*),
- bend the knees and open the kua (*qu xi kai kua*),
- relax the waist and round the crotch (*song yao yuan dang*), and so on,

are directed at fangsong for qi to sink to the dantian (*qi chen dantian*) and support the formation of dantian's central status.[8] In short, the mind and body discipline of Taijiquan is to cultivate and maintain dantian centrality.

The phrases in Chen Xiaowang's principle are not new, but appear in one form or another in the classical literature. For example, in *Elucidation of Thirteen Postures* there is:

Yi dong wu you bu dong 一动无有不动
Yi jing wu you bu jing 一静无有不静

One part moves, no part is not set in motion
In stillness, no part is not still.

Like the beguilingly simple ideas of meditation, the deep meanings of the principle sink in only when insight is experienced. Only through the time and effort of practice, by tempering the many layers of the body, can internal balance and Taiji principles be infused. Then the body achieves Taiji balance, and jin is everywhere. In encountering an attack, the jin responds with "springlike" spontaneity, changing between yin and yang, *rou* and *gang*, to absorb, deflect and counterattack. That is, one responds at will in kungfu (*cong xin suo yu*).

Principle of Three Unities (Sanhe)

The discussions above reduce the theory of Taiji balance to the concepts of full dantian qi and dantian centrality. However, in practice, the daunting task of resolving imbalances at the myriad joints remains. There are hundreds of bones and more of muscles, and miles of nerves in the body. Fortunately, not knowing anatomical details did not stymie Traditional Chinese Medicine (TCM) nor did it hamper Taiji masters of old.

Fortuitously, at the time I was pondering on the problem of the "hundred joints," Zhu Tiancai was our house guest.[9] So I asked him about it, and he readily directed me to Chen Changxin's *Ten Essential Principles of Taijiquan* and gave me an exposition of the theory. The essay expounds the *Principle of Three Sections (Sanjie)* and the *Principle of Three Unities (Sanhe)*, which address the pragmatics of the "hundred joints."

Principle of Sanhe 三合 provides a formula to discipline movements by simplifying the frame structure into three correspondences of the major joints or parts:

1. the shoulders and kua (hip joints)
2. the elbows and knees, and
3. the hands and feet.

The picture of the "Single Whip" (Danbian) pose illustrates the three correspondences (fig. 7.1).

Shoulder-Kua

Elbow-Knee

Hand-Foot

Figure 7.1 Three Correspondences

One works through the fangsong process systematically, a correspondence at a time. The fangsong resolution of the kua-shoulder correspondence relative to the dantian sets the foundation of training, which extends to the elbow-knee correspondence and then to the hand-foot correspondence. Covering the major joints builds perceptiveness of the frame structure upon which fangsong skills are refined to work on the secondary joints.

To realize the unities is to gain cognition of the correspondences and to cultivate qi connectivity between them. The "three unities" of the principle regulate the harmony of motion among the correspondences with respect to structural integrity, between left and right, front and back, and upper and lower parts of the body. The poise of balance of a posture manifests the unities of the three correspondences.

The unities are critical to generating coordinated power (*he jin* 合劲) necessary in kungfu techniques from locking joints of qinna to the power actions of fajin (explosive release of jin). For example, waist-power action relies primarily on the unity of shoulder-kua correspondence.

Additionally, there are three *auxiliary correspondences*: between head and hands, hands and body, and body and feet. The unities of these correspondences regulate movements of the limbs relative to the trunk of the body. An application is "chest and waist folding" (*xiong yao zhe die* 胸腰折叠), a front-and-back undulating motion of the torso that transmits power from the base to the upper body.

As the above correspondences are referenced externally, their unities are called *External Three Unities (Wai Sanhe* 外 三 合 *)*. Complementing them are the three internal correspondences:

1. heart (*xin* 心) and mind (*yi* 意),
2. qi 气 and force (*li* 力), and
3. tendons-muscles (*jin* 筋) and bones (*gu* 骨)

The *Three Internal Unities (Nei Sanhe* 内三合*)* regulate muscle actions and qi flow—the internal dynamics.

The unity of mind and heart (yi and xin) gives clarity, tranquility and equanimity. This draws meditation into the practice. An undisciplined mind, beset by worries and agitating thoughts, distracts easily. Desires and emotions tug at the mind and afflict stress. Chinese and Hindu cultures have long held the belief that psychology (the mind) affects physiology (the body) and vice versa. Medical science now studies the mind-body connection, led by Dr. Herbert Benson's pioneering clinical study in 1975, which has found that meditation elicits a "relaxation response" that benefits both mind and body.[10]

Taijiquan's soft methodology disciplines the mind—moving slowly inculcates attentiveness that moderates thoughts flitting in and out. The dictum of using yi (mind) not li (force) induces meditation. As the body is tempered in fangsong, perceptiveness sharpens and consciousness deepens. The mind quiets and murkiness clears, creating the conditions for heart and mind to be one. (More of meditation is discussed in chapter 10.)

The correspondence of tendons-muscles (jin 筋) and bones (gu 骨) refers to the factors of muscle actions. Disunity of "muscles and bones" corresponds to internal imbalance of muscle actions. Fangsong relaxation and *shen jin ba gu* (stretching the tendons and bone) tune the imbalance, which clears the impedance to the flow of bioenergies and qi. In other words, the unity of tendon-muscles and bones is the fangsong discipline of reducing jin errors towards Taiji balance.

The unities of "heart and mind" and "muscles and bones" cultivate tranquility and internal balance, which are the conditions for qi to develop fully and for dantian qi to mature to fullness. The dantian may then assert its centrality to drive motion internally by dantian qi. Motion thus is unified with qi dynamics and the force (li) derived therefrom is jin. In short, the internal unity of li (force) and qi sums to jin.

I remember well Chen Xiaowang's early lessons. I was completely mesmerized by the power of his fajin, and hung on to every word he said about jin. Not in so many words, he expounded that jin power is a combination of qi and li. He explained that qi by itself cannot generate power, and li ("muscle force") without qi is crude like an unpolished sword. The crispness of his signature fajin finds its basis in the unity of qi and li.

Principle of Sanhe refers yet to another set of internal unities, which regulates the internal organs under the wuxing classification of wood, fire, earth, metal, and water (table 3.2). Chen Changxin's essay discusses the internal organs in *Principle of the Five Organs (Wu Zang 五脏)*, which follows the TCM explication of holistic health.

The internal unities here refer to the yin-yang balance of the correspondences between heart (fire) and eyes, spleen (earth) and flesh, lungs (metal) and body, kidneys (water) and bones, and liver (wood) and tendons. (The wuxing correspondence is in parenthesis.) They represent holistic harmony of the organs and robust qi flow in the network of meridians.

Kinetic Sequence (Dige)

The mechanics of energy transmission through the segments of a body in motion is like linked rail freight-cars. When the locomotive pulls the first car, the cars behind do not move together at the same time. Rather, the head car pulls the second, which then pulls the third, and so on, car by car, in sequence, groaning at each link. Falling dominoes is another example of sequential motion, which is called a *kinetic sequence (dige* 递个, "one by one").

Kinetic sequence in body motion is not as forbidding as it seems. We have all made use of the principle to save many a broken ankle. If you jump from a height and land solidly as a rigid frame, you would surely break a few bones. To break the fall, the body instinctively lands on the balls of the feet first, then the heels, bending at ankles then knees for the legs and thighs to absorb the impact, followed by the waist and the rest of the body. This sequential breaking of the fall takes advantage of the principle of kinetic sequence. The same principle applies when catching a basketball—the hand draws the ball in with the fingers first.

Transmission in kinetic sequence defines a coherence of motion critical to body performance. This is evident in a professional ball player's pitch: Waist power transmits up the back through shoulder, elbow, and hand to the ball, in sequential order, all while balanced and supported by the base. If the sequential kinetics is broken, the throw loses power.

The picture of Andy Pettitte of the New York Yankees captures the waist power passing through the shoulder to the upper arm, as it is being transmitted to the hand and fingers to the ball (fig. 7.2).[11] A good pitch is relaxed and balanced at each point of the delivery, and energy transmits in sequential order. The throw appears smooth and the motion fluid, the characteristics of "soft power."

Sequential motion in the body-frame is not linear as in the linked rail cars. Also, body segments have their own muscles to move. Generally, only parts of the body in motion engage in kinetic sequence but may not be coordinated. As such, body motion is "noisy" and lacks sequential coherence. The concept of wholebody motion is to engage the segments to move coherently in kinetic sequence.

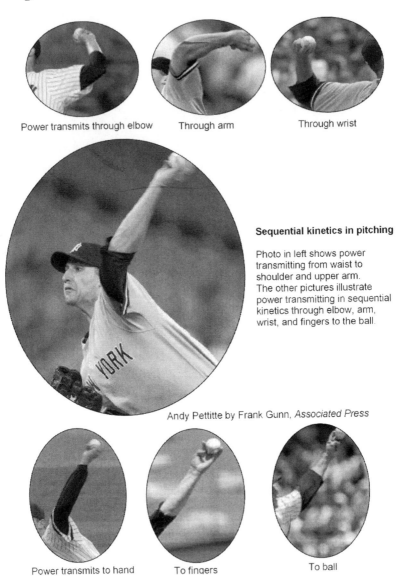

Power transmits through elbow   Through arm   Through wrist

Sequential kinetics in pitching

Photo in left shows power transmitting from waist to shoulder and upper arm. The other pictures illustrate power transmitting in sequential kinetics through elbow, arm, wrist, and fingers to the ball.

Andy Pettitte by Frank Gunn, *Associated Press*

Power transmits to hand   To fingers   To ball

Figure 7.2 Kinetic sequence of power from the waist to the ball.

In kinetic sequence one can see the mechanics of how a frame structure is rendered both soft and hard. The coherence of kinetic sequence takes out the languidness in the soft-frame. That is, functionally, kinetic sequence threading the soft-frame integrates the frame structure as a whole, and renders the hard-frame. At the same time, the energy threading through the joints in sequential order in the hard-frame necessarily softens the structure, and renders the soft-frame. Therefore, the principle of kinetic sequence resolves the conundrum of being both soft (yin) and hard (yang).

The theory of sequential motion—together with the two modes of rotational motions to be discussed in chapter 8—was first explained to me by Zhang Zhijun who credited it to his teacher, Chen Zhaokui.[12]

Locally, sequential coherence is a timely transmission of motion at the joints. However, internal imbalance impedes motion transmission. So training to move in kinetic sequence rides on the same foundational practice of resolving imbalances, but the timeliness in transmission adds more precision to the fangsong process. Still, one encounters the same problem of the myriad joints. Chen Changxin's *Principle of Sanjie (Three Sections)* provides a formula to view the "hundred joints" in "sections of three." Ingeniously, more than a simplification, the principle in practice induces a smooth transmission of qi through the joints to generate sequential motion.

Principle of Three Sections (Sanjie)

The principle of *sanjie* 三节 *(three sections)* prescribes a division of the frame structure into sections of three—*top, middle, and base,* or *root, middle,* and *extremity*—depending on the context of application. Each section may be subdivided further into sub-sections of three, so that the minutest motion of each elemental part can be captured.

To start, the body sections into three parts: head as the top, torso as the middle, and legs as the base. The torso subdivides with chest as the top, belly as the middle, and dantian as the base. The leg section subdivides with kua (hip joint) as the root, knee as the middle, and foot as the extremity. Likewise, the arm divides with shoulder joint as the root, elbow as the middle, and hand as the extremity. To study hand motion, the model places the wrist as root, the palm as middle, and the fingers as extremities. In this way, from head to feet, the body gains incremental cognition of the motion of every elemental part.

For several years from 1998, I traveled as a translator and assistant to Chen Zhenglei in his workshop-tours in the United States. The many repetitions of the same translations have burnt the theories into my memory banks, much of which are being distilled in the present exposition. I remember well the recitation from the *Principle of Sanjie*, which warns of the ill effects of not knowing the "Three Sections."

> *Shang jie bu ming, wu yi wu zong* 上节不明，无依无宗
> *Zhong jie bu ming, man qiang shi kong* 中节不明，满腔是空
> *Xia jie bu ming, dian fu bi sheng* 下节不明，颠覆必生

> If top section is not clear, one's adrift with no purpose,
> Middle section not clear, abdomen is hollow [of qi],
> Base section not clear, one is sure to fall.

With no clarity of the head section, internal imbalance of muscle actions is unclear, and qi cannot settle. To cultivate clarity, point the crown upward to activate awareness but without causing the neck to stretch—imagine a string attached to the crown and tugging at it, but with "no tension" (xu ling ding jin). This creates an awareness of the top section that lifts the spirit of the form and heightens relaxation at the waist for qi to sink, as expressed in the following verse of *Taijiquan Classics*.

> *Xu ling ding jin* 虚领顶劲
> *Qi chen dantian* 气沉丹田

Point the crown upwards with empty tension
Qi sinks to the dantian.

With no clarity of the base, the support cannot be sound, and the body wavers under pressure. Clarity of the leg's three subsections enables the base support to be strengthened: The kua, as the root, drives force to anchor the feet, as extremities, on the ground, and the knees, in the middle, negotiate in between to bolt down the support.

With no clarity of the trunk in the middle, qi in the midsection scatters, and the top and bottom cannot connect. Fangsong resolution of the shoulder-kua correspondence tempers the trapezius and latissimus dorsi of the back and the pectoralis major and the rectus abdominis of the front (concealed as they may be by fatty tissue), and builds cognition and clarity of the torso. As qi fills the torso, attention to its sub-divisional refinement induces qi to collect at the lower abdomen and to concentrate at the dantian.

Principle of Three Sections regulates the dynamics of body segments by the rule: "Extremity leads, middle follows, and root drives." (*Shao jie ling, zhong jie sui, geng jie cui* 梢节领，中节随，根节摧). The mechanism of this rule induces sequential kinetics in the body. In practice, the rule reduces to: "Extremity leads the jin" (*yi shao jie ling jin* 以梢节领劲).

Extremity Leads the Jin (Yi Shao Jie Ling Jin)

Yi shao jie ling jin 以梢节领劲 prescribes that the extremity leads in initiating action. This gives directional clarity to the energy driven at the root to transmit smoothly through the middle section. Without directional guidance, the motion can be wild like an unsecured shower head darting about when the water is turned on. Directing the shower head to the body is the idea of leading jin.

Let us examine the rule applied to the arm—shoulder as root, hand as extremity, and elbow as middle section. Consider two extreme cases: one, the arm is frozen stiff, and the other, the skeletal arm is stripped of muscles. In the first case, the arm is like a rod; the motion of one end controls the motion of the other end, and the middle section has no relevance. In the second, the driving action at the shoulder cannot determine the motion of the hand, as it depends on the transmission at the elbow joint. The uncertainty of the motion may be reduced by tugging at the hand to give direction. The directional tug at the extremity (the leading jin) aids the driving power at the root to pass through the elbow to the hand.

Of course, the hand's motion is powered by the many muscles of the arm. The driving power comes from the muscle actions at the shoulder (the root). Transmission of energy at the elbow (the middle section) is critical to the delivery of power by the hand (the extremity). If the hand jumps ahead before the energy from the shoulder muscles arrives at the elbow, then not only would the hand be deprived of the energy, the upper arm would have to be pulled along. On the other hand, were the forearm tardy, the power of the upper arm arriving at the elbow would jam into the forearm's inertia. In either case, the kinetic sequence breaks and the power delivered is interrupted.

The prescription of *yi shou ling jin* (hand leads the jin)—*shou* (hand) being the *shao jie* (extremity) here—sets the directional clarity of the hand action. The leading jin is just enough to guide the action in the direction intended, but not so much as to cause the hand to jump ahead of the rest of the arm. The leading jin of the hand guides the driving jin from the shoulder to pass through the elbow smoothly. In this way, the rule of yi shou ling jin induces coherence of kinetic sequence in the arm's motion.

However, the concept of extremity leading the jin is often a source of confusion. It has the implication that jin or qi begins at the extremity, which contradicts the Taiji tenet that the source of power comes from the interior. The confusion clears once the driving jin at the root is distinguished as the source from the leading jin at the extremity.

The leading jin at the extremity and the driving jin at the root together form a "pull-and-push" to harmonize jin transmission through the middle joint, which refines the fangsong of internal stretching and relaxation. The rule of "extremity leading the jin" thus facilitates and adds precision to fangsong, and reinforces jin connectivity between extremity and root. By extending the formula to other subsections, motion is disciplined to thread through joint by joint (*jie jie guan chuan*) in coherence of sequential kinetics.

Principle of Four Extremities (Sishao)

The maturing fullness of qi has an inner aspect, more than qi filling the body to the top as a container. The *Principle of Four Extremities (Sishao* 四梢*)* in Chen Changxin's essay expounds an inner fullness of qi extending to "four extremities" (*sishao*), but not the obvious ones of the hands and feet.

The principle refers to qi residing in the internal organs, blood, flesh, bones, and tendons, extending to the four extremities: hair, tongue, teeth, and nails. Only if qi reaches these extremities can the fullness of qi be considered substantial inside. Below is a translation of the principle.

> The power of the boxing system is issued from the interior to the exterior. To use qi in application, qi must be full in the whole body, that is, qi extends to the extremities. If not, then qi is said to be *xu* 虚 (insubstantial) and not *shi* 实 (substantial). If qi does not reach the extremities, the body may appear solid, but is insubstantial inside. The extremities referred to are not the hands and feet.

Hair is the extremity of blood. Qi swimming in the sea of blood has to be full. If not, it cannot rise and leave the blood to reach the hair. If qi in the blood does not reach its extremity, then qi in the body is not full inside. If qi reaches the hair—blood's extremity—then hair can be raised to stand like a bird's crest.

Tongue is the extremity of flesh. Qi residing in the flesh has to be full for qi to be considered substantial in the body. If qi is not fully charged in the flesh and tissues, it cannot extend to reach the tongue. Only when qi reaches the tongue can qi be considered full in the flesh. Fully charged in the flesh, qi reaches the tongue, and the tongue can "break teeth" (*cui chi* 摧齒).

Teeth are the extremities of bones, and nails are the extremities of tendons and sinews. If qi is not full inside, then qi in the bones cannot reach the teeth, and qi in the tendons and sinews cannot reach the nails. The inner fullness of qi in the bones and tendons means that qi reaches the teeth, which can "sever tendons," (*duan jin* 斷筋), and qi reaches the nails, which can "pierce through bone" (*tou gu* 透骨).

This is the theory of the inner fullness of qi. Inner fullness of qi is established by qi extending to the four extremities. Only thus can one avoid mistaking that qi is full (shi) when it may still be insubstantial (xu)!

Taijiquan's methods to imbue the body with Taiji balance and yin-yang principles are embodied in Chen Changxin's *Ten Essential Principles,* particularly, the Principles of Sanjie (Three Sections), Sanhe (Three Unities), and Sishao (Four Extremities).

Self-regulating Balance

An average Taijiquan practitioner may not have the dramatic skills of withstanding the push of several strong men. But the body is so ingrained in training to move with Taiji balance that one responds naturally to keep balance. So when one falls, the danger of being hurt is mitigated by the natural response of Taiji balance, even when accidentally stepping on ice.

Our body has a self-regulating mechanism to maintain balance but only within a range of normal activities. If we are hit with a pillow or bumped by a small child, our balance remains intact without conscious effort. But pushed suddenly from behind we lose our balance. This says that the self-regulating mechanism of balance functions well only within certain parameters of routine activities.

The principle of dantian centrality can enhance the body's self-regulating balance so that one can treat the charge of a fearsome muscular hulk as that of a child. Dantian centrality dresses the body in a web of jin connectivity centered at the dantian. The elasticity of jin responds spontaneously to keep the dantian center intact by internal self-adjustment. So when attacked unexpectedly, the dantian center is not breached, as if only hit by a pillow.

I recall Zhu Tiancai's story of Chen Jixia, a luminary in the pantheon of Chen family masters. Chen Jixia, a twelfth-generation master, lived in the latter part of the reign of Qing Emperor Qianlong (1735 – 1796). His martial fame had spread widely. Chang Sanzhai lived in Sishui to the east of Chen Village along the south side of the Yellow River, and was also a well-known martial artist, as well as a scholar. Hearing of Chen's extraordinary kungfu, Chang traveled to Chen Village to check him out.

Kungfu challengers had not been known to observe etiquette, not even of salutation. Chang found Chen, who was also an artist, engrossed in painting a Buddha image for the old village temple. Without ceremony,

Chang pounced at Chen from behind. The ferocity of the charge seemed certain at least to ruin the art work. But instead, Chang was flung over several meters to the front of the drawing table. Chen betrayed not the slightest sign of being ruffled and continued on to finish his brush stroke. Chang was left unceremoniously to wonder what had just happened to himself. So consummate was Chen's internal kungfu that the attacking force barely affected his dantian center, and his "hidden" shoulder jin in spontaneous response propelled the intruder over.

Chen Jixia's kungfu exemplifies the finest manifestation of dantian centrality and the balance of "the skin and hair"—a feather landing or a fly alighting is reflected in the dantian center. The jin connectivity renders the whole body elastic and springlike—one characterized by "not a part of the body that is not a circle, and not a part that is not a fist" (*wu chu bu shi quan* 无处不是圈 *wu chu bu shi quan* 无处不是拳). Chen Jixia's kungfu was truly at the rarefied heights that would inspire the generations to come.

The Chen family record goes on to say that Chang Sanzhai and Chen Jixia became very close friends, learning from one and another, and exchanging kungfu skills.[13] Chang Sanzhai was also known as Chang Naizhou, the originator of the Chang Boxing System.[14]

Zhang Zhijun was our house guest in Fall 2001

Zhang Zhijun and Mingwei

Mahla and Zhang Zhijun

Soaking in the glorious pencil peaks
of Zhangjiajie, Hunan

Zhang Zhijun took me on this
memorable trip when I visited him in
2002.

Zhang An Ning, author, Zhang Zhijun, Zhang Peng

*Zhang Zhijun's openness to discuss Taijiquan in terms of
biomechanics has been very encouraging to the author.*

8
Theory of Chansi Jin

Fundamental to Taijiquan is the *chanrao* 缠绕 ("coiling") energy that powers motion. Coiling is present in the body's curvilinear and rotational motion. One sees it in wringing a towel, twisting a bottlecap, or turning a screwdriver. Coiling energy powers the legs and arms when working against a load. The power in swinging a racket or bat comes from the rotational energy of the waist coiling up the torso, through the shoulders, arms, and hands to the fingers. The grappling techniques of judo, aikido, and other martial arts all rely on the coiling energy of the waist. Whether it be work, recreation, sports, or kungfu, coiling energy is utilized in one form or another.

Generally, the body can only mobilize coiling energy partially unless it is highly trained. The training to harness coiling energy cohesively is the practice of *chansi* 缠丝 ("silk-reeling") motion. (*Chan* 缠 means "to twine or coil" and *si* 丝 means "silk.") The motion twines like silk being drawn from a cocoon without breaking. The training of chansi is implicit in all Taijiquan, but explicit in the Chen Style system.

The study of chansi does not introduce a new or special kind of motion. Chansi is a discipline of rotational motions, which are inherent in body motion.

Two Kinds of Motion

The motion of an object is described by two modes: the trajectory of its center of mass[1] (CM) and the rotation about an axis through its CM. For example, the earth revolves around the sun and spins on the north-south axis. A football spins as it traverses a path in flight. In springboard diving, the diver's CM traces out a parabolic path, similar to that of a stone projectile, as the body twists and somersaults (fig. 8.1).

Figure 8.1 Diver's CM traces a parabolic path[2]

The two modes of motion are linked. The speed of the earth's rotation (the hours in a day) is tied to its orbit around the sun. A top's precession —the revolving motion described by its axis sweeping out a cone—is supported by its spinning motion. A football's flight depends on the spinning speed about its principal axis. If the football does not receive enough spin, it cannot slice very far through the air. Worse still, if the football does not spin on its principal axis, the motion is erratic. This illustrates the importance of the rotational component in motion.

Body motion is more complex than that of a solid object because body-frame is a structure of linked segments. The motion is a composition of the rotational motions of the torso, arms, legs, hands, and feet. Each segment, while constrained by structural linkages, has its own two modes of motion as a simple object. Aesthetics, agility, power and strength in the art of body motion lie in the discipline of the rotational components of body segments.

Taijiquan describes two kinds of motion of the body complex, which parallel the two modes: (1) *self-rotation (zi zhuan* 自转 *)* as representing the "spinning" motion, and (2) *general-rotation (gong zhuan* 公转*)*, which is analogous to the motion of the CM.

For example, when an arm draws an arc, its circular motion is the general-rotation, and its twisting motion is the self-rotation. (The self-rotation is suppressed in the action of wiping a blackboard.) The arm's motion is actually a combination of the self and general rotations of upper arm, lower arm, and hand.

In the hand's motion, we see the fingers turning relative to the wrist in self-rotation and the wrist turning in general-rotation. As the fingers turn, the end of the phalanges play to connect to the thumb sequentially, starting with the small finger in one orientation, and with the thumb in the opposite orientation. Also, the hand is not limp, but sits on the wrist (*shou zuo wan*) to nurture cognition of the fingers.

For the body as a whole, general-rotation is the motion of its CM, as when the body moves side to side, front and back, or up and down, from posture to posture, in fixed or moving steps. Self-rotational motion is the body turning on an axis through its CM, which in Taiji postures is primarily the vertical axis in line with the spine. The waist turning generates a series of rotational motions of the limbs. So body motion is a series of self (zi zhuan) and general (gong zhuan) rotations of body segments.

Chansi motion describes the body's series of self and general rotations in coherence. This adds another degree of precision to the internal dynamics of the frame structure. The training of chansi integrates these rotational motions in sequential kinetics towards the cultivation of Taiji balance. The torque and leverage generated in sports and martial arts derive from this integration to harness the body's coiling energies cohesively. The ping-pong or tennis player, golfer, pitcher or quarterback all use the rotational action of the fingers and wrists integrated with the rotation of the waist for the right grip and power. The effectiveness of qinna joint-locking techniques relies on the coherence of the self and general rotations.

Chansi Gong (Practice of Silk-Reeling Energy)

Ode to Chansi gong

Hidden in the depths of I-Ching,
Mystic energies are said to delve.
But to seek the dharma of Taijiquan,
Walk the path of chansi gong.

At the heart of the Chen Taijiquan system is the training of silk reeling (*chansi*), called *chansi gong* 缠丝功. Chansi gong cultivates the body's fluency of the two kinds of motion. The training methodology applies fangsong and sequential kinetics to self-rotation and general-rotation at the outset to forge the chansi elements in yi-qi-motion. This steeps the rotational modes in the fangsong resolution of yin-yang imbalance of body motion.

In other words, the Chen system inculcates chansi at the foundational training of Taiji balance, and chansi gong is guided by the formulas of "three sections" (sanjie), "three unities" (sanhe), and "four extremities" (sishao). Thus, by the methodology, chansi motion is regulated by yin-yang principles, and the force arising is jin—the jin of chansi motion, called *chansi jin* 缠丝劲 ("silk-reeling energy"). Chansi jin is not regarded as a special category of jin in Taijiquan. The terminology merely points to the chansi element in jin. Chansi jin is the basic energy that powers Taijiquan motion.

The mechanics of chansi may be viewed from the motion initiated at the kua junction: the waist-kua turning drives motion up the torso, through shoulders, elbows, and wrists, to the hands, generating a kinetic sequence of self and general rotations in the upper body; at the same time, the kua-groin drives motion down the thighs, through the knees and ankles to the feet, generating rotational motions in sequence through the lower body. This produces the characteristic "coiling" or "spiraling" (*luoxuan* 螺旋) motion of chansi.

Chansi motion is far less complicated in practice than in theory. The practice of chansi is built into the Chen Taijiquan form routines. In particular, the practice of the "first routine form" (*yilu* 一路), consisting of some seventy movements, develops chansi jin as the body's core strength. That is why the first routine is regarded as the basic kungfu form (*gongfu jiazi* 功夫架子). Traditionally, chansi gong is the training of the form routines. However, the chansi elements may be obscured in the general form practice. Chapter 11 introduces a set of basic exercises that brings out the essentials of chansi.

Chen Xin (1849-1929) describes the different kinds of coiling (*chan*) motion in *Theory of Chansi*:[3] advancing *chan*, retreating *chan*; moving up and moving down *chan*; left and right *chan*; inward and outward *chan*; large and small *chan*; *shun chan* (coiling with the flow) and *ni chan* (against the flow). The fundamental of these are *shun chan* 顺缠 and *ni chan* 逆缠, which describe the two opposite orientations of self-rotation of the limbs.

Orientations of Shun and Ni

The turning motion of the arm has two orientations: *shun chan* 顺缠, when turning from palm down to up, and *ni chan* 逆缠, when turning from palm up to down. *Shun* 顺 means "with the flow," and *ni* 逆 means "going against," the opposite of *shun*. For instance, flowing downstream is shun, while moving upstream is ni. The rotations are supported by the pair of ulna and radius of the forearm. Turning in the ni orientation, the ulna and radius cross, and turning in the shun orientation, the ulna and radius uncross.

The orientation is also characterized by whether the thumb or little finger leads in the turning. The little finger leads the motion when the palm turns from face down to up in the shun orientation. In the ni orientation, the thumb leads as the palm turns from face up to down.

Likewise, in silk-reeling of the leg, when the little toe leads, the foot is turning in shun chan, and in ni chan when the big toe leads. But chansi of the legs, supported by the pair of tibia and fibula, is more subtle as both legs are usually still planted on the ground while in motion. For example, on the waist turning to the right, friction on the ground holds both the feet from turning. To simulate silk-reeling of the foot, relax to let the toes find the ground, and as the waist turns to the right, the small toe of the right foot leads the jin to the big toe as the turn completes, to grasp the ground in shun chan. At the same time, on the left foot, the big toe leads the jin to the small toe in ni chan.

In the terminology of chansi, Taijiquan is a practice of silk-reeling motion, coiling in arcs of varying sizes and changing from shun to ni and ni to shun. Zhang Zhijun captures this eloquently in the verse:[4]

Yi shun yi ni zou luo xuan 一顺一逆走螺旋
Kai he zhi chu wei zhuan guan 开合之处谓转关
Shou fang tun tu Taiji jin 收放吞吐太极劲
Zhe die wang fu sheng miao xuan 折叠往复生妙玄

Alternating in shun and ni, the motion coils.
Opening and closing play to enliven the joints.
Reeling in and out, sync with qi, and Taiji jin arises.
Wondrous skills are born from the ease of folding and turning.

Versatility of Chansi

The body enjoys tremendous versatility in maneuvers with chansi by
coiling in smaller or larger arcs and changing orientation to advance or
retreat, to move left or right, or up or down. By coiling, one can follow
and adhere to an opponent's action to neutralize or to attack. Chen Xin
expresses the ubiquitous application of coiling in maneuvers:[5]

Ji yin ji chan 即引即缠
Ji jin ji chan 即进即缠

In drawing in use coiling (*chan*)
In advancing use coiling.

For instance, when pushed and pressed by an opponent, rather than
resisting, chansi jin responds by coiling in smaller spirals to draw in and
neutralize the force. When the attacking force ebbs, chansi jin reverses
and coils in larger spirals to advance and pressure the opponent in
offense. When armlocked in qinna, by coiling in the right circle and
direction, one can follow and break the opponent's action and counter
attack. The coiling energy of the hands reads and follows the "light
and heavy" (*qing zhong*) of the opponent's actions. Dantian, at the
center of the body's jin connectivity, detects the subtlest differences
between light and heavy of the opponent's intentions, and initiates
response accordingly in defense or offense.

By changing the coiling radius and orientation, the response of chansi
jin becomes soft and hard. Thus chansi jin is both *rou* and *gang*, supple
and strong, yin and yang, penetrating and unstoppable. Chen Xin
writes (translation):[6]

Unless a long time is spent in the quest, one cannot fathom the depths of Taijiquan. The posture, with shoulders relaxed and elbows dropped, comports the elegance of a delicate maiden. But in confronting an opponent, one is unrestrained like a fierce tiger descending a mountain. The hands become a scale, detecting the slightest change in light and heavy (qing zhong). With chansi instilled in body and soul, the response is spontaneous, coiling accordingly to the opponent's actions. So no matter how the opponent attacks, whether advancing or retreating, fast or slow, one's spirit remains centered and dantian intact. One maneuvers with natural ease as if practicing the form, and the kungfu skills emerge effortlessly. The key is in the divine scale of the hands, reading with clarity the light and heavy (of the opponent's actions), and in the chansi jin responding accordingly. Such truly are the hands of divine wonder.

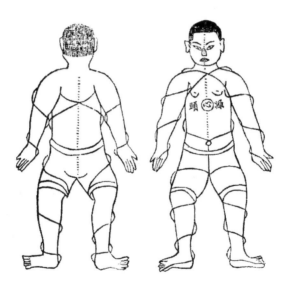

Figure 8.2 Coiling energy of chansi motion emanates from the dantian.[7]

The Leverage of Chansi Jin

A screwdriver may be ordinary and we take for granted the remarkable leverage of the turning motion. Its action is present in all kinds of tools, from nuts and bolts, to drills and car jacks. A screwdriver accords control and precision that a hammer does not. A body thoroughly fluent in chansi can simulate the action of a screwdriver by the groin-waist (dang-yao) acting as the handle in generating the leverage power to bore into an opponent. The torque power of chansi jin is initiated at the dantian center and reinforced by the series of self and general rotations of the body segments in kinetic sequence to the hands and feet. The magic of Taijiquan kungfu stems from the overwhelming advantage of this leverage principle. The dang-yao control is an assertion of the principle of dantian centrality.

It was this advantage that Steve C. was up against when he armlocked Chen Xiaowang, as recounted in *Qinna Manifestation of Rou Jin*, chapter 5. Chen Xiaowang did not struggle against Steve's armlock, but his jin was adhering to the latter's action. So when Chen turned his dantian, as one would the handle of a screwdriver, it generated a tremendous torque against the armlock. It was as if Steve was holding the tip of a screwdriver against the master's control of the handle. Little wonder then that at such a mechanical disadvantage, Steve, strong as he was, stood no chance of holding the master in the armlock and was effortlessly disposed of.

The qinna skills of Taijiquan kungfu are always enthralling because the chanrao (coiling) leverage is unexpected and not apparent. The skills bespeak of the body's fluency of chansi jin in generating the proper leverage with precision.

The practitioner and martial arts historian, Gu Liuxing (1908 – 1991), in an essay echoing his predecessor Tang Hao, cites the methodology of *chanrao* 缠绕 (coiling) as seminal in martial arts.[8] Chen Wangting's insight of chanrao is hailed as a creative contribution to Chinese Martial Arts.

Jin Division at the Dantian

We do not pay attention to muscle actions in routine activities. In standing up, we are not attentive of the muscles straightening the body nor of those balancing the posture. In walking up a long flight of steps, we may feel aches at the knees but notice little of the dynamics at the hips and ankles.

We pay no heed to the muscle actions between those supporting the upper body and those the lower. Yet coordinating the muscle actions between upper and lower body is critical to waist power. In swinging a golf club, the whole body does not turn in the direction of the swing. The hands and arms turn with the swing, but the legs and feet remain "fixed," aided by ground friction. (The body's follow-through occurs after the club's impact). That is, the arms and upper body turn in one direction as the lower body and legs turn in the opposite direction. This creates a junction in the body where the turning motions divide. The power output in the action depends on where this division occurs. The waist is the natural division for maximal power.

If the division occurs at the knees, then the thighs would add to the mass of the upper body in the turn, which would have to be supported by the lesser mass below the knees turning in the opposite direction, notwithstanding that the knees are not designed to turn much in the first place. This would not only destabilize balance but severely strain the knees and ankles, often the cause of injury. If the division were at the chest, as when using only the upper arms and shoulders in the swing, then there would be underutilization of the body's muscle mass.

Force generated in the upper body must be supported by sufficient muscle mass in the lower body, a consequence of Newton's Third Law of Motion (Action equals Reaction). Thus, physics and distribution of the body's muscle mass determine that the division be at the kua (hip) junction for optimal power output. Hence waist power is used in all the body's power actions—a further validation of the kua's paramount status.

More precisely, from the viewpoint of jin, the division of jin actions is at the dantian center, as the source of motion coiling throughout the body to the extremities. The training is to initiate the jin division at the dantian—the action-reaction of jin at the dantian—in generating the coiling motion.

Taijiquan's Waist Power (Dang Yao Jin)

Taijiquan's terminology for waist power is *dang yao jin* 裆腰劲. *Yao* 腰 refers to the waist, and *dang* 裆, to the crotch or groin area, so dang yao jin conveys the product of the muscle actions above and below the kua junction.

Taijiquan's dang yao jin derives from chansi jin initiated at the dantian center where the action-reaction of jin occurs to power the motion. With hands leading the jin, the driving jin of the kua-waist spirals up the torso, through shoulders and arms to the hands, in kinetic sequence, and in balance between the left and right. At the same time, with the feet (as extremities) directing jin to anchor on the ground, the opposite jin at the kua-groin winds down, through the knees (in correspondence with the elbows) to the feet (in correspondence with the hands), in effect, bolting the feet down to secure firm and solid support for the waist-power action. In this way, the myriad muscles of the body, from top to bottom, are delineated between those supporting torque of the upper body and those supporting opposite torque of the base. Thus, with the fluency of chansi jin, the entire muscle mass of the body is recruited in generating dang yao jin.

The Chinese term for initiating waist-power action is: *zhuan yao kou dang* 转腰扣裆 "turn the waist, close the groin inward." Turning the waist (*zhuan yao*) generates torque action of the upper body, and closing by turning the groin inward (*kou dang*) generates the opposite torque reaction to secure support of the base. The terminology thus conveys both the mechanics of waist power and the division of torque action and reaction at the kua junction. Try throwing someone (gently) to the side. The need to keep the base fixed as you turn the waist becomes clear.

Another Chinese term commonly encountered in discussing waist power is *yuan dang* 圓裆 "round crotch," mentioned previously.[9] The "roundness" refers to the ease of the kua-waist turning as an axle with agility and liveliness. Lack of roundness means that the kua is tight and unable to turn freely, which hinders the output of waist power. Fangsong, in cultivating internal balance at the kua, keeps the waist-groin (dang yao) "round and lively" (*yuan huo* 圓活) and breathes clarity into the muscle actions between those of the upper body and those of the lower. This comes from enlivening the internal motion of the ball-and-socket joints at the hips.

The images (fig. 8.3) show the waist-power actions of swinging a bat and a tennis racket, illustrating the graceful balance of the upper-body torque fully supported by the counter-torque of the lower body.[10]

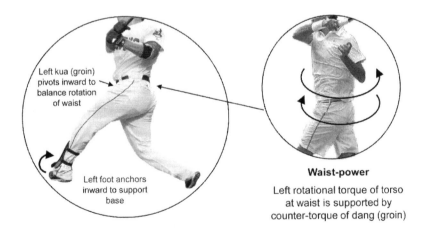

Left kua (groin) pivots inward to balance rotation of waist

Left foot anchors inward to support base

Waist-power
Left rotational torque of torso at waist is supported by counter-torque of dang (groin)

Figure 8.3. Torque and counter-torque actions at the waist.

Dang yao jin, sequential kinetics, and the paramount status of the kua junction are conveyed in the following stanza of *Taijiquan Treatise.*[11]

Qi gen zai jiao 其根在脚
Fa yu tui 发于腿
Zhuzai yu yao 主宰于腰
Xing yu shou zhi 形于手指
You jiao er tui er yao 由脚而腿而腰
Zong xu wan zheng yi qi 总须完整一气

The roots are at the feet
Force springs from the legs
Control center at the waist
Form expressed at the fingers.
From feet to legs through waist,
The whole motion must unify as one.

Although the mechanics of control at the waist is not clearly specified, the energy transmitting sequentially through the body segments is implicit in the verse. Note that the usage of "root" here is different from that used in the Principle of Sanjie (chapter 7), where "root" refers to the source of driving power in "the three sections."

Cover Hand Punch (Yan Shou Gong Quan) and Fajin

Among the movements in the Chen Taijiquan form, "Cover Hand Punch" (Yan Shou Gong Quan) stands out—its explosive action, like the crack of a whip, is uncharacteristic of the uniformly slow motion of Taijiquan. The power-action movement appears four times in the form routine to train explosive release of jin (*fajin* 发劲) from the dang yao (waist-groin).

The punch is practiced in all fighting arts but to harness the full power of the body in a punch is not easy. Often, a practitioner is preoccupied with speed and power, which causes the fist to jump ahead of the rest of the body. Disconnected from the waist, the punch is deprived of the lower body's horsepower. To pun, such a punch lacks *punch*.

In "Cover Hand Punch" the torque power of the upper body is supported by the counter-torque of the lower body, and the left and the right are balanced—the right fist balanced with the left elbow.

In practicing the fajin movement, the focus is not on speed or power, but on the state of internal balance in fangsong to enliven the kua. The fajin action is executed by accelerating the motion. With the right fist and the left elbow leading the jin, the driving jin from the kua-waist (reinforced by the lower left and right back muscles in balance) spirals up the torso through shoulders and arms to release simultaneously in balance at the extremities. At the same time, the opposite jin at the dang (groin) winds down the legs, through the knees to anchor the feet to the ground in support of the action. The practice of "Cover Hand Punch" is to hit all the notes in the kinetic sequence of self and general rotations.

Figure 8.4 Fajin action in "Cover Hand Punch"

A stanza of *Elucidation of Thirteen Postures* describes the prerequisites of fangsong in fajin:

Fajin xu chen zhe song jing 发劲须沉着松净
Zhuan zhu yi fang 专主一方

To fajin one must relax completely to let qi sink,
And release energy fully in one direction.

The power of fajin is fruit borne of the soft-training methodology that tempers the body to develop jin connectivity centered at the dantian. With jin elasticity, the body can issue fajin with the readiness of an arrow awaiting release from a drawn bow. Chen Changxin says it poetically:[12]

Shen si gong xian shou si jian 身似弓弦手似箭
Xian xiang niao luo xian qi shen 弦響鸟落显奇神

Body as the bow and string, and hand as an arrow,
The string sounds and a bird falls—how divine the skill.

Chen Xin elaborates in the verse:[13]

Shen si gong 身似弓
Shen jin si xian xue ru de xi 身劲似弦穴如的兮
Shou ru jian an shi gui xi 手如箭按时癸兮
Xu cun zheng 须忖正
Qian wan mo yao yu xue pian 千万莫要于穴偏

Body as a bow
Jin as in the bowstring drawn
(Energy aligned through acupoints)
Hand as an arrow awaiting release
Must assess correctly
Must not be misaligned in the acupoints.

Another verse in *Elucidation of Thirteen Postures* also likens fajin to the release of an arrow:

Xu jin ru kai gong 蓄劲如开弓
Fajin ru fang jian 发劲如放箭

Store jin as in drawing a bow,
Issue jin as in releasing an arrow.

The analogy does not imply that the body stores energy for fajin like potential energy in a drawn bow, but rather likens the body to the elastic and tensile qualities of the bow. An untrained body is like a crude bow with uneven arm and coarse bowstring. The disciplined Taiji body issues jin in a natural and unforced manner, like a well-crafted bow shooting an arrow.

The body mechanics of fajin is the same when other parts of the body are simulated as extremities for strikes. With the soft-frame any part of the body—elbows, knees, shoulders, and hips, head, as well as chest and back—can be summoned to strike in situations when an opponent is too close in with no room for the feet or hands to extend in use. The power of the fajin comes from dang-yao jin spiraling to the extremities in sequential order. The reader may enjoy a series of fajins by Chen Xiaowang and also by his cousin, Chen Yu, posted on YouTube.[14]

The Chen system has two form routines for training. The First Routine is predicated on softness (*yi rou wei zhu*), and is primarily to temper and infuse the body with the Taiji principles. The Second Routine complements the First to train jin explicitly in fajin. So the Second Routine practice is more driven by "hardness" (*yi gang wei zhu*). Because of the prevalence of explosive movements, the Second Routine also goes by the moniker, Cannon Fist (Paochui).

Chen Zhaokui, son of Chen Fa'ke, had left Chen Village as a young boy to live with his father in Beijing. Later, he returned to Chen Village to teach on several occasions. In 1975, Wenxian County (which administers Chen Village) organized the *Wenxian Wushu Tournament* following the resurgence of Chinese martial arts at the close of Cultural Revolution. Chen Zhaokui was invited as a guest of honor. To mark the occasion, he choreographed a set of 32 fajin movements, which was performed by the then-emerging stars of Chen Village: Chen Dewang, Chen Xiaowang, Chen Zhenglei, Wang Xi'an, and Zhu Tiancai. These "tigers" moved in patterns of squares and plum-flower circles, letting fajins thunder out in unison—a stunningly brilliant performance unmatched since. The set survives as a 42-movement fajin form taught by Zhu Tiancai.

Dantian Internal Rotation (Dantian Neizhuan)

In a nutshell, Taijiquan cultivates dantian as the center where jin initiates coiling through the joints in kinetic sequence to the extremities. Thereby the whole body is engaged in chansi coherence as one. How jin initiates at the dantian source is the study of the internal motion of dantian—*dantian neizhuan* 丹田內转 ("dantian internal rotation").

The body's rotational motion can be referenced by three axes running through the dantian: the vertical axis running along the spine and two horizontal axes—one from side to side, and the other from front to back (fig. 8.5).

An ice-skater spinning rotates on a vertical axis. A forward-rolling somersault rotates on a side-to-side axis. In a cartwheel one rotates on a front-to-back axis. In springboard diving, one may see a combination of twists and turns in all three axes. However, these rotations are external, not the internal motion of dantian.

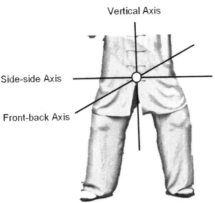

Figure 8.5 Three axes of rotation

Dantian internal rotation is also described with reference to the principal axes but in a way the body appreciates and initiates internal motion. Following Chen Xiaowang's exposition, the three kinds of *dantian neizhuan* are:

1. Left and right rotation (*zuo you xuan zhuan* 左右旋转)
2. Front and back rotation (*qian hou xuan zhuan* 前后旋转)
3. A combination of the first and second kinds invoked when there is a change of internal energy (*huan jin* 换劲)

Taijiquan motion is initiated at the dantian by one of these internal rotations.[15]

Dantian neizhuan of the first kind draws upon the body's natural distinction between left and right in turning. It encompasses rotational motions of two principal axes: the vertical axis and the front-and-back axis. On the vertical axis, turning to the left or right is clear. Along the front-back axis, by thinking of a steering wheel, turning to the left or right is also clear. This turning is usually aided by the waist rotation turning in the same direction.

Motion generated by dantian neizhuan of the first kind is very clear in chansi. The internal rotation of dantian to the left or right initiates the waist's rotational motion: The rotation coils from kua up torso through shoulders and elbows to hands in sequential order, and coils down from kua to legs through knees to feet. That is, the coiling motion of chansi is visibly generated in left-right dantian neizhuan.

In dantian neizhuan of the second kind, internal rotation from front to back or back to front on the side-to-side axis produces a "folding motion of the chest and waist" (*xiong yao zhe die* 胸腰折叠). For example, dantian turns internally from front to back as both the hands are raised in the beginning movement of the Taijiquan form.

The motion may not be coiling externally in dantian neizhuan of the second kind, but the energy in the arms and legs is coiling internally. The motion from the hips to the feet is twisting internally by the pair tibia and fibula to find balanced support at the joints. Similarly, chansi jin is also implicit by the radius and ulna of the upper limbs twisting internally when both hands push forward in the same direction.

When motion changes between left and right or front and back, there is a change of energy. A change of jin (*huan jin* 换劲) is initiated by a combination of left-right and front-back internal rotations, namely, dantian neizhuan of the third kind. Whenever there is a change of chansi orientation, from shun to ni or ni to shun, in the form movements, dantian neizhuan of the third kind is invoked. Coiling energy is also visibly generated in dantian rotation of the third kind as in the first kind.

Complementing dantian neizhuan is the theory of jin division at the dantian—the action and reaction of jin. The jin bifurcates at the dantian: neizhuan of one direction initiates jin to the upper-body action while neizhuan of the opposite direction initiates jin to the lower body in mutual support.

The concept of the division of jin to mutually support actions between upper and lower body, left and right, and front and back is implied in the following verse of *Taijiquan Treatise*:

You shang ji you xia 有上即有下
You qian ze you hou 有前则有后
You zuo ze you you 有左则有右
Ru yi yao xiang shang 如意要向上
Ji yu xia yi 即寓下意
Ruo jiang wu xian qi 若将物掀起
Er jia yi cuo zhi zhi li 而加以挫之之力

In up, there is down,
With front, there is back,
For left, there is right,
In mutual accord and support.
Intent to move up is
Aided by intent to move down.
To lift something up,
Press down to add reaction force.

The idea of mutual support in an action is clearer in the following stanza from Chen Changxin:[16]

Shang zuo xu jin you 上左须进右
Shang you xu jin zuo 上右须进左
Fa bu shi zu gen xian zhu di 发步时足根先著地
Shi zhi yao pa di 十指要爬地
Fa yao wen dang 发要稳裆
Shen yao zhuang zhong 身要莊重
Qu shi sa shou 去时撒手
Zhu ren cheng quan 著人成拳

To act on the left, dig in on the right.
To act on the right, dig in on the left.
When stepping, first anchor the foot.
All toes must grab the ground.

To issue power, waist-groin must be balanced,
Body centered and composed,
Then let the hands fly forth.
One who can do this has attained kungfu.

The division of jin action and reaction in the dantian is invoked by dantian internal rotation, which requires that the central status of the dantian be formed (through the fangsong training of internal balance to cultivate full dantian qi). In contrast, a stiff body is poor in internal dynamics and devoid of dantian internal rotation.

Chen Xiaowang is quick to add that the classification of dantian neizhuan is not intended to be complete—the theory cannot be fully expressed in words—but to provide a formula of practice to exploit the principle of dantian centrality. One cannot be too fixated with theory. In his words, "half mind, half practice," that theory be grounded with practice. The art of Taijiquan is conveyed in three languages: one, body language by demonstration; two, theory by the intellect of words; and three, experiential knowledge by a master's hands-on adjustments and interactions.

The Comprehension of Jin (Dong Jin)

The term *dong jin* 懂 劲 means "understanding jin." This understanding is more than an analysis of jin, but rather the body comprehending how to train for and generate jin in use. It is the body's knowledge of jin that translates the rou-gang (soft-hard) of jin to the vector properties of force and the principle of leverage in application. Comprehension is nurtured by fangsong tempering that infuses the body with Taiji principles. Dong jin is realized by the maturing of the central status of the dantian.

By achieving dong jin one attains "divine insight" (*shen ming* 神明) and mastery of the art:[17]

You zhe shu er jian wu dong jin 由着熟而渐悟懂劲
You dong jin er jie ji shen ming 由懂劲而阶及神明
Ran fei yong li zhi jiu 然非用力之久
Bu neng huo ran guan tong yan 不能豁然贯通焉

As the art matures, gradually comes comprehension of jin.
With comprehension of jin, arises divine insight.
Unless one puts in the requisite time and effort,
One cannot gain thorough and insightful understanding.

In other words, dong jin crystallizes only by the kungfu process of Taiji practice. The insight manifests in the body comprehension of the "insubstantial" (*xu* 虚) and "substantial" (*shi* 实) and the response of change with ease. Dong jin equips the body to read the slightest disturbance to balance even by a feather or fly as in the verse below:[18]

Yi yu bu neng jia 一羽不能加
Ying chong bu neng luo 蝇虫不能落
Ren bu zhi wo 人不知我
Wo du zhi ren 我独知人

A feather cannot be added
Nor can a fly alight.
Thus I know well the opponent
While he knows me not.

Double Weightedness (Shuang Zhong)

Taijiquan kungfu relies on one knowing the opponent's sudden weakness and responding timely to take advantage (*de ji de shi* 得机得势). The problem, of course, is that one may not sense an opponent's weakness nor take advantage. One's body may be unable to turn freely—obstructed or trapped in its own structure—a symptom of the illness of "double weightedness" (*shuang zhong* 双重).

Instances of this occur often when one is pushed. One instinctively pushes back to prevent from being pushed over. The reaction of pushing back locks up the body structure, causing it to be "double-weighted." The waist is impeded from turning by double actions—the opponent's action and one's own reaction. How can one take advantage of an opponent's sudden weakness if one is unable to turn at the waist to maneuver? The following lines from *Taijiquan Treatise* point to the flaws of internal structure and scattered qi in the body.[19]

Xiang qian tui hou 向前退后
Nai neng de ji de shi 乃能得机得势
You bu de ji de shi chu 有不得机得势处
Shen bian san luan 身便散乱
Qi bing bi yu yao tui qiu zhi 其病必于腰腿求之

If able to move forward or step back with ease,
Then only can one seize upon a sudden opening.
If unable to take advantage when an opportunity presents,
Then 'tis the body that be confused and scattered.
To cure the illness, look to the waist and legs.

Important as it is, the symptoms of double weightedness are not clearly understood. The simplest and most prevalent interpretation of double weightedness is that it is the effect of the body weighted evenly between the two feet. So a posture of equal weight distribution at the feet is flawed as being double-weighted.

This interpretation has evolved into a practice rule to avoid postures weighted evenly between the feet and adopt postures with more weight on one foot. This has led to a similar interpretation of *xu shi fenming* 虚实分明 ("the clarity between the insubstantial and the substantial"), to mean that a posture should be distinguishable between a "substantial" (*shi*) side of more weight and an "insubstantial" (*xu*) side of lesser weight. However, these interpretations are an external reference, which say nothing about the internal structure of the posture.

Whether a posture weights equally at the feet or not, if it suffers from internal imbalance, it has defects. Defects of imbalance are not addressed by avoiding postures of equal weight distribution at the feet, but only by the fangsong resolution of yin-yang imbalance. Chen Xiaowang often remarks that if Taijiquan training is simply to avoid equal weight distribution at the feet, then it would be easy to teach and learn. Moreover, it is technically impossible as the body has to move through a posture of equal weight distribution in transition from one stance to another.

If there is internal imbalance, motion is obstructed, and its flow becomes sluggish. The body cannot turn freely, like a wheel that is jammed—it is double weighted.[20]

Li ru ping zhun 立如平准
Huo si che lun 活似车轮
Pian chen ze sui 偏沉则随
Shuang zhong ze zhi 双重则滞

Stand as a balance scale
Then one can turn freely as a wheel
And motion flows as fluid
If it stagnates, t'is double weightedness.

Double weightedness refers to an internal condition of the body. One may stand in balance, but if the body is stiff, then like a faulty scale, the arms cannot weigh clearly the xu (insubstantial) and shi (substantial) of the opponent's intentions. This affliction of shuang zhong is caused by internal imbalance in the posture.

Taijiquan Classics warns of the futility of practice unless one grasps and cures the illness of shuang zhong. If not, one could practice for years to no avail of the art's wonders.

Mei jian shu nian chun gong 每见数年纯功
Bu neng yun hua zhe 不能运化者
Shuai zi wei ren zhi 率自为人制
Shuang zhong zhi bing wei wu er 双重之病未悟耳
Yu bi ci bing xu zhi yin yang 欲避此病须知阴阳

Many have put so many years in training
Yet cannot effect change to neutralize
And end up subdued by an opponent
The ill of double weightedness is not yet grasped
To shield it, inoculate with the principles of yin and yang.

The inoculation is the tempering of the body to infuse the yin-yang principles—the fangsong process to cultivate Taiji balance. The dantian can then assert centrality to read the xu (insubstantial) and shi (substantial) with clarity, that is, xu shi fenming. In short, the formation of dantian's central status immunizes the body against the illness of double weightedness.

Therefore, double weightedness is not about weight distribution at the feet, any more than the sensitivity of a scale is about the weights on the scales. It is about the defects of internal imbalance of body structure. Cure it or forever suffer defeat! *Taijiquan Classics* adds,

Fang wei dong jin 方为懂劲
Dong jin hou 懂劲后
Yu lian yu jing 愈练愈精
Mo shi chuai mo 默识揣摩
Jian zhi cong xin suo yu 渐至从心所欲
Ben shi she ji cong ren 本是舍己从人

It all comes down to understanding jin.
Once comprehension of jin is grasped
The more one practices, the more exquisite the art.

Ponder deeply this gem of knowledge
In time, one can use Taiji skills at will
By the stratagem of "giving up self to follow."

That is, by "giving up self to follow" (*she ji cong ren* 舍己从人), one can follow an opponent's action without struggling against it—the principle of yielding.

"Yield, Do Not Push Back"

When two persons push against each other, the instinct is to push hard, believing that pushing harder will prevail. But beyond the huffing and puffing the winner is the one who maintains balance, not necessarily the one who pushes harder or is the bigger or stronger. Yet, in the tussle, one usually thinks only of pushing the opponent off and not of keeping balance.

Pushing hard against the opponent is in fact a bad strategy. The harder the push, the more the body stiffens up, causing double weightedness. The body becomes less responsive to change and less able to maneuver, and thus, more vulnerable. In pushing and fighting back hard, one may end up an unwitting partner to one's own defeat. The Taiji strategy is to focus on balance and avoid pushing back.

The practice dictum is to "yield and not push back." Try it, and of course you would get pushed off by a strong person! It is easy to yield, but to do so without losing balance is the hard part. No matter, treat it as a lesson. As the erudite Cheng Manching put it, it is an "investment in loss."[21]

When we push at a tree, we feel the reaction force. The harder we push, the greater the reaction force, but the tree is not doing anything to "push" back. The tree is actually supporting our balance in the push— we would fall hard if the tree-support was suddenly taken away.

Practicing to yield is not to give in, but to induce a response that does not react with force against force, so that the body learns to maintain balance under pressure. That is, yielding serves to forestall the body from pushing back rashly and lets the structure align internally to anchor the feet on the ground. To find the anchor, let the body be pushed gently by your partner. By having the partner graduate the push, the body learns to align the segments between the point of push and the feet, and effectively creates a jin path to the ground. Mike Sigman, a pioneer in introducing body mechanics to neijin, refers to this as the "ground path."[22] Taiji balance keeps the jin path lively to root the feet and to neutralize and direct the partner's force to the ground.

"Give Up Self to Follow" (She Ji Cong Ren)

The underlying ethos of Taijiquan kungfu—yielding and not fighting force with force—is summed up in the phrase, "giving up self to follow" (*she ji cong ren* 舍己从人). This does not mean to surrender with a white flag—one is only giving up the reactive response to counter force with force in order to follow.

The strategy of *she ji cong ren* is to maintain control of the combat situation by following the opponent's action so that at the moment of his weakness, one may take advantage to dispose of him. This entails the skill to "stick, connect and adhere to and follow" (*zhan nian lian sui* 沾连黏随) the opponent's action.[23]

She ji cong ren evinces a philosophy of fighting that is quintessentially Taoist: to fight by not fighting but to "accommodate" the enemy. The prescription is not to struggle against (*ding* 顶) but to receive the force of attack, and not to lose contact (*diu* 丢) when the opponent pulls back but to follow and stick to his action.

Implicit in the stratagem of "giving up self to follow" is one's core strength built on internal balance without which it would be hollow. Balance in the action of *zhan lian nian sui* ("stick and follow" for short) is underscored by the three characters *bu diu ding* 不丢顶 ("neither lax nor resisting") that append the phrase in the *Push-hand Song*: *Zhan lian nian sui bu diu ding* 沾连黏随不丢顶. *Bu diu bu ding* characterizes the state of Taiji balance.[24]

Therefore, with Taiji balance underpinning zhan lian nian sui, the actions between upper and lower body, left and right, and front and back are in mutual accord and support (*zhou shen xiang sui* 周身相随).[25] Also, by dantian centrality—the body's jin connectivity centered at the dantian—the jin response is lively (linghuo) and "changes accordingly to the situation" (*sui ji ying bian* 随机应变).[26]

The body's jin cushions the opponent's force like a shock absorber. It adheres to and follows the opponent's action by a natural ease of change between the *rou* (soft) and *gang* (hard) of jin: the rou absorbs the attack's "hardness," and the gang buttresses the body in balance, as described in the verse of *Taijiquan Classics*.

Ren gang wo rou wei zhi zou 人刚我揉谓之走
Wo shun ren bei wei zhi nian 我顺人背谓之黏
Dong ji ze ji ying 动急则急应
Dong huan ze huan sui 动缓则缓随
Sui bian hua wan duan 虽变化万端
Er li wei yi guan 而理为一贯

Counter hardness with softness, the way I respond.
Whatever his actions, I follow, is how I stick.
Fast he moves, fast I move,
Slow he moves, slow I follow.
Throughout the myriad changes,
The principle of response is the same.

By zhan lian nian sui, Taiji balance can read the opponent's intention, so one can respond preemptively, as in the verse of the *Elucidation of Thirteen Postures*:

Bi bu dong ji bu dong 彼不动己不动
Bi wei dong ji xian dong 彼微动己先动

If he does not move, I move not.
But when he does, I move first.

The techniques of zhan lian nian sui are, operationally, jin coiling in the appropriate circles and directions. The jin adheres to and follows the opponent's force by changing the turning radius or direction accordingly to the action—the mechanics of jin coiling in large-medium-small circles.

Large to Medium to Small to No Circles

The progression of Taijiquan practice is often described as follows: At the beginning phase of training one moves in large circles (*da quan* 大圈), advancing to medium circles (*zhong quan* 中圈) at the middle levels, to small circles (*xiao quan* 小圈) at the higher levels, and to "no circles" (*wu quan* 无圈) at the highest. That is, the higher the level of one's practice, the smaller the circles. Articulating movements in small circles can be interpreted as rendering the form compact, which suggests a denseness of qi motion, implying internal power. Does it then mean that as one advances, Taijiquan is practiced in smaller and smaller movements, eventually becoming almost motionless with no circles?

At the early phases of training, movements are extended and articulated in large arcs to express the external form. Also, yin and yang are more clearly distinguished in the large movements. So at the beginning, one practices moving in large circles, but under the admonition of "using yi (mind-intent) not li (force)."

As practice progresses with fangsong softening the frame structure, the body becomes more perceptive of the soft-frame. One gains awareness of the motion articulated at the joints. This elevates training to the intermediate levels where one becomes cognitive of medium-circle motion at the joints. For example, in the movement of "Hands Waving Clouds," one has perception of the elbows drawing medium arcs and the hands drawing large arcs.

Training at the higher levels to move in smaller circles (*quan lian xiao*) does not mean to articulate smaller circles uniformly in motion. It refers to cognition of the smaller circles closer to the center of rotation. In the example of "Hands Waving Clouds," it is the perception of the small-circle motion of the shoulders. Moving in large-medium-small circles refers to the body perception of the large circles of the extremities, the medium circles of the intermediate joints, and the small circles of the base joints. More succinctly, it refers to the training of inculcating body fluency of the series of self-rotations and general-rotations in a range of circle sizes.

At still higher levels of training, the focus shifts to the motion at the dantian center, namely, dantian internal rotation (*dantian neizhuan*). The practice of moving in "no circles" is to initiate motion at the dantian center to drive the body's motion.

In other words, the training to move in large-medium-small-no circles represents the progressive softening of the frame structure to instill the body's cognition of the turning radii in the coiling motion. This, of course, is just chansi motion—the series of self and general rotations—in kinetic sequence, from "no circles" initiated at the dantian center to the largest arcs at the extremities.

The kungfu skills of qinna (locking joints) and close-quarter fighting depend on one's ability to maneuver in small circles. For instance, when locked in close combat, one might not be able to move, like a blocked wheel. However, with chansi jin one can coil in smaller arcs. The smaller radial turn allows one to move more tangentially to the opponent's force, making it easier to escape from a qinna hold or to recover from a disadvantageous position. On the other hand, if the opponent suddenly falters, one can coil in a larger radial turn of chansi jin to pressure the opponent.

In this theory of fighting, by using coiling leverage, a smaller force can overcome a larger force, that is, "the weak can defeat the strong" (*ruo sheng zhuang* 弱胜壮). Also, by closing in to intercept an opponent's punch at an intermediate part of his arm, one can neutralize the action at a speed lesser than his fist. Thus, "the slow can beat the fast" (*man sheng kuai* 慢胜快).

Last but not least, maneuvers by changes of small circles within the internal structure are less detectable by the opponent, compared to the arm struggling at the point of contact. At the highest levels of kungfu, the jin change initiated at the dantian center is imperceptible in *wu quan* (no circles), until the opponent is struck down, as if by a thunderbolt of invisible jin.

How can mortals stand against one of divine insight whose jin flows in large-medium-small-no circles in accord with the Tao of Change!

I first met Chen Yu in 2005.
I take lessons from him whenever I stopover in Beijing.

Between a break in training with Chen Yu in Beijing (2008)

Chen Yu has helped me gain insights into Taijiquan.

9
Methods of Taijiquan Kungfu

Three Ranges of Engagement

The hands and feet are most readily summoned in punches and kicks, and they reach furthest and fastest. This reach represents the first line of engagement where fighters strike at one another predominantly with the hands and feet. Combatants often step back as the other advances to keep the distance of this engagement.

Instead of stepping back, a fighter may dodge a punch or kick by closing in. When fighters close in on each other, the fighting space becomes crammed. The closer proximity puts one in the second range of engagement where kungfu techniques rely primarily on the use of elbows and knees as there is not enough room for the limbs to extend fully in a punch or kick. The fighters may get closer still, for example, as in judo or wrestling, where the bodies come into contact. Indeed, fighters often lean on each other, appearing to be hugging, but they are actually taking a little respite—they are constrained in the limited space to maneuver strikes.

At the proximity of the bodies in contact—the third range of engagement—combat techniques may recruit the shoulder, hip, head, chest, or back. For example, in judo, the hip is used to pivot a throw. However, the use of the shoulder, hip, chest, or back to strike is rarely seen as it is a highly trained skill. This contact-range technique is in the kungfu arsenal of Taijiquan, called *kao* 靠 (literally to bump). Struck by the power of *kao* fajin in the close proximity, the opponent is propelled as if by an invisible force.

The strategy of the three ranges of engagement is expressed in the Chinese literature as:[1]

Yuan yong zhou 远用手
Jin yong zhou 近用肘
Tie shen yong kao wu chu zou 贴身用靠无处走

Far—use the hands
Close—use the elbows
Body in contact—use kao
Nowhere to escape.

Muay Thai boxers train in ranges of proximity to strike with the "eight points"—two hands, elbows, knees, and feet. Wrestlers grapple each other in the second and third line of engagement but they are generally not trained to hit. One trained in the submission techniques of jujitsu engages in close-quarter fighting right away. Mixed martial artists are training more and more in techniques that cross over among the varying ranges of proximity.

It is relatively easy to throw a punch or kick, not as easy to draw out the same power with the elbows or knees, but to summon the shoulder or hip in a power strike of *kao* is most difficult. It requires that the body be well tempered by fangsong for it to be cognitive of the soft structure and to be fluent with the rou-gang (soft-hard) of jin in order to transmit dang yao jin (waist power) to the *kao* action.

Kungfu styles tend to be biased in their preferred ranges of fighting by training. But in Taijiquan, the core training to cultivate Taiji balance equips one to execute fighting techniques with equal proficiency at the varying ranges of proximity.

The same body mechanics of Taiji balance applies in the fajin power of a punch, elbow strike or shoulder *kao*, as well as the ease of change between the actions according to the opponent's proximity. Indeed, Taiji balance underlies the "ten thousand" kungfu techniques—the principle of *wan fa gui yi.*

In essence, all kungfu techniques are maneuvers in large, medium, or small circles. For example, a shoulder fajin articulates in small circles, an elbow strike, in medium circles, and a punch, in large circles. Taijiquan's push-hand exercise (as well as Wing Chun's chi sau—sticky-hand play) engages primarily in the medium range of proximity. It drills the responsiveness of coiling jin in large-medium-small-no circles, thus all the ranges of combat, and complements the soft solo training of form routines.

Push-hand Exercise

Tuishou 推手, a two-person push-hand exercise, is Taijiquan's methodology to train proficiency in martial art skills, by cultivating the four cardinal jins: *peng, lü, ji, an.* The drill consists of two partners engaged in various patterns of pushing, starting from single hands to double hands, from fixed steps to moving steps, and then changing to freer foot work. The push-hand patterns may vary among schools but are essentially the same. The reader may check the many postings on YouTube to get an idea.[2]

Push-hand exercise, like form practice, is enigmatic to the uninitiated as it does not directly train the speed and power necessary for fighting. It appears choreographed and not aggressive, nothing like two persons engaged in combat. However, as innocuous as it may seem, the rather domesticated exercise drills the four basic jins of *peng, lü, ji, an*, on which Taijiquan kungfu techniques are based.

In essence, the two-person exercise drills the "giving and receiving" of each other's force in alternation. When one pushes in offense, the other receives the incoming force, but in turn pushes back when the force ebbs. In this way both partners follow and stick to each other's actions, establishing a connection analogous to two persons sawing a tree trunk. However, unlike the linear back-and-forth saw motion, the push-hand pattern is circular to draw out the coiling jin in the interactions of *peng, lü, ji, an*.

At the basic level, the exercise trains one's responsiveness and balance, which are fundamental in combat. If balance is breached, then techniques are compromised, and one becomes vulnerable as well. If one cannot respond with timeliness or maneuver at ease according to the combat situation, then the kungfu techniques become ineffective. If balance is intact and response spontaneous—the pragmatic elements of neijin—then kungfu techniques can be both offense and defense (*gong fang* 攻防).

In the solo practice of the Taijiquan form, one builds the core strength of neijin. In push-hand exercise, one consolidates the body's fluency of jin by testing the interaction of jin between one another. If one's jin cannot neutralize the partner's force, then one is cornered and is vulnerable. If one's jin cannot take advantage of the partner's weakness, then one cannot prevail. The push-hand drill thus exposes the shortcomings in one's practice and comprehension of jin, which reaffirms the importance of form practice to build the core strength of neijin. Push-hand exercise and form practice go hand-in-hand in the training of Taijiquan kungfu. Chen Changxin expresses this symbiosis as:[3]

Cao lian shi mian qian ru you ren 操练时面前如有人
Dui di shi you ren ruo wu ren 对敌时有人若无人

One practices the form as if there is an opponent,
But in combat, one moves as if there is none.

Song of Push-hands

The verse that resonates most with Taijiquan players, young and old, at any level of practice, is *Song of Push-hands*.[4] The forty-two characters encapsulate the spirit and essence of the kungfu art of Taijiquan.

Song of Push-hands

Peng lü ji an xu ren zhen 掤捋挤按须认真
Shang xia xiang sui ren nan jin 上下相随人难进
Ren ta ju li lai da wu 任他巨力来打吾
Qian dong si liang bo qian jin 牵动四两拨千斤
Yin jin luo kong he ji chu 引进落空合即出
Zhan lian nian sui bu diu ding 沾连黏随不丢顶

Be attentive to the energies of *peng lü ji an*
Upper and lower in mutual accord, the enemy cannot enter.
No matter how much force comes at me,
With "four ounces" I repel "a thousand pounds."
With his force guided into "emptiness," I follow to dispatch.
Sticking to and following his action, I keep intact my balance.

The phrases in the song: *yin jin luo kong* (guide force to emptiness) and *si liang bo qian jin* (four ounces repel a thousand pounds) express the canons of Taijiquan kungfu. *Shang xia xiang sui ren nan jin* means that an opponent cannot penetrate and breach the dantian control center—a consequence of Taiji balance. No matter how great his force of attack (*ren ta ju li lai da wo*) one yields to follow (*she ji cong ren*) by sticking to and following (*zhan lian nian sui*) his action in the jin response. Using the leverage of coiling jin, a little effort of "four ounces" repels "a thousand pounds" of attack. Guiding the force away causes the opponent to overextend and falter. Thereupon, one immediately takes advantage (*de ji de shi*) to dispatch him using his faltering momentum (*jie li da ren*). All these skills are applications of the cardinal jins of *peng lü ji an.*

For generations the children of Chen Village have recited an almost identical push-hand song, called the *Seven Character Ballad.*[5]

Seven Character Ballad

Peng lü ji na xu ren zhen 掤捋挤捺须认真
Yin jin luo kong ren ren qin 引进落空任人侵
Zhou shen xiang sui di nan jin 周身相随敌难近
Si liang hua dong ba qian jin 四两化动八千斤

Be attentive to the energies of peng lü ji na
No matter the attack, all are guided to "emptiness."
Whole body in mutual accord, the enemy cannot enter.
With "four ounces" I deflect "eight thousand pounds."

The textual difference of deflecting *ba qian jin* 八千斤 (eight thousand pounds) and *bo qian jin* 拨千斤 (repelling a thousand pounds) between the two versions is not significant as both texts convey the enormous leverage of the action. In the architecture of the body frame, this huge leverage can only be achieved by coiling (chanrao) jin.

Accompanying the Chen Village ditty is a second song, which makes no bones about the deadly intent of Taijiquan's kungfu applications.

Second Ballad

Shang da yan hou xia da yin 上打咽喉下打阴
Zhong jian liang lei bing dang xin 中间两肋并当心
Xia bu liang lian he liang xi 下部两臁合两膝
Nao hou yi zhang yao zhen hun 脑后一掌要真魂

Above, target the throat; below, aim for the crotch.
In the middle, through the ribs, and into the heart.
Lower, go for the shanks and the knees.
[When he is down,]
Pound the back of his head to dispatch his soul.

How wrong one would be to think of Taijiquan only as gentle and civil! There is a movement in the form called, "Striking the Ground Fist" (*Ji Di Zhui*), a punch down towards the ground. This is to deliver a blow to the back of the head of an enemy falling down to shatter the brain.

Eight Gates of Energies—Eight Jins

The four cardinal jins, *peng, lü, ji, an,* are also known as the four primary jins (*si zheng fang* 四正方). Together with the four auxiliary jins (*si xie jiao* 四斜角) of *cai, lie, zhou, kao* they form the "eight gates of energies." The eight energies are listed in an appendix to *Taijiquan Classics.*[6] The standard translations of *peng, lü, ji, an* are "ward-off, roll-back, press, and push," and of *cai, lie, zhou, kao* are "pluck, split, elbow, and shoulder," respectively.

We retain the Chinese terms for the eight jins since they are vocabulary specific to Taijiquan. The translations, if used, are only for reference. The jins are taught by hands-on demonstration and best understood through practice. The explanations in the literature are surprisingly brief. For instance, the four primary jins are categorized relative to directions, which though simple, does capture the essence of the energies in push-hand play. Grandmaster Feng Zhiqiang summarizes the four primary jins:[7]

> *Peng* means energy goes up; *lü*, back (left or right side); *ji*, forward; *an*, down. But *peng* is also expressed in *lü, ji,* and *an. Lü* is back *peng. Ji* is forward *peng. An* is down *peng.* If you don't have *peng* energy, you are too soft. *Peng/lü/ji/an* are just variations of *peng*: left/right, up/down, forwards/backwards.

Although the four cardinal jins may be regarded primarily as defensive, offense is built into the actions as well. Comprehension of these jins grows from training response not to fight back or resist, but to follow and adhere to the opponent's action. This keeps the dantian intact and puts one in an ever ready mode to unleash any of the eight jins in offense, particularly the four auxiliary jins, at the opportune moment. That is, the practice of these jins in push-hands tests and consolidates the comprehension of the rou-gang (soft-hard) of jin and the central control at the dantian.

Peng (Ward-off) 掤

Peng jin is the mother of all jins, indeed of all Taijiquan kungfu techniques. Peng jin is the jin of Taiji balance brought into focus in the context of push-hand practice and kungfu application. In push-hands, the jin does not resist (*ding*) the opponent's force, nor does it lose (*diu*) him in action. Thus, peng jin is also the jin of *bu diu bu ding* (neither lax nor resisting). Peng jin is developed as a natural consequence of the foundational training of cultivating Taiji balance and establishing dantian centrality. Push-hand exercise unfolds the dynamics of peng jin.

The quintessence of peng jin is the *ziru* (natural) responsiveness that regulates balance not just in one's form practice, but under pressure in combat. Peng jin has the buoyancy of water, and responds in the manner of a compressed spring or air pressure. It absorbs an opponent's force without resisting. Thus, peng jin embodies the essence of Tao, omnipresent and in control without seemingly doing anything.

Enveloping the body, peng jin protects and supports on all "eight sides" (*zhi cheng ba mian* 枝撐八面).[8] The jin cushions attacks from disrupting the control at the dantian. Peng jin neutralizes the opponent's force by internal changes managed at the dantian center. As long as dantian centrality is not breached, peng jin is maintained.

Peng jin is the expression of the jin connectivity of the body centered at the dantian. Peng jin in the body follows and sticks to the opponent's action, so that one may deploy any of the other jins appropriately in defense or offense. For example, if captured in a joint-locking technique (qinna), lacking peng jin, one is trapped in pain and unable to escape, even though not all the joints are locked. Struggling against the qinna increases the pain and exacerbates the situation. Peng jin cushions the qinna so that one can initiate change internally (the soft structure) to follow the qinna pressure and escape, and counterattack.

The response of peng jin is not active—it is passive but spontaneous like a spring. For example, the harder one pushes at a Taiji master, the stronger his natural jin response. The master's jin response is not an action of pushing back. He seemingly does nothing, but his peng jin constantly adjusts internally to break the push. So no matter how hard one tries, the hands keep slipping away and are unable to find a grip on the master's center. Furthermore, more strenuous exertion only causes one to have less control.

Peng jin is not all defense. The opponent may falter when his force is neutralized or spent. At this point, one's peng jin turns into offense. By extending the arms still adhering to him upward, a gush of force springs forth from peng jin to propel him off. Thus, in push-hands, peng jin projects upward and outward to uproot the opponent—the force comes from the waist (dang yao).

While writing this chapter, I asked Master Chen Xiaowang again about peng jin. "Come," he said, to go at him. I cautiously refrained from any aggressive move as I knew that the more force I used, the harder I would be beaten back. So I gently rested my hands on his arms in an attempt to "listen" to his jin. As he finished saying, "This is peng jin," I found myself tossed with my back to the wall. As slightly as I rested on his arms, the force was certainly greater than that of a feather. Despite my caution, he instantly caught my center, broke my root, and merely by extending his arms, sent me flying with his peng jin. The incident bespoke of Master Chen's far superior gongli (core strength).

In form practice, the term peng jin is also used to refer to the inner strength of one's posture or motion. A form is critiqued as lacking in peng jin if it appears limp. If the form is scattered or lacking cohesiveness in motion—not having sufficient energy to connect the movements of the diverse parts—it is also said to be weak in peng jin, like a hose not having enough water pressure.

Peng jin may not show physically as in the appearance of a sculpted body. But peng jin is evident in good Taijiquan form to a discerning eye. The form with peng jin is spirited and vibrant like water pressure in a fireman's hose. Peng jin reflects the maturity of one's practice.[9]

To sum up, peng jin is the intrinsic strength, developed by infusing the body with the principle of Taiji balance. The ziru (natural) response and the buoyancy and springlike flexibility (tan xing 弹性) of peng jin are derived from the fullness of dantian qi establishing the central status of the dantian. From the Song of Ward-off (Peng):[10]

> How can we explain the energy of Ward-Off (Peng)?
> It is like water which supports a moving boat,
> First make the ch'i (qi) in the tan-tien (dantian) substantial,
> Then hold the head as if suspended from above.
> The whole body has the power of a spring.

Lü (Roll-Back) 挒

Lü primarily draws inward but away from one's center to divert an opponent's incoming force, causing him to overextend and falter. The receiving action of *lü jin* complements peng jin in defense, but relies on peng jin to follow and stick to (zhan lian nian sui) the opponent. However, lü does not receive the force in a straight line, but moderates it by coiling it out of harm's way to the side without confronting it directly.

In lü action, peng jin absorbs the attacking force as a first order of defense but changes to lü jin by turning at the waist in order not to resist or struggle against the force. The turning generates the coiling jin of chansi to moderate and divert the force. The arm coils in appropriately smaller circles according to the strength of the force, absorbing and drawing it away to the side. With the loss of its target, the attacking force falls into "emptiness," leaving the attacker with nothing for the effort except to falter. This is the skill of *yin jin luo kong* (guiding attacking force to emptiness).

The chansi of the lü action is generated by the waist's rotational energy initiated by left-right dantian neizhuan (internal rotation).[11] The coiling energy transmits from the dantian through the jin connectivity to the hands to express lü jin. The efficacy of lü relies on the peng jin of Taiji balance, without which, one may get uprooted before the lü action comes into play.

Peng and lü work in mutual support not only to shield against attacks, but to lure in the opponent for him to overextend while one's dantian center remains intact. The moment the opponent falters, one may immediately take advantage (de ji de shi) to launch an offense with any of the eight jins. From the *Song of Roll-Back (Lü):*[12]

> How can we explain the energy of Roll-back (Lü)?
> We draw the opponent towards us by allowing him to advance,

While we follow his incoming force.
Continuing to draw him in until he overextends,
We remain light and comfortable, without losing our vertical posture.
When his force is spent he will naturally be empty,
While we maintain our center of gravity,
And can never be bested by the opponent.

Ji (Press) 挤

Ji follows an opponent's "returning" force by coiling outward in a growing spiral to squeeze and pressure his body structure, to make him lose balance. The action of *ji*, like that of *lü*, is a chansi jin and reliant on peng jin. As the opponent pulls back, the peng jin of the adhering arm changes to ji jin by widening the spiral to squeeze into his body structure. Thus, ji jin is a forward jin.

In the push-hand drill, ji jin counters the partner's lü action. As one's action is deflected by the partner's lü jin one may be led to overextend and falter. But by dantian centrality keeping one's balance, one can turn at the waist to change peng jin to ji jin by widening the chansi spiral to follow his lü action. The enlarging circle of the coiling arm pressures the partner's body structure to break his lü jin. One would have faltered from the partner's lü jin if peng jin was lacking.

The methods of lü and ji utilize the waist's rotational energy initiated by left-right dantian neizhuan (internal rotation): ji spirals outward in widening circles to threaten, while lü coils inward in smaller circles to lure in. The efficacy of the methods lies in the natural responsiveness of peng jin by adjusting the coiling radius and direction accordingly to the partner's force. This responsiveness is a measure of the maturity of dantian centrality.

An (Push) 按

An presses down into an opponent's center to stall him from making changes in his internal structure, and thereby seal his motion. Directed at the opponent's center, the action of *an* jams into the body structure to inhibit internal change, and corners to fell him. In essence, *an jin* disrupts his dantian center to break his peng. *An jin* does not push against an opponent's force. Nor does it flow with the force like lü or ji. Rather, *an jin* cuts across the direction of the force to break the opponent's action. In other words, *an jin* threatens to breach his dantian center so that he cannot root. While *an jin* prevents the opponent from rooting, *ji jin* breaks his roots by squeezing into his body structure. However, without peng support, *an jin* cannot form efficaciously.

The push-hand pattern trains *an jin* to counter a partner's *ji* action. As the partner's *ji jin* squeezes into the body, one applies *an jin* to cut across the direction of his coiling *ji jin* and into his center to disrupt his peng. Threatened thus, he has to pull back the *ji* action to maintain his peng or be pushed off.

An jin seems the easiest to use but is the most difficult to master as it entails both highly developed peng jin to read the opponent's changes and the kungfu skill to maneuver in small circles. Think of pushing a basketball hard against a wall with one hand. The ball will slide away unless the push is aligned with the ball's center and its contact point at the wall. The alignment breaks easily by the ball's varying air-pressure reacting to the push. The action of *an* controls the ball from sliding. Given the myriad changes that can occur internally within the body structure, it is indeed difficult to "lock" the dantian center of a Taijiquan gaoshou (expert)—his peng responds spontaneously from being captured.

A movement in the Chen Style routine that brings out *an jin* is "Six Sealing, Four Closings" (*Liu Feng Si Bi*). The nomenclature of "six-four" expresses a "wholeness" in the arithmetical sum of ten. The pressing action of the movement depicts a complete sealing off of the routes of escape. This movement appears seven times, followed by "Single Whip," in the Chen Style Taijiquan First Routine.

In summary, peng and lü shield against attacks—peng cushions the force and lü diverts it. More importantly, by receiving and luring in the attacking force, peng and lü cause the opponent to overextend and falter, and thus be uprooted by his own action. *Ji* and *an* emerge from zhan lian nian sui (stick to and follow) to breach the opponent's dantian center to uproot him.

The defining characteristic of the jins' operation is that they do not fight or struggle against the attacking force. The jins stick to and follow (zhan lian nian sui) the opponent's action to avoid his strength (*shi*) but attack his weakness (*xu*) (*bi shi ji xu* 避实击虚).[13] More than avoiding the *shi* (substantial), peng and lü work together to neutralize and sap the opponent's strength to render it *xu* (insubstantial) for one's offense to follow.

Turning in "No Circles"

How effective the cardinal jins in application are depends on how refined the maneuvers are—coiling in large-medium-small circles to accommodate the myriad changes in zhan lian nian sui (sticking to and following). The smaller the circle of maneuver, the less detectable the jin technique is to the opponent, and thus the higher the level of kungfu. *Peng lü ji an* emerging from zhan lian nian sui that flows from coiling in *wu quan* (no circles), give rise to *shenmiao* kungfu—kungfu of divine wonder.

An example of this kungfu is the technique of *zhan* 粘 (glue) that seals an opponent's motion. Through dantian qi, the gaoshou (expert) reads the slightest change of the opponent's action and maneuvers jin accordingly to prevent him from moving, effectively sealing his motion (*zhan zhu bu neng zou* 粘住不能走).[14] If the dantian scale is so fine as to tip by a proverbial feather and the maneuvers so refined as in wu quan (no circles), then the kungfu of *zhan* manifested is shenmiao of the divine order.

The rare kungfu of *zhan* 粘 featured in the challenge match between Chen Fa'ke and a well-known shuai jiao (wrestling) master. Chen's fame had attracted many challenges in Beijing not long after his arrival in 1928. In the match, the wrestler placed his hands on Chen Fa'ke, and Chen, likewise, did the same. Both were in position to throw each other, but they just stood there. Neither one moved. To the onlooking students, the seconds of non-action were agonizingly long. Suddenly, the challenger let out a laugh, and the two parted. The next day, the shuai jiao master returned bearing drinks and food. They both ate and drank heartily like old friends. Seeing the perplexed looks of the students, the shuai jiao master praised not only Chen's superior kungfu, but his martial virtue as even greater. He explained that he had tried to throw their master the instant they held each other, but he found himself unable to do so, nor could he move to escape. He had realized the height of Chen's skill and of his own vulnerability of being disposed of at will, and so he let out a laugh of joy to have met a truly peerless master. The technique Chen used was *zhan* maneuvered in wu quan.

Arsenal of the Auxiliary Jins

One may uproot the opponent with the four primary jins, but without seizing the chance to counterattack, he may recover. "Listening jin" (*ting jin*), inherent in peng, picks up the opponent's strength as well as his weakness. So with peng, one can immediately take advantage of his sudden weakness (de ji de shi) to inflict a decisive defeat. "It must not be missed, as it may not present itself again," Chen Xin advises.[15]

This is where the arsenal of the four auxiliary jins of *cai, lie, zhou, kao* comes in. Any of these can be summoned to emerge from the corners of the four primary jins to blast the opponent away. The four auxiliary jins are offensive in nature, but, with basis also in peng jin, have a built-in defense as well. Their actions require the jin to be coordinated (*he jin* 合劲)—between up and down, left and right, and front and back in mutual support—in order to bring out the power and leverage.

Cai (Pluck) 採

The action of *cai* is a coordinated force of leverage that produces the effect of "plucking" the opponent's arm from the shoulder socket. To save the arm from being dislocated the body yields in pain and tumbles under *cai jin*. The lü action transforms to cai by securing the opponent's arm, one hand at the wrist and the other by the elbow; both hands combine in *he jin*—one up and the other down to lock and control the opponent's arm—to prevent escape. So when the leverage of chansi jin is applied by "turning in small circles with a short burst of energy" (*quan xiao jin duan* 圈小劲短),[16] the opponent is readily taken down by the cai action. Caught in the grip of cai jin, the big and strong will fall without grace! While used mostly on the arm, the cai action can also be applied on the leg.

"Lie" (Split) 挒

The action of *lie* produces a tangential force at the extremities by a burst of jin from the waist's rotational motion (dang-yao jin). Such a force is like being struck by the rim of a turning wheel. The opponent, caught by the hands glued to him, is flung off like a pebble coming into contact with a flywheel, as conveyed in *Song of Split (Lie).*[17]

> How can we explain the energy of Split (*Lie*)?
> Revolving like a flywheel
> If something is thrown against it,
> It will be cast off at a great distance.

Zhu Tiancai explains that the terminology of *lie* comes from the Chen Village farming colloquialism in the winnowing of wheat harvest. After threshing, the grains are collected in a mound. The task of separating wheat from chaff is a collaborative work done on a clear, sunny day with a light breeze by a crew of three or four shoveling wheat into the air. As the grains fall back to the ground, the lighter chaff in the air is swept aside by a highly skilled farmer with a broad broom cutting across. The village farmers call this action, *lie*. *Lie jin* is the product of the same body mechanics produced by a short burst of dang yao jin.

Zhou (Elbow) 肘 and Kao (Shoulder) 靠

The actions of *zhou* and *kao* rely primarily on the coiling power of the waist initiated by left-right dantian internal rotation (neizhuan). They are powered by dang-yao jin (waist-groin energy) just as in the fajin action of "Cover-hand Punch." *Zhou jin* is generated by accelerating body motion to project jin at the elbow. Fajin can also project from other parts of the body simulated as an extremity—shoulder, chest, back or hip—to explode out in a strike at a close-in opponent inches away in a *kao jin*. Certain *kao* action, especially of the chest or back, is powered by "folding energy" (*zhe die* 折叠) at the waist initiated by front-back dantian internal rotation.

The technique of *kao* calls for dang-yao jin to transmit up the torso, balanced between left and right, and front and back, in a maneuver of small circles, which is a higher level kungfu.

Transformation of the Eight Jins

High-level kungfu skills are not culled from preconceived scenarios of applications, but flow from the spontaneity of jin response. The kungfu is the body summoning the eight jins at will, according to combat needs (cong xin suo yu).

The jins transform from one to another with ease as the combat situation dictates. For example, if *cai* action is evaded by the opponent, it can change to *lie*; if *lie* cannot be executed effectively, it can change to *an*, and so on. When the opponent closes in, bodies almost in contact, an intended *zhou* (elbow) can change instantly to *kao*.

The eight jins transform from one to another by changes in the internal structure, like the yao-lines changing in the trigrams of the bagua. The transformation manifests the yin-yang alternation between soft and hard (*rou gang* 柔刚), insubstantial and substantial (*xu shi* 虚实), folding and extending (*qu shen* 屈伸), retreating and advancing (*tui jin* 退进), reining in and letting go (*shou fang* 收放), luring and attacking (*yin ji* 引击), and so on.

At the heart of the transformation is the quintessential jin of Taiji balance, without which the eight jins have no legs to stand on. The magic of the hidden jin is the maneuver of change in small-to-no circles initiated at the dantian center.

Ode to the Eight Jins

No matter how formidable the offense
Coil to stick and follow his action.
With dantian center intact,
The attack cannot penetrate
The shield of *peng* and *lü*.

No matter how strong the defense
Ply the primary jins with diligence,
He will falter under *ji* or *an*.
Seize the moment,
Let the four corner jins fly out:
Cai to dislocate,
Lie and *kao* to fell,
And *zhou* to injure internally.

Coiling in large-medium-small-no circles,
The eight jins transform
As in the trigrams of bagua.
How can one not triumph?

Bagua Representation of Jins

The eight trigrams of bagua aptly represent the eight jins, but the correspondence described in the Taijiquan literature is not consistent. One reason is that there are two arrangements of bagua, one, the pre-heavenly arrangement (xiantian 先天), and the other, post-heavenly (houtian 后天).[18] The following table lists three versions commonly found in the literature.

The Eight Jins and Bagua

	PHA	CWM	YCF
Peng	*Qian*	*Kan*	*Kan*
Lü	*Kun*	*Li*	*Li*
Ji	*Kan*	*Zhen*	*Dui*
An	*Li*	*Dui*	*Zhen*
Cai	*Xun*	*Qian*	*Xun*
Lie	*Zhen*	*Kun*	*Qian*
Zhou	*Dui*	*Gen*	*Kun*
Kao	*Gen*	*Xun*	*Gen*

PHA: Pre-heavenly arrangement
CWM: Post-heavenly, in *The Art of Taijiquan*, by Chen Weiming.[19]
YCF: Post-heavenly, in *Self-defense Applications of Taijiquan*, by Yang Chengfu.[20]

To see a derivation of the correspondence of the pre-heavenly arrangement, align the jin energies in the I-Ching axis, with *Peng* at the Qian trigram and *Lü* at the Kun trigram. The change of the middle yao-line in Qian and Kun, begets the trigrams of Li and Kan. *An* energy seeks to break *Peng* by changing its internal structure, so is identified with the Li trigram. *Ji jin* breaks *Lü jin* by a change of radial spiral, so is matched with the Kan trigram. Thus the correspondence of the four cardinal energies is derived.

Moving the middle yao-line of Qian and Kun:

Qian	☰ *(Peng)*	Li	☲ *(An)*
Kun	☷ *(Lü)*	Kan	☵ *(Ji)*

Changing the top yao-line of the four trigrams Qian, Kun, Li, and Kan begets the trigrams of Xun, Zhen, Gen, and Dui that represent the four auxiliary energies. The yao-lines can also be moved in various positions to produce the combinations of the trigrams.

Moving the top yao-line of the four cardinal jins yields the four auxiliary:

Qian	☰ *(Peng)*	Xun	☴ *(Cai)*
Kun	☷ *(Lü)*	Zhen	☳ *(Lie)*
Li	☲ *(An)*	Gen	☶ *(Kao)*
Kan	☵ *(Ji)*	Dui	☱ *(Zhou)*

Moving the bottom yao-line of the four cardinal jins:

Qian	☰ *(Peng)*	Dui	☱ *(Zhou)*
Kun	☷ *(Lü)*	Gen	☶ *(Kao)*
Li	☲ *(An)*	Zhen	☳ *(Lie)*
Kan	☵ *(Ji)*	Xun	☴ *(Cai)*

Producing the appropriate jin by transforming the trigrams in accord with Tao requires, of course, the pragmatics of the body's fluency of frame structures, trained by tempering in form practice and push-hands. Neglecting the Tao can turn a strong position into an unfavorable situation. Likewise, in an adverse situation, do not despair nor act rashly but seek change in the bagua. Stick to and flow with the opponent's action, or, as Bruce Lee famously said, "Be like water." Patiently ply the four cardinal jins. When the enemy contravenes the Tao and falters, a right jin will fly out in offense by a change in the bagua. How can victory not be assured?

The Thirteen Postures

The term "Thirteen Postures" (*Shisan Shi* 十三势) appears in two of the titles of the Five Classical Canons of Taijiquan: *Song of Thirteen Postures* and *Elucidation of Thirteen Postures*. The number "thirteen" is a footprint of I-Ching—the sum of bagua's eight trigrams and wuxing's five elements. The bagua represents the eight jins, and wuxing, the five directions of stepping: forward, backward, left, right, and center (stationary). Thus, Taijiquan, braced by the concepts of bagua and wuxing, is often identified as Thirteen Postures (*Shisan Shi*).

The wuxing correspondence has variations, too, in the Taijiquan literature, but the one listed below is consistent with the standard directions (facing south, back to the north, east on the left, and west on the right):

Correspondence of Wuxing Elements and Directions

Wood	Fire	Earth	Metal	Water
Left	Forward/Advance	Center	Right	Back/Retreat
Zuo Gu	*Qian Jin*	*Zhong Ding*	*You Pan*	*Hou Tui*
East	South	Center	West	North

The term *Shisan Shi* also appears in the boxing routines taught by Chen Wangting, the 17th century founding patriarch of the Chen Village art. The art then was disseminated in seven routines: a set of "Five Boxing Routines" (*Wu Tao Quan*), one "Long Fist" routine (*Changquan*), and one "Cannon Fist" routine (*Pao Chui*). The first of the "Five Boxing Routines" is called *Shisan Shi*. By the time of Chen Changxin, the 14th generation Chen Family patriarch, these routines were consolidated into two routines, called *Yilu* (First Routine) and *Erlu* (Second Routine), which are still practiced today. Chen Xin divides the First Routine movements into thirteen sections to adhere to the revered count of thirteen.[21]

Sports Training and Taijiquan

In sports science one reviews actions in slow motion to find the flaws in body mechanics. In Taijiquan one moves in slow motion to temper and imbue the body with Taiji principles, so that the errors of body mechanics are avoided in actions. Instead of analyzing balance, Taijiquan infuses the principle of Taiji balance into the body, so that the motion it generates is balanced and forged in unity—in mutual support between upper and lower body, left and right, and front and back. Athletes experience this unity of motion at peak performance, which is often characterized by "softness" and a calm oneness of the body, grounded in relaxation and harmony, a condition opposite to the brute exertion of force.

The power of a long drive in golf may share the body mechanics of dang-yao jin (waist power), but it is not neijin. In golf, the player is not concerned with the body's mechanics after the ball is struck except to follow through. In contrast, the Taiji player is attentive to Taiji balance at all times so that neijin is maintained in a state of ever readiness.

Taijiquan training is philosophically different from sports. The training goal in sports is to excel in performance which can be directly measured by how strong, fast, long, high, or points gained. The goal of Taijiquan is not set by measurable records. The prize is the insight of Taiji balance, manifested in a mind of tranquility and a body full of impenetrable peng jin.

Five Levels of Taijiquan Kungfu

Taijiquan is a *gongfu* 功夫 (pinyin spelling for kungfu) art, which means that mastery is attained only through a process of time and effort. Embarking on a journey of Taijiquan requires no initiation rites but only the commitment for the practice to take root. When it does, it will only be a matter of time that it grows. As the practice matures, the shroud of mystery will lift, uncovering the gems of the art.

Five milestones guide the practitioner's journey, similar to the stages of education, from primary and secondary schooling to undergraduate and graduate studies in university. They mark the five levels of kungfu achievement, and pragmatically, they also characterize the margin of errors in practice (*wucha*).

The five gradations are defined by a pair of yin-yang notional values that convey the relative states of yin-yang imbalance.

> Level 1: 9 Yang 1 Yin (External)
> Level 2: 8 Yang 2 Yin (Cultivating the Internal)
> Level 3: 7 Yang 3 Yin (Internal Driving the External)
> Level 4: 6 Yang 4 Yin (Miaoshou—Expert)
> Level 5: 5 Yang 5 Yin (Shenmiao—Divine Mastery)

The exposition here elaborates on essays about the five levels of kungfu by Chen Xiaowang[22] and Zhu Tiancai.[23]

Level 1 (External):

At level 1, the training is primarily external and, except for its slow motion is like any physical exercise. However, the exercise is not totally physical because the methodology urges one to use "mind-intent (yi) not force (li)."

The objective is to prepare the ground—the tempering of the body by fangsong—for Taijiquan's internal practice to develop. Moving by "not using muscle force (li)" induces relaxation and develops qi. Using yi (mind) cultivates awareness of the body and qi, and sows the seed of internal training, which germinates into the soft training of Taijiquan.

In essence, the body is physically tempered to prepare it for qi cultivation—one of "tempering the external to cultivate the internal" (*cong wai dao nei* 从外到内). In the process the body gains awareness of its internal structure.

The nascent qi is rejuvenating and spurs the practice on. Just by following the prescription of practice one enjoys a lift of well-being even at an early phase.

At level 1, the errors of practice can swing widely. The mistakes in the movements and the correctional adjustments are physical and not clearly understood by the practitioner. In the notional values, the margin of error is "plus or minus 4." So unless guided, one's efforts of correction may make the errors worse.

From kungfu perspective, the practitioner at level 1 is stiff and tense like a wood block devoid of internal dynamics, so the body tumbles easily to a push.

Level 2 (Cultivating the Internal):

Moving up to the 8 yang-2 yin level is only a matter of time once the practice takes hold. The body becomes sufficiently tempered—the "1 yin" is improved to "2 yin"—for the internal phase of training to cultivate qi.

At level 2, the body has an understanding of its internal structure and begins to have a clarity of the large-medium-small circles in motion. More importantly, it begins to discern the connection between jin errors and qi flow. This helps the development of qi in the fangsong process of resolving jin errors. But because the qi build-up is uneven, the fangsong resolution is still mainly physical.

The objective at this phase is for the internal training to form through the continual fangsong tempering of the body—the cultivation of qi. This includes the development of the fangsong skills as well.

Qi development at this stage opens up new experiences as the practitioner stumbles into all kinds of qi phenomena. Beguiled, the practitioner may be easily misled into taking the wrong turns as the mind can play tricks. Distracted thus, the practitioner may lose sight of the objective of practice.

The practice must stay grounded in fangsong to resolve internal imbalances and let qi develop on its own accord, not chase after it. A common mistake at this level is to put too much effort into building qi. The emphasis to get more qi may create anxiety and cause the energy flow to stagnate instead. This is the error of "putting yi (mind-intent) on the qi" as noted in *Elucidation of Thirteen Postures.*

> *Quan shen yi zai jing shen* 全身意在精神
> *Bu zai qi, zai qi ze zhi* 不在气，在气则滞

> Put your mind completely on the spirit,
> Not on qi; emphasis on qi causes stagnation.

By persistently staying with the mantra of "using yi and not li" and the recipe of fangsong, one's form gradually gains the Taijiquan flavor of fluidity. Practice at this stage can be very rewarding. The practitioner enjoys tremendous health benefits derived from qi. Indeed, a large majority of practitioners are quite content to stay with the qi development of Taijiquan and keep refining the qi practice for a very long time.

At level 2, the margin of errors in practice improves to "plus or minus 3." But corrective adjustments may not improve the errors unless guided by an expert.

At level 2, the kungfu is one of "scattered hands" as jin cannot coordinate (*he jin*). The practitioner's qi may not be sufficiently developed for the diverse parts of the body to connect cohesively in action.

While one may have cognition of the medium circles in motion, the response in combat occurs predominantly in large circles, and is easily detected by the opponent. There is insufficient clarity of the insubstantial (xu) and substantial (shi), so the kungfu techniques cannot utilize the internal changes between soft (*rou*) and hard (*gang*). For example, when pushed or cornered, the body traps itself under pressure—lacking in yin the frame structure is too yang to change internally. So the only alternative is to fight back, meeting force with force, as yielding would only cause one to be shoved off.

Level 3 (Internal Driving the External):

Elevating to level 3 requires the guidance of a good master or exposure to good Taijiquan and kungfu skills. The practice at level 3 is primarily internal—the body has greater clarity of the connection between qi and motion, ushering in the phase of "internal driving the external," where motion is more and more driven by qi dynamics. This leads to the actualization of the yi-qi-motion paradigm: Yi (mind-intent) activates qi, and qi drives motion.

In the internal practice, the fangsong tool relies more on qi to remedy jin errors. Also, the fangsong tool is being refined to work on the more subtle jin errors, which entails the discipline of the mind (meditation) to sharpen one's perceptiveness.

At some point, the practitioner is driven by a sense of imminent breakthrough. This spurs him to undergo a prolonged period of uninterrupted and intense practice to realize the unification of qi and motion, centered at the dantian—the experiential comprehension of the central status of the dantian (dantian wei hexin). This gives the practitioner a first insight into Taiji balance and dantian centrality, which represents a breakthrough of the art. The body becomes sufficiently tempered to manifest the yin-yang principles.

From a kungfu standpoint, the body can maneuver in small circles and is no longer at the mercy of its own frame structure being trapped inadvertently in combat. When cornered in a tight spot, the body can undergo change in qi dynamics in the relative softness of 3 yin to recover and counterattack. The practitioner has sufficient clarity of the soft (*rou*) and hard (*gang*) of jin to effect the use of "the soft to overcome the hard" (*yi rou ke gang*). However, the response is predominantly in medium circles, which is adequate for most kungfu maneuvers, but there still remains some yang-hardness in the skills. Nevertheless, the body can *he jin* (coordinate jin) and fajin in offense. This represents a functional mastery of the kungfu skills of Taijiquan and one is said to have achieved kungfu (*xia gongfu* 下功夫).

More significantly, at level 3, the margin of error in practice reduces to "plus or minus 2," meaning that the practitioner can self-correct errors of practice without making it worse. At level 3, with diligent attentiveness, the fangsong process of reducing jin errors will stay within the cone of convergence towards Taiji balance. The practitioner is on path to establish dantian centrality (yi dantian wei hexin), the main objective of this phase of training.

The practitioner enters a phase of self-cultivation, which continues on to the next levels. Further development depends less on what is taught, but more on one's own diligence and perceptiveness to pick through the skills and knowledge of the masters. Towards the end of the level, poised to enter level 4, practice of the art comes of age as one's own, and the title of "master" is earned.

Level 4 (Miaoshou—Expert):

At the 6 yang-4 yin level, one's form is fully integrated with qi. The margin of error reduces to "plus or minus 1," and jin errors no longer mar the flow of qi and motion. The errors can self-adjust to maintain the integrity of Taiji balance. At level 4, dantian qi becomes full, establishing the central status of the dantian—qi and motion unify to define the body's jin connectivity centered at the dantian. Jin is everywhere in the body.

The body can summon the eight jins as one wishes (cong xin suo yu) in offense and defense. Jin response is spontaneous. And shielded by peng jin of Taiji balance, one's actions betray no "holes" that can be exploited by an opponent. Maneuvers, initiated at the dantian, occur in small-to-no circles, so are not visible until manifested. The kungfu skills of a master at level 4 are superlative. This is the exclusive club of the *miaoshou* 妙手 (wondrous hands).

Level 5 (Shenmiao—Divine Mastery):

At the level of 5 yang-5 yin, jin errors no longer have external dimension. The yin-yang changes are internal: The rou-gang changes of jin are spontaneous and occur in "no circles" (*wu quan*). Kungfu maneuvers are neither visible nor detectable. "No part of the body is not a circle, and no part of the body is not a fist" (*wu chu bu shi quan* 无处不是圈 wu chu bu shi quan 无处不是拳). As a result, wherever the attacker strikes, the target becomes empty and, at the same time, is propelled on contact. The level 5 kungfu is "wondrous of divine order" (*shenmiao* 神妙).

Development at this stage is a self-cultivation of Tao—the holistic and spiritual harmony of yin and yang. Of the body, it is the dynamics of qi in the flesh, blood, bones, and marrow consolidating fully in the harmony of the internal organs and wuxing (five element). Of the mind, it is tranquility and equanimity, fostering an insight that sees things with penetrating clarity, without bias, for what they are of the moment. One is no longer fettered. One strives to return to spiritual purity in the re-generative transformation of "essence, energy, and spirit" (*jing qi shen* 精气神).

At level 5, one ascends to the pinnacle and the Tao unfolds. Mind and body become one in the embodiment of the Tao. Just as the "ten thousand kungfu techniques" trace to the principle of yin-yang change in the art of Taijiquan, the meditation of Tao leads to the experiential comprehension of the returning of yin and yang to "non-being" (*wuji* 无极). One experiences the all-embracing Tao: nothing is so large that is not contained and nothing so small that is not reached. At this rarefied height, one is in the company of the Taoist immortals!

The Journey of Taijiquan

In the thicket of yin-yang maze,
Shrouded in the densest of mists,
Is the holy grail of Tao.

The occult rears its head
With promise of magical powers.
Succumb not to the lure,
For neijin resides not in
The realm of the mystical.

Fangsong lights the path of the middle way.
Tend to the dang-yao garden, and
Diligently weed away the jin errors.
In time the Gordian knot of the kua yields,
And dantian assumes the central seat.

Dantian qi matures,
Lifting the fog of mystery.
Enlightenment seems at hand,
But reach out to touch it,
As a rainbow it recedes.
Stray not from the path.
As the mind sharpens,
Delusions melt before its gaze.

Amidst the gems of wisdom,
Dawns the prize of Tao.
What more is at journey's end
In the promised land of the sages?

Celebrating Master Chiang Yun-chung's 90th birthday 6/9/2012. With his
wife, Liu Hui (top). Rose (holding painting middle), Cheng Fu-tung (above)
and author were the Master's early students in Guangping Taijiquan.
(Photos by Donald Battershall)

After the induction ceremony as Chen Xiaowang's disciples (from the U.S.) in
Chen Village in March 8, 2006
Back row: James Cravens, Bill Helm
Middle row: Chris Forde, Allison Helm, Derryl Willis, Angela & Jim Criscimagna
Front row: Betty Dong, Chen Xiaowang, Kim Ivy, C.P.Ong

Double Broad Sword training in Chen Village
Master Chen Xiaowang adjusting author's posture

10
Breathing & Meditation of Taijiquan

Breath and Qi

The creation of Taijiquan was inspired by the ancient practice of *daoyin tu'na* 导引|吐纳. Daoyin tu'na is the precursor of qigong, the art of nurturing qi or qi energetics. Daoyin refers to calisthenics to induce qi; and tu'na refers to breathing methods to take in the fresh and expel the stale.

The Chinese character 氣 (qi) is the same for both qi as air or breath and qi as the quasi-physiological life-force energy. Within the character is *mi* 米 (rice), which indicates that qi is composed of air and food. The two concepts—qi as breath and qi as energy—are intertwined in qigong. They are identified as two different things by the body at first, but they harmonize in the practice of daoyin tu'na.

Although the same character is used for the two concepts of qi, two different characters, *li* 力 and *jin* 劲, describe body strength. Strength is distinguished between "physical strength" (li) and "internal strength" (jin). Unless trained, the body cannot tell the difference between the two kinds of strength. An untrained body can only express physical strength (li). Internal strength (jin) is developed by the methods of internal energetics. The etymological composition of the character for jin 劲 (巠 and 力) conveys that the strength of jin is highly refined and cultured as a result of training. Thus, jin is aptly distinguished by a different character. Jin is the fruit of Taijiquan training.

Surprisingly, Taijiquan, with its roots in daoyin tu'na, does not seem preoccupied with the discipline of breathing in training. The advice on breathing by the Chen Village masters is quite ordinary: Be natural, breathe in through the nose and exhale through the mouth, which is disappointing to say the least for one expecting something profound to unlock the mystery of qi. Sometimes, the masters may elaborate that the tip of the tongue should be placed at the palate just behind the upper teeth, to connect the channel *ren mai* in the front with the *du mai* channel running along the back of the meridian circuit.[1]

Natural Breathing

The advice of "natural breathing" (*ziran huxi* 自然呼吸) does seem underwhelming in a practice so steeped in the "internal." As simple and non-specific as it may be, natural breathing turns out to be most effective and functional—it melds with the fangsong process of qi development and grows into a discipline of abdominal breathing.

Breathing in Taijiquan form practice may follow a pattern, such as to inhale with this movement or to exhale with that, but it is not rigid. A breathing regimen may be helpful to regulate breath, but strict adherence can become a hindrance as one has to adjust readily to a change of tempo. Breath changes according to the pace and execution of movements.

If breathing is unregulated, one runs out of breath easily. Breath may not keep up with the demand of exercise, or one's breath may be chronically shallow. The idea of natural breathing is to maintain an ease of breathing in practice.

Naturally, one breathes heavily when short of breath. But in heavy breathing, the body heaving up and down affects form and internal balance. Heavy breathing may be natural in the circumstances, but it is not the natural breathing of Taijiquan.

In regulating breath we immediately think of deep breathing. We take a deep breath when asked to in a medical checkup, or when imbibing a natural scenic wonder. However, when taking a deep breath, the chest muscles may inadvertently raise up the ribcage and hollow the abdominal region. This may expand the thorax but the body becomes top-heavy and topples easily with a push—a symptom of internal imbalance. Taijiquan's natural breathing incorporates deep breathing, but is careful not to cause internal imbalance.

The rationale of natural breathing in Taijiquan practice is for the breath to follow the fangsong relaxation of nurturing qi. The rule is for breathing to follow the demands of practice, rather than for practice to be dictated by the demands of a breathing regimen.

In throwing a punch (a fajin), breathing out is natural with the action, sometimes accompanied with a cry of exertion, like a *kiai* in karate. So, one breathes out in executing a power action and breathes in to gather energy—*xu xi fa hu* 蓄吸发呼 (inhale in collecting energy and exhale in discharging power). Also, generally, one inhales in rising and exhales in lowering, and breathes in to open and breathes out to close.

By being natural and not burdened in breathing one can be more attentive of motion that it is not rushed or of breath that it is not shallow. And in the slow motion, one can learn to adjust breath accordingly to the demands of fangsong practice. By letting breath follow fangsong, one becomes more aware of fangsong. And mindfulness of fangsong guides natural breathing. As perceptiveness grows by the attentiveness of "using yi (mind) not using li (force)" in practice, natural breathing in turn reinforces mindfulness of fangsong. In the iteration, breath gradually becomes in tune with the qi dynamics of the fangsong process, and breathing progressively harmonizes with the body's qi.

How natural is natural breathing? The chest movements may seem natural in breathing, but as noted, the muscle actions can cause internal imbalance. The practice rule to guard against this is:

Hanxiong tayao 含胸塌腰

"Contain the chest and settle the waist."

To contain the chest means to let it settle and relax, the opposite of bracing the chest up. The consciousness of hanxiong (containing the chest) keeps the chest from moving needlessly in breathing. The chest can expand to fill the lungs on inhale, but "containing the chest" acts to reduce the excessive muscle actions. With fangsong at the kua (hip) and the abdomen relaxing, the breath following the qi collecting in the lower abdomen leads to "abdominal breathing." In other words, the mechanics of hanxiong tayao in fangsong induces natural breathing to grow into abdominal breathing.

Abdominal Breathing

In abdominal breathing (*fu shi huxi* 腹式呼吸), the abdomen expands and distends on inhale, and the diaphragm pushes down to increase the lung capacity. On exhale, the abdomen contracts, pushes up the diaphragm and expels the stale breath. Abdominal breathing thus increases the efficiency of diaphragmatic breathing.

Nevertheless, in Taijiquan, the emphasis is on natural breathing not abdominal breathing, which is deferred for the following reasons. First, the preoccupation with the mechanics of abdominal breathing may undermine fangsong. Second, natural breathing grows into abdominal breathing as the practice advances. Third, the discipline of abdominal breathing in Taijiquan involves "reverse abdominal breathing."

The problem with abdominal breathing is that, on exhale, the contraction of the abdomen can cause the abdominal region to hollow and render the body top-heavy. This would introduce internal imbalance, subverting the development of Taiji balance.

The abdominal breathing of Taijiquan is not a simple function of the abdomen expanding and contracting like a bellows. Let us review the action of a punch. One breathes out with the punch, but the abdomen does not hollow. Rather, in the power action, breath pushes down into the lower body. That is, the abdomen is substantial, not hollow, in the exhale cycle. Try pushing the breath into the legs as you execute the punch, and you will find that the punch comes out stronger. Pushing the breath down aids the jin at the dantian connect to the ground to support the jin action of the upper body. The breath on exhale accompanying the power action is thus pushed down—the reverse of the abdomen contracting—to render the lower abdomen substantial in qi.

In order to execute power actions with the full support of the base, the expanding and contracting phases of abdominal breathing would have to be reversed. But that would affect the efficiency of diaphragmatic breathing. The abdomen is more versatile than a bellows in managing expansion and contraction—there are more ways. For example, an accordion can open on one side and close on the other in drawing in and expelling air at the same time.

Reverse Abdominal Breathing

In "reverse abdominal breathing" (*ni shi fu huxi* 逆式腹呼), Chen Zhenglei explains that the abdomen is regarded as of two parts: the large abdomen above the navel, and the small or lower abdomen below, containing the dantian. The reverse of the expanding and contracting phases in abdominal breathing applies only to the small abdomen so that qi remains substantial in the base to support the issuance of jin power. The large abdomen maintains the efficient diaphragmatic breathing in regular abdominal breathing.

On the inhale cycle, the large abdomen expands to draw in air while the small abdomen contracts, pushing the dantian to the back and compressing qi into the seat of the tailbone. Therefore, qi is substantial in the lower abdomen. On the exhale cycle, the large abdomen contracts to expel breath as the small abdomen expands, pushing the dantian forward and still compressing qi downwards. That is, qi stays substantial in the lower abdomen. The thrust of reverse abdominal breathing in Taijiquan is to ensure that on both inhale and exhale cycles, dantian qi remains substantial to maintain connectivity of motion and energy (jin) between the dantian and the legs.

Reverse abdominal breathing seems anything but natural. But it evolves from natural breathing, impelled by the pragmatics of full dantian qi and the issuance of jin power. So Taijiquan practice does not impose reverse abdominal breathing, but adheres to the rule of *hannxiong tayao* (含胸塌腰) in natural breathing to follow fangsong.

The implementation of the rule is part of the training process to be cognitive of the internal mechanics of hanxiong tayao. Externally, hanxiong (containing the chest) reduces the excessive movements of the chest. Internally, hanxiong relaxes the chest for the diaphragm to move down and up in tandem with the abdomen expanding and contracting in breathing. Externally, tayao (letting the waist and back settle) settles the torso into the seat of the pelvis, and internally, it induces qi collecting in the abdomen to reach the tailbone and to break through the kua to the knees and ankles in developing full dantian qi.

The qi breakthrough at the kua is critical to the development of dantian qi and qi connectivity to the legs. Reverse breathing of the lower abdomen and hanxiong tayao work to keep qi substantial to connect to the legs. The lack of this qi connectivity is what hampers the development of full dantian qi and progress to the higher levels of kungfu.

Breathing Methods in Classical Literature

The classical literature of Taijiquan does not say much about breathing methods, but the discipline of breathing is implicit in qi development. The fangsong methodology externally tempers the muscles, bones and skin, and internally induces breath to be in tune with qi.[2]

Nei lian yi kou qi 内练一口气
Wai lian jin gu bi 外练筋骨皮

Internally, one trains connectivity of qi
Externally, one trains muscles, bones, and skin

Only when breath can follow fangsong, can the discipline of abdominal breathing be implemented to support the development of dantian qi; only with the fullness of dantian qi can dantian assert its centrality and jin be lively and spontaneous. This is observed drily in *Elucidation of Thirteen Postures*:

Neng huxi ran hou neng ling huo 能呼吸然后能灵活
Only if one can breathe, can then one be lively.

To reiterate, the discipline of breath grows with practice. Taijiquan's reverse abdominal breathing is not forced, but evolves from natural breathing as breath follows fangsong in developing dantian qi. So whenever the discussion of breathing gets complicated, simply revert to the rule of hanxiong tayao and natural breathing to support and follow the fangsong mechanics, guided by the principles of three sections (sanjie), three unities (sanhe), and four extremities (sishao). That is to say, whatever the breathing methods are, do not lose sight of the core training of fangsong to cultivate Taiji balance.

"Breathing with the Heels"

Breath following qi through the joints in the fangsong process induces "breathing" into the joints. With qi breaking through kua, knees and ankles to feet, and breath following, one thus "breathes with the heels." The Taoist sage Zhuangzi (369 – 298 B.C.) had noted the practice of breathing with the heels. In Taijiquan, it affirms that qi is reaching the feet, establishing qi connectivity of the whole body.

Reverse abdominal breathing actually derives from Taoist breathing that emulates the way the fetus breathes in the womb. The rationale of fetal or prenatal breathing is to nurture "prenatal qi," which is believed to be of the purest essence in rejuvenation, in contrast to "postnatal qi" for growth and maintenance. Prenatal qi is the Taoist elixir of life.

Influenced by the Taoist belief, reverse abdominal breathing has been used in qi energetics for health and for martial arts since the beginnings. The breathing discipline cultivates mindfulness and lifts the spirit. The internal motion of abdominal breathing massages the organs. The fullness of qi penetrates the organs, blood, bones, flesh, and skin, to promote their functions in holistic balance. The practitioner reaps a bountiful harvest of health benefits. And for the martial artist, the prize is neijin.

Role of Meditation in Taijiquan

Shaolin lore has an iconic image of the sixth-century Indian Buddhist monk, Bodhidharma, sitting in meditation facing the wall of a cave for nine years. In Taijiquan, meditation is not as ascetic but is inherent in the slow and attentive nature of the exercise.

Taijiquan prescribes that one simply follows the slow-motion exercise. Meditation enters through the mantra of using yi (mind), not li (force) to move. The meditation discipline works right away: More than giving pause and restraining the body from its habitual mode of producing motion, the mantra cultivates mindfulness. This allows the body to find itself and learn to regulate motion internally by yin-yang principles.

Also, the mindfulness of yi nurtures attentiveness, which keeps the mind from being distracted. This cultivates a quietness of the mind conducive for perceptiveness to grow, and awakens the mind's eye to discern the body's own motion, qi, and internal structure. The development of the roles of yi and qi in the paradigm of yi-qi-motion rests on the meditation discipline to build cognition.

Attentive observation in meditation does not mean to ponder or hang tenaciously onto what is being observed, but rather to let go. One does nothing specific except to attentively note and let the observed pass. In this way, thoughts are being "emptied" by attentive observation, and the heart and mind lighten (*xu* 虚). The body relaxes, the mind calms, and qi settles to fill the lower abdomen to render it full and substantial (*shi* 实). Thus it is said in meditation: "light is the heart, full is the abdomen" (*xu qi xin shi qi fu* 虚其心实其腹).

Meditation is not stressed in Taijiquan practice at the initial phases, but the meditation component works in the background without burdening the practitioner. The physical but soft exercise prepares the ground for the meditation discipline to take root. However, at the higher levels of practice, one has to consciously cultivate meditation.

Meditation and Perceptiveness

The mind, by nature, is restless and tends to wander. Thoughts zip in and out, and the object of concentration keeps slipping away. The wanderings clutter and cloud the mind, frustrating efforts to focus. This inattentive and fickle state of the mind is described in Chan or Zen meditation as "the mind of a monkey" (*xinyuan* 心 猿). Meditation discipline tames the mind to gain clarity and insight.

One may set out with resolve to restrain the mind from wandering. But the problem is that one may not be aware of the wandering to begin with. Taijiquan's meditation is ingeniously pragmatic. Under the constant admonition of "using yi (mind) not li (force)," at some point, one becomes aware that the mind is wandering. The awareness itself marks a turning point in the practice. One learns to use the act of awareness to trigger an arrest of the wandering and bring the mind back to the task of attentive observation. This creates a feedback loop of awareness reining in the wandering mind, which in turn refines consciousness to be more aware of wandering. The mind, thus sharpened, wanders less, catches the wandering sooner, and becomes clearer and more perceptive.

With perceptiveness, the practice moves to the internal phase of regulating qi dynamics to drive motion. Thus, the practitioner acculturates to yi-qi-motion and works in the qi medium to resolve jin errors. However, the practice may falter and stall—the fangsong tools may not be fine enough to resolve the jin errors that are more subtle at the higher levels. The role of meditation is crucial to keep the fangsong tools continually refined in order to weed out the increasingly subtler jin errors.

Qi can then grow more robustly to break through the joints to fill the body. In the fuller qi medium, one gains experiential comprehension of the body's structural integrity—one part moves, the whole body moves; and in stillness, no part is not still—and of the paramount status of the kua junction—the division of motion between the upper and lower body. The focus at the kua junction induces the qi buildup to concentrate at the dantian (qi chen dantian). As dantian qi matures to fullness, the body experiences the unity of qi and motion and the fruition of dantian centrality—the jin connectivity centered at the dantian.

Meditation plays a crucial role at each step of the way, particularly at the higher levels. In the tranquility of meditation, the mind unifies with the form—the unity of the internal and external.[3]

> *Xin shen ru jing xing shen he yi* 心神入静形神合一
> Heart and form unify spiritually in meditation.

Tranquility of Meditation

The above section discusses meditation from the pragmatic viewpoint of Taijiquan—developing perceptiveness to regulate qi and motion in the fangsong process. Basically, meditation nurtures a culture of tranquility of the mind, which complements the harmony of Taiji motion. So Taijiquan builds not only a core strength of neijin but an inner sanctum of calmness through the "internal unity of the heart and mind" (*xin yi he* 心意合).[4]

Meditation may seem remote to the mundanities of life, but far from it, we are constantly subject to stress, both physical and emotional, which builds up without us knowing. When we are angry, we are not aware of the anger until after it has erupted. Even with the body shaking with anger, we may still be unaware as the mind is too agitated. Envy, greed, and hatred are not simple failings that can be readily unwound or rectified. Ominously, such emotions can fester and consume to the point of overwhelming one's thinking and actions. Not many ills, pains, or sufferings do not trace to thoughts and actions driven by negative emotions.

If one could reason not to be angry, hateful, greedy, or jealous, or control emotions like turning down sound volume, then social and inter-relational problems would be less intractable. Worse still, the mind is unaware of the emotions until after they have manifested and taken their toll. How can one be cognizant of the emotion when one is so consumed by it? How can one be calm when one is already in a state of anxiety, worrying, losing sleep, or suffering migraines?

Meditation builds a reservoir of serenity and nurtures the heart as the center of tranquility. This keeps one steady and calm amidst the waves of emotions. The serenity is cultivated by taming the "wild monkey" of the mind by meditation. This builds a radar of mindfulness that picks up emotions. The awareness moderates the emotion and forestalls it from getting worse or becoming consuming. In so doing, meditation elicits a relaxation and thus a relief of stress. This is the relaxation response that Dr. Herbert Benson was referring to in his pioneering study of meditation.[5]

With mindful awareness, one learns to react less with uncontrolled emotional outbursts, just as the Taiji body learns not to fight force with force. At the higher planes of meditation, the refined consciousness becomes aware of the emotion as it arises, not after, and arrests it before it manifests. By arresting and eradicating unwholesome thoughts, ills and sufferings are thus mitigated. This opens the mind to the bliss of tranquility.

The meditation here may seem more abstract than the pragmatics of fangsong, but the practice principle is the same: to cultivate mindfulness of unwholesome thoughts and to weed them out. It tempers and quiets the mind, giving more clarity and concentration to better discern and dissolve more unwholesome thoughts. This creates a positive feedback loop as in fangsong, which tempers and refines consciousness, much as water in a running brook polishes a rock. Meditation renders the mind inhospitable for unwholesome thoughts to take root, and thereby consolidates inner tranquility. By harmonizing heart and mind, meditation nurtures the "heart" (*xin* 心) as the "moral center" of the mind, analogous to the central status of the dantian.

"The Moral Heart"

In the Chinese psyche, the heart has been co-opted as a "thinking" organ since antiquity. The characterization of feelings as coming from the heart is universal. However, the ancient Chinese thinkers had made the philosophical distinction that thinking with the heart—to have feelings for others—makes one human. The mind with a feeling heart—the moral heart—subsumes a consciousness of humanity and righteousness.

The Confucian sage Mencius or Mengzi (c. 372 – 289 B.C.) propounds that human nature is innately good, based on the moral heart. He further expounds that the "goodness" of the heart may be nurtured by qi energetics (daoyin tu'na) and meditation. By infusing qi with the Confucian virtues, qi becomes cultured with humanity (ren 仁), righteousness (yi 义), decorum (li 礼), and wisdom (zhi 智). Menzi calls this qi, *haoran zhi qi* 浩然之气 ("the magnificent and noble qi"). He describes the tranquility as an imperturbable heart, ensconced in the fullness of haoran zhi qi. It was said that he mastered it at age 40.

Mengzi's contemporary, Zhuangzi (369 – 298 B.C.), of the rival Taoist philosophy, also propounds that through the self-discipline of daoyin tu'na one may embody the Tao and become a "genuine person" (*zhenren* 真人), whose spirit is free and in tune with nature and humanity, but unfettered by the artificiality and vainglory of social constructs, and who may ascend the heavenly realms.

Zhuangzi had realized that human lifespan was short and knowledge in the books was limited, but knowledge itself was inexhaustible and boundless. It dawned on him that to embody the Tao, the mind and spirit had to be free to transcend the constraints of expressed knowledge. Did he come close to the liberation when he dreamed that he was a butterfly, flitting and fluttering freely, and upon awakening, wondered if the butterfly was dreaming it was Zhuangzi?

Chen Taijiquan and Meditation

The attainment of Taijiquan at the higher levels is marked by the inner fullness of qi in the blood, flesh, bones, and sinews.[6] "Blood-qi" (*xue qi* 血气) refers to blood "saturated" with qi in this context. Chen Xin (1919), in *Essence of Chansi* (*Chansi jing* 缠丝精), writes of infusing blood with the qi of chansi (silk-reeling) energy. The circulation of blood-qi purifies the heart, and the heart imbues the blood-qi with the virtues of humanity to render the "qi of morality" (*zheng qi* 正气), which is the *haoran zhi qi,* the noble and magnificent qi.[7]

The development of haoran zhi qi from silk-reeling energy and meditation is encapsulated in Chen Xin's diagram (fig. 10.1). The essence of silk reeling is illustrated by the concentric spirals of black and white paths winding towards the central small circle containing the Taiji symbol, a representation of Tao. The following paraphrases Chen Xin's exposition of the diagram.

The diagram as a whole symbolizes Taiji theory: Wuji ("Nothingness") is represented by the unfilled outermost circle. It gives rise to Taiji, the mother of yin and yang, represented by the first outermost pair of white and black paths respectively (*Taiji zhi yin yang* 太极之阴阳).

The second pair of white and black paths symbolizes Taiji giving rise to "two forms" (*liang yi* 两仪) of yin and yang, and the cosmogony of Taiji: the birth of heaven represented by the yang white path and earth by the yin black path (*tian di zhi yin yang* 天地之阴阳). Thereafter, all the myriad things come into being, multiplying in series of yin and yang.

The third pair of paths symbolizes humankind: the Taiji principles of yin and yang and wuxing (five phases or elements) that govern the life-force energy (qi) and humankind (*ren sheng zhi yin yang* 人生之阴阳).

The fourth pair symbolizes the theory of qi energetics: The white path represents Mengzi's magnificent qi (*haoran zhi qi* 浩然之气), and the black path represents blood-qi (*xue qi* 血气). Infused with humanity (*ren* 仁) and righteousness (*yi* 义) in accord with Tao, blood-qi gives rise to the qi of morality (*zheng qi* 正气), which is Mengzi's magnificent qi.

Figure 10.1 Illustration of the Essence Silk-reeling Energy

The fifth is the symbol of Taiji itself, which represents Tao. The white part depicts the "heart of Tao" (*dao xin* 道心) as the control center that regulates and refines qi in accordance with Taiji principles. The black part depicts human nature, regarded by the sages as one of "selfishness" (*si xin* 私心). However, within the black part is a white dot, which represents "discipline of restraint" (*kenian* 克念), and within the white part is a black dot, which represents "delusion" (*wangnian* 罔念).

The unwholesome thoughts of *wangnian* deceive the heart, feeding selfishness and smothering the heart's innate goodness. The example of *wangnian* cited by Chen Xin is human nature's appetite for the "food of sex" (*shi se xing ye* 食色性也), the phrase used by the philosopher, Gaozi, in his dialogue with Mengzi to counter the latter's proposition of the heart's innate goodness. The unwholesome *wangnian* are deep-seated, and the discipline of restraint and perceptiveness to reach and uproot them leads to sagehood. Once eradicated, the heart is free from the fetters of selfishness and delusion and one gains spiritual purity. Chen Xin concludes that with this attainment, one's Taijiquan becomes sublime. One's actions and responses are spontaneous and natural, and flow in accord with the principles of Taiji.

Taoist and Buddhist Approaches

Although Taijiquan is of Taoist origin, the above exposition of meditation draws from the author's practice of Insight Meditation (*Vippassana*) of the Buddhist tradition.[8] The Buddhist meditation practice, in essence, is to sit in stillness for a long duration, concentrating on something specific like the breath, observing it without bias to develop mindfulness to be with the present as the observed phenomena come and go in the stream of time. The process of mindfulness weeds out unwholesome thoughts and extinguishes all cravings, rendering the mind pure with penetrating clarity. One attains equanimity and insight unfolds. With the insight of meditation one often sees solutions beyond that of reasoning or analysis. The noble goal is nirvana, the extinction of all the causes of *dukkha* (sufferings): the extinction of *lobba* (greed), the extinction of *dosa* (hatred), and the extinction of *moha* (delusion). Through nirvana one gains deliverance from *samsara*—the wheel of existence in the cycle of rebirths that traps one in perpetual wandering and suffering. The path to nirvana is through enlightenment by meditation. Enlightenment and wisdom are the fruits of mindfulness and concentration (*samadhi*) in meditation, which are cultivated on *sila* (morality).[9]

The goal of Taoism, on the other hand, is motivated by the quest to return to the origin of the myriad things and formations of the universe—the primordial void. According to Taoist evolution, the "void" (*xu* 虚) gives rise to "spirit" (*shen* 神); the spirit gives rise to "energy" (*qi* 气); and qi gives rise to "essential fluids" (*jing* 精) from which life is formed.

Through the self-discipline of meditation and qi energetics, the Taoist seeks to traverse the journey of this evolution in reverse—by purifying *jing* (essence) to generate prenatal *qi*, by purifying *qi* to generate *shen* (spirit), and by purifying spirit, ultimately to return to the Taoist void.[10]

> *Lian jing hua qi* 錬精化气
> *Lian qi hua shen* 錬气化神
> *Lian shen huan xu* 錬神还虚

> Forge essence to transform to qi
> Forge qi to transform to spirit
> Forge spirit to return to void.

The mind-and-body process of the regenerative transformation of *jing qi shen* 精气神 (essence, energy, and spirit) is referred to as "inner alchemy" (*neidan* 內丹) that produces the "elixir of immortality." Alongside this is the practice of "external alchemy" (*waidan* 外丹), a proto-chemistry to produce pills or herbs of longevity. Alas, the formulas of both inner and external alchemies remain the secrets of Taoist immortals.[11]

Taoist philosophy embraces the preciousness of the body to be nourished with qi and food for longevity. By contrast, Buddhist philosophy views the body with suspicion, as a gateway of pleasures and wantonness, fed by desires, greed, and unwholesome thoughts. The body, therefore, must be denied and starved so that passion, greed, anger, and delusion cannot take root. Initially, following the Hindu tradition, Buddha (before he became Buddha) went through a period of extreme asceticism. He eventually realized that rather than enlightened, he was getting emaciated. This led him to the middle path to Enlightenment. The ascetic tradition is not completely abandoned in Buddhist practice as some monks still choose to live in seclusion in the forests or mountains.

The Chinese Buddhist adept Daoan 道安 (314 – 385) once noted of this fundamental difference between the Buddhist and Taoist practices: "The Buddhist teaching sees the emptiness of life, thus abandoning the body to liberate all sentient beings. The Taoist teaching sees the body as the ultimate, thus cultivating food and medicine for longevity."[12] However, the meditation discipline of both philosophies cultivates the moral center of the heart by rendering it pure, so one becomes a moral person. Thus, the moral compass of the heart is inculcated by meditation of moral precepts, in contrast to morality by dictates or dogmatic beliefs.

Standing Meditation

Taijiquan reinforces the internal practice by standing or sitting still in meditation. Standing meditation tempers the mind and body to gain insight of Taiji balance. Not moving may be simple, but stay still in a posture for a duration of time and you will find how challenging it can be. Keeping a posture stationary is not devoid of physical activities; rather, the muscles are constantly working to maintain the posture in balance.

The body also has to contend with a restless mind. Thus, standing in a stationary posture tempers and conditions both the mind and body.

Let us practice meditation in the standing-post posture (fig. 10.2). Feet are shoulder-width, toes point straight, knees bend slightly, and hands are held level in front between chest and abdomen, as if holding a beach ball. First, check the physical form of the posture—head, torso and legs are centrally aligned and upright, not inclining or leaning to the left or right, front or back (*li shen zhong zhen bu bian bu yi*). This can be done in front of a mirror or preferably with the guidance of a teacher.

The practice is to stand in the posture for 30 minutes. The idea is to let the mind and body relax and quiet down to nurture comprehension of the soft structure—the joints and internal dynamics. However, the mind cannot be still and attentive for long, getting distracted, bored or restless, exacerbated by aches, pains or fatigue. So getting through the first 10 minutes of standing can be very challenging. At the initial phase there is no clarity except discomfort and restlessness, but persevere to let the practice develop.

Check the fangsong relaxation of the three sections—head (the top), torso (the middle) and legs (the base)—to gradually gain clarity of the posture:

- **Head**. Use yi (mind) to point the crown of the head skyward. Take your time to let the body find the crown, and then point it vertically up. The pointing action simulates a tugging at the crown as if by a string but with no tension (xu ling ding jin). It holds up the head, keeping it from inclining without stretching the neck, and raises the spirit of the posture. Look far into the distance. One can lower the eyelids about three-quarters down to block visual distractions but not shut, to stay alert. Place the tip of the tongue against the palate behind the upper teeth (to connect the ren mai meridian in the front with the du mai running along the back).

- **Torso**. Let the torso settle at the seat of the pelvic girdle. This settling can be simulated by sitting on an imaginary stool—the muscles holding up the posture lessen a little, giving a sense of the torso. Note the shoulders and kua (hips) defining the torso in the relaxation, nurturing clarity of the shoulder-kua correspondence. Relax the chest so that it does not brace up like a soldier at-attention pose. Be cognizant of the fangsong mechanics of "containing the chest and settling in the waist" (hanxiong tayao) and qi building up in the abdomen. The substantial qi in the lower abdomen ameliorates the internal imbalance of "top heavy and base light" (shang zhong xia qing). In holding up the hands, let the arms drop to hang like cables suspended at the shoulders. This relaxes the muscles of the arms, allowing the shoulders and elbows to drop (chen jian jia zhou). The relaxation nurtures clarity of the hands, elbows and shoulders, and the left and right sides of the lower back in balance.

- **Legs**. Bend slightly at the knees and "open the kua" (*qu xi kai kua* 曲膝开胯) to let the torso sink into the hips. Simulate sitting on a stool again to lessen the muscle actions supporting the body-frame. This nurtures clarity of the base support—the weight at the feet and the division between the upper and lower parts of the body. Fangsong at the kua and ankles to stimulate relaxation at the knees for qi to break through. The clarity unveils the mechanics of the base support—the driving force at the kua (the root) transmitting through the knees (the middle section) to anchor the feet (the extremities) on the ground.

One can scan the body from the head down to build comprehension a layer at a time. One may apply Chen Changxin's *Principles of Three Sections* and *Three Unities* (chapter 7) to refine the clarity of each subsection. However, like nurturing a plant, it takes time for the body to cultivate the awareness of the many elements of the posture.

As noted earlier, the biggest obstacle is the restless, fickle, and fanciful mind. The mind gets bored and restless as one is not engaged in some form of activities. Staying still and quiet is a direct challenge to the "restless monkey" of the mind. But meditation does not confront the monkey mind in a test of will to tame it. The strategy of meditation is to focus on something simple. The idea is not to burden the mind but to let it nurture attentiveness and concentration, thus providing a grip on the practice.

Following a method of *vipassana* (insight meditation),[13] take breath as the principal object of meditation. Focus on the breath and simply observe the body breathing. After a while, one registers the breath of inhaling and the breath of exhaling. Keep observing to gain clarity of the inhaling and the exhaling. When it is clear, focus at the nostrils: Observe the air passing through the nostril at inhale and exhale. Stay with the task of observing the breath passing through the nostrils to develop awareness, and not be concerned with anything else—let distractions pass.

Whatever thoughts that arise, just let them be and only observe. Inevitably the mind wanders off unawares. At some point you realize that you are no longer observing the breath. Apply the awareness-trigger: The moment you become aware of the mind wandering, learn to let it trigger a return to the task of observing the breath. Observe again the breath passing through the nostrils at inhale and at exhale. You realize later that, again, your mind has been wandering a while. Awareness triggers a return to the task again. In time the meditation skill develops. You can stay longer with the observation of the breath and catch the mind's wandering sooner. The aim is not to prevent the mind from wandering, but to cultivate the sharpness of observation to catch it the moment it occurs, and thereby reduce its frequency. In this way, one develops will power without a confrontational test of will.

Fig. 10.2 Standing-post Meditation Posture

The discipline of observing or noting is a foundation of meditation practice. It develops a cognitive tool to penetrate the internal structure of the body. However, sustaining the stationary posture is a physical endurance as well, and when aches, pains or fatigue set in, it disrupts the meditation. The pain can be excruciating, especially if the posture is low or one is sitting in a cross-legged position.

When pain occurs, observe the pain and let it be. It may subside or it may intensify. The pain can surge and be so overwhelming that one wants to give up. Giving up right away is easy, but it does not advance the practice. To persevere does not mean to fight the pain head-on, but again only to note it. The awareness of wanting to give up brings a spurt of energy. Use that to overcome the urge and go on a little longer. In this way, one learns to ride the pain a little longer with perseverance at each meditation session. In time, the pain intensity reaches its hump, and it is subdued and no longer overwhelms the practice. The meditation will then take root.

It is very tempting to chase after the sensations of qi. But this can distract and lead the practice astray. To avoid the mistake, stick to the discipline of observing and let whatever thoughts that arise flow by in the stream of time as petals floating down a stream. In short, stay grounded on fangsong to develop Taiji balance.

Practice of Stationary Posture (Ding Shi)

The practice of standing meditation by using the postures of a Taijiquan form is referred to as *ding shi* (stationary posture) training. Though each form posture has its nuances, the principles of centrality and balance are the same. The immediate objective is to tweak the soft structure and to tune the internal dynamics of qi through fangsong relaxation to settle the posture towards Taiji balance.

The practice can be very taxing on the body, even for the very strong, a point merrily brought home in Chen Xiaowang's workshops.[14] There is often a session on stationary-posture training, where the master adjusts the participants' postures individually. The posture after the teacher's correction is decidedly more settled and stronger to the eye, even though one cannot see the internal mechanisms of adjustment.

Chen Xiaowang does the posture-tuning at three levels: light, medium and deep. After a light adjustment, the student is comfortable in the relatively easy and high stance, and is clearly seen to be content with the ease. The master then asks the student if he wants to go more deeply into the posture, explaining that the light adjustment is like eating soup, and that the next level of adjustment will be like eating spaghetti. The medium adjustment sets the student in a lower stance. After the master is satisfied with the tuning, he steps back to let the work be admired like a sculpture. The posture is amazing transformed. It is solid and exudes power. As the class enjoys the posture, he asks the student again if he wants to go even more deeply into the posture, explaining that it will be like loading the meal of soup and spaghetti with pizza. With the student nodding eagerly, the master proceeds with more tuning. Before long, the student is pouring sweat and his legs are shaking as he valiantly tries to hold the posture, but then collapses to a burst of laughter. The muscles are clearly burning in the deep stance. So participants are always egged on to take the "pizza" treatment, as the class has fun seeing the body crash to the ground without fail.

"Single Whip" (Danbian)

In the "Single Whip" (*Danbian*) posture both arms are extended to the sides. The palm of the left hand sits on the wrist and the fingers of the right hand facing down are closed to form a hook. The posture is like a rider using a whip in a Chinese opera, hence the name. Of the vast differences in the form among the various schools of Taijiquan, the danbian posture is easily the most recognizable. The movement recurs most number of times in the Taijiquan form routine. Here we look at the essential elements of the danbian posture from the Chen Family form (fig. 10.3).

Danbian posture is a left "bow-stance." *Bow-stance (gongbu)* is a basic kungfu stance, where the body's weight is more substantial on one side. In the left bow-stance, weight is more on the left, and in the right bow-stance, more on the right. The weight distribution is roughly 60-70 percent on the substantial side, and can be more if the stance is lower.

In left bow-stance, the left toe points outward at 45-degree angle and the right toe points straight. The legs, relaxed at the hips, knees and ankles, form a support like the arch of a bridge. By sitting into the kua, the left knee is kept from extending beyond the toe even in low stances.

Standing stationary in the danbian posture is more demanding than the standing-post posture, but the practice of meditation is the same—to build awareness of the soft structure and internal dynamics in the development of Taiji balance. Go through the checklist in the standing meditation: lift the crown with no tension, sink the shoulders and elbows, contain the chest and settle the waist, and anchor the feet to the ground. Stay the course and one will in time go past the initial phases of aches and pain to comprehend the internal dynamics.

Let us review the fangsong play at the kua. To stimulate and enliven the internal motion of the hip-joints, "open from the inside and close from the outside" (*nei kai wai he*). This renders the "roundness" at the crotch (*yuan dang* 圆裆), which describes the strength and liveliness (linghuo) of the arch support.

In conjunction with hanxiong tayao (contain the chest and settle the waist), fangsong at the kua junction induces qi to sink to the dantian (qi chen dantian). This develops the dantian as a level bubble to gauge the internal balance of the body. As dantian qi matures to fullness, qi breaks through the joints and penetrates to the far reaches of the body. The body experiences the centrality of the dantian—the insight of Taiji balance.

Fig. 10.3 Single-Whip Danbian Posture

A passage in the *Art of War* by Sunzi (Sun Tzu) of the sixth century B.C., compares a skillful tactician to *shuairan,* a remarkable snake from the Chang Shan mountains:[15] "Strike at its head, and you will be attacked by its tail; strike at its tail, and you will be attacked by its head; strike at its middle, and you will be attacked by head and tail both."

A Chen Village poem in Chen Xin's book likens the Taiji body to the *shuairan* snake:[16]

Single Whip Posture

Single Whip strikes a majestic pose
Unobstructed are the meridian passageways
The spirit perked, the form is stirred
Arms like a shuairan snake span east to west
Attack the head, the tail swings to defend
Attack the tail, the head springs to counter
Attack the center, head and tail coil in to act.
All four sides, from top to bottom are connected
In readiness as a stretched bow.
Where is the source of this ingenious marvel?
Study the axis of the spine to the dantian center.

Other Stationary Postures

An iconic posture of the Chen Taijiquan form is "Lazy Tying Coat" (Lan Zha Yi) (fig. 10.4). This is a standard posture for tweaking the soft structure of a right bow-stance in ding shi (stationary posture) training. Another common stationary posture for meditation is "Oblique Form" (Xiaxing) (fig. 10.5), where the left-bow stance is oriented obliquely at 45 degrees to the left.

Fig. 10.4 Lazy Tying Coat (Lan Zha Yi)

Fig. 10.5 Oblique Form (Xia Xing)

Transition to "Buddha Pounding Mortar Board"

Transition to "Oblique Form"

11
Silk-reeling Exercises

Chansi Gong (Practice of Chansi Silk-Reeling)

Chansi gong 缠丝功, the discipline of *chansi* (silk-reeling) motion, is at the heart of the training of Chen Family Taijiquan. The practice develops chansi jin as the body's core strength. This is the inner strength of chansi motion, harnessed by the coherence of the series of self and general rotations of body segments moving in sequential kinetics—the *chanrao* (coiling) energy discovered by Chen Wangting in the 17th century, which led to the creation of the Chen family art.

Chanrao power is the source of coiling leverage essential in high-level kungfu. As such chansi motion is implicit in the practice of all martial arts. Zhu Tiancai once told me of a kungfu master in Singapore[1] who, upon learning the *chansi gong* exercises, keenly observed that it was like the secret of kungfu was being revealed. Indeed, the power actions generated in sports share the same body mechanics of chanrao power.

In Chen training, traditionally, the practice of form routines constitutes chansi gong. That is, chansi discipline is embodied in the First Routine (Yilu) form. The silk-reeling exercises practiced today are a modern innovation of basic movements that bring out the chansi elements to complement regular form practice. The explicit emphasis of chansi gong distinguishes Chen Taijiquan from other forms of Taijiquan.

In 1980, Chen Xiaowang was plucked from the relative obscurity of Chen Village and appointed officially as a Taijiquan instructor in the Henan Physical Education Department in Zhengzhou, the capital city of Henan Province. There had been a revival of *wushu* (Chinese Martial Arts) after the Cultural Revolution (1966-1976). To come up with basic exercises (*jiben gong*) needed in the teaching curriculum, Chen Xiaowang devised a set of *chansi gong* exercises. Soon, other contemporary Chen instructors also incorporated similar basic chansi exercises in their classes. The exercises described below are a combination of the methods taught by Chen Xiaowang, Chen Zhenglei and Zhu Tiancai.

The first set of chansi gong exercises is a series of arms moving in circular arcs, coordinated with the body turning and shifting weight from one side to the other in fixed steps. The second set introduces the practice in moving steps. The many elements in chansi gong may seem many to remember, but the body absorbs them through practice. The reader is urged to practice the drills as they are presented. The body will gain the fluency of chansi motion by following the exercise recipe.

Moving Between Bow-stances

Recall that a bow-stance is a stance where there is more weight on one side. The bulk of the motion in Taijiquan consists of the body moving from one bow-stance to another—left to right and the right to left. Practice moving slowly between right bow-stance (fig. 11.1 A) and left bow-stance (fig. 11.1

B) 20 times. Be attentive that the posture stays upright and in balance as the efforts in shifting weight can cause the body to incline. Check the movements in a mirror, but it is important to build awareness of the body.

Take a medium stance, about twice shoulder width. It may be impressive to practice in a low and wide posture, but if the body is not ready for it, done improperly, it can be very taxing on the knees. Moreover, the excessive efforts needed to hold a low posture cause the structure to be stiff (*jiang*), and obscure one's perception of the motion. The posture should not be so low as to be unduly taxing, but not so high as to be without effort. The objective is to build an awareness of the motion.

Note the two modes of motion: (1) general-rotation—the motion of the body shifting weight between right and left (motion of the body's center of mass) and (2) self-rotation—the waist turning (the trunk turning on the vertical axis).

Starting at the right bow-stance (posture A), turn torso at the waist to the right about 45 degrees; as the body shifts weight to the left, the waist turns back to face front at the left bow-stance (posture B). At the left bow-stance (posture B), turn 45 degrees to the left; as the body shifts back to the right bow-stance, turn waist back to face front (posture A).

Fig 11.1 A Right Bow-stance   Fig 11.1 B Left Bow-stance

Note that the side-to-side motion is not a lateral swing as in a pendulum. Relax at the kua, imagine sitting on a bench and glide along it. As the body shifts weight in the relaxation, the butt draws a back-lower arc (*zou hou xia hu* 走后下弧).

Two Basic Single-Hand Silk-Reeling Patterns

The two basic single-hand silk-reeling patterns are 1) cloud-hand and 2) reverse-hand. The name of cloud-hand is taken from the movement, "Hands Waving Cloud" of the Taijiquan form routine. The reverse-hand is the reverse of the cloud-hand pattern. They form the fundamental building blocks of silk-reeling motion.

1. Cloud-Hand Silk-Reeling

In *cloud-hand silk-reeling,* the arm is drawing a circular motion as the body shifts weight from side to side in the bow-stances, as in postures A, B, C, and D (fig. 11.2). Do the movements 20 times paying attention to the lower and upper arcs of the circular motion. Be mindful of posture balance as the movements can cause the body to incline. Then repeat the exercise with the left hand (fig. 11.3). Note the self and general rotations: The trunk is turning as the body shifts weight side to side; and the arm is self-rotating in its circular motion as the trunk turns. Let us review the motion of the right hand in detail.

Fig 11.2 A Start Cloud-hand Silk Reeling

Fig 11.2 B Count 1 Hand to waist level

Fig 11.2 C Count 2 Shift weight left

Fig 11.2 D Count 3 Hand to shoulder leavel

a) Weight Shifts, Arm Motion Follows

The circular motion of the arm follows the body shifting weight side-to-side. The motion of the hand consists of two arcs: the right-lower arc which starts with the hand to the side (posture A) and ends with the hand at the abdomen center line (posture C), and the left-upper arc which starts at posture C and ends at posture A. In the side-to-side motion, the body shifts weight from one bow-stance to the other. As the body shifts from the right bow-stance to left (posture A to posture C), the arm follows in the lower arc, and as it shifts from the left bow-stance to right (posture C to Posture A), the arm follows in the upper arc.

Be attentive to the relaxation of the waist-kua and the turning motion of the waist (self-rotation) as the body moves side-to-side (general rotation). Let the weight-shifting motion induce the arm's circular motion, in the lower arc from right to left (A to C), and in the upper arc from left back to right (C to A). Do the exercise again to gain clarity of these rotational motions.

However, the hand can be impetuous, causing it to jump ahead in the motion instead of following the waist. Invoke the practice mantra of using "*yi* (mind) not *li* (muscle force)" to initiate and internalize the motion. In the "soft and relaxed" motion, the body learns to move accordingly. Keep the waist relaxed so that the torso remains settled at the kua to maintain posture balance.

Do the exercise at least 20 times, and then repeat with the left hand, to let the body absorb the information.

b) Self-rotation of the Hand

The hand is turning in self-rotation in the arm's circular motion. Recall the arm's self-rotational motion: The palm of the hand turns from facing down to up and from up to down. With the little finger leading, the right hand turning clockwise is rotating in the *shun* orientation, and with the thumb leading, the hand is turning anti-clockwise is rotating in *ni*.[2]

Constrained by the joint structure, the hand can only turn a little over 180 degrees in either the *shun* or *ni* orientation. For convenience, *shun chan*, reeling in *shun* orientation, is referred to as "*in-reeling*," and its opposite, *ni chan*, as "*out-reeling*."

Using the silk-reeling terminology, in the right-lower arc motion from posture A to posture C, the arm is self-rotating in in-reeling motion (*shun chan*), and in the left-upper arc motion from posture C to posture A, the self-rotation is out-reeling (*ni chan*). Do the exercise with attentiveness to the orientation: the *shun* orientation of in-reeling (little finger leading), and the *ni* orientation of out-reeling (thumb leading). Keep in mind that the arm motion follows the weight shifting, the waist turning induces the arm's circular motion, and always the posture balance. Do the exercise again 20 times for the body to understand the *shun and ni* orientation. Repeat the exercise with the left hand, giving attentiveness to the same elements.

c) The change between the *shun and ni* orientation

The orientation of the hand's self-rotation has to change because the motion is limited by the arm's anatomical structure. Be attentive of the in-reeling motion ending, the change occurring, and the out-reeling motion beginning, and vice versa. To instill body awareness of the change of orientation, slow down the motion as the change occurs. Do the exercise again with diligence to the change of the *shun-ni* orientation. Repeat the exercise with the left hand.

d) Tracing through the silk-reeling motion in the 4 postures

Let us trace through the details of cloud-hand silk-reeling in the 4 postures A, B, C, and D. Posture A is a right bow-stance and posture C, a left bow-stance. Posture B shows half the self-rotation of the hand (90 degrees) in in-reeling (*shun*), and posture D, half the rotation in out-reeling (*ni*).

Count 1 Posture A to B. Start with right bow-stance (posture A). Relax at the waist-groin. Turn at waist 45 degrees to right. Arm follows and hand at shoulder level in-reels (shun chan) with little finger leading 90 degrees from palm (wrist) facing down to facing front at waist level to the side in half of the right-lower arc to posture B.

Count 2 Posture B to C. Be mindful of the relaxation at the waist-groin. Shift weight to left bow-stance, trunk turns 45 degrees to face front. Arm follows and hand continues in-reeling another 90 degrees, to complete the lower arc motion, ending with palm (wrist) facing up at the front of abdomen (posture C). In the shifting motion, the buttocks describe a back-lower arc (*zou hou xia hu*).

Count 3 Posture C to D. Relax at the waist-groin. Turn waist to the left 45 degrees. Arm follows in half of the right-upper arc and hand out-reels (ni chan) 90 degrees with the thumb leading to posture D, where palm (wrist) faces front of chest at shoulder level, and weight is still on the left.

Count 4. Posture D to A. Be mindful of the relaxation at the waist-groin. Shift weight to right bow-stance as torso turns to face front. Arm follows and hand continues out-reeling another 90 degrees to complete the upper arc motion, ending with the palm (wrist) facing down, back to posture A. As before, in the shifting motion, the buttocks describe a back-lower arc.

At the start of the exercise, do a few rounds tracing through the counts to build up the clarity of the in-reeling (*shun chan*) and the out-reeling (*ni chan*), the change of orientations, the weight shifting, and the arm motion following the waist. Then let go and relax for the motion to flow smoothly.

Always be attentive to the relaxation (*fangsong*) at the *kua* to maintain posture balance and ease of movements. The focus at the kua cultivates the *dang-yao* (waist-groin) as the hub of motion and develops dantian qi.

Do the left cloud-hand silk-reeling motion, tracing through the postures A, B, C and D (fig. 11.3), paying attention to the same details as in the right hand.

Fig. 11.3 A Start Cloud-hand Silk Reeling Left

Fig. 11. 3 B Count 1 Hand to waist level

Fig. 11.3 C Count 2 Shift weight right

Fig. 11.3 D Count 3 Hand to shoulder level

The body is not expected to absorb the many elements of silk-reeling right away. It helps to start at the beginning again, and go through the instructions in a), b) and c). Just as it takes time to gain fluency in a foreign language, the body needs practice to express *chansi* motion.

Note the coherence of the rotational motions in the chansi exercise. In the in-reeling motion of the right-lower arc (posture A to C), the hand's rotational motion is matched with the arc motion of the arm; the arc motion of the arm is matched with the trunk's rotational motion; the trunk's rotational motion is matched with the body shifting from the right to the left bow-stance. Likewise, the exercise trains coherence of the rotational motions from posture C to A.

Caution: There is a tendency to be too intense in attentiveness, which can cause one to tense up. However, without attentiveness, the body cannot cultivate coherence of the rotational motions. Be attentive but relax and let go for motion to flow.

The practice of attentive relaxation nurtures *qi* energy. The practitioner can use the *qi* flow to consolidate the silk-reeling practice, by tracing through the *qi* route. Chen Xiaowang describes the route of the qi flow in the counts accompanying the four postures (fig. 11.2):

1. Qi moves from hand along the arm, through shoulder down to the right side of waist.
2. Qi moves along the side of waist to the dantian.
3. Qi traverses up the back along the spine from dantian to shoulder.
4. Qi traverses along the back of the shoulder to arm, through elbow and wrist to hand.

2. Reverse-Hand Silk-Reeling

Reverse-hand silk-reeling motion is the reverse of the cloud-hand pattern. In cloud-hand of the right hand, the circular motion is clockwise. In reverse-hand, the right hand draws an anti-clockwise circular motion, which consists of two arcs: (1) the right-upper arc from posture A (fig. 11.4) to C in *shun chan* (in-reeling) cycle, and (2) the left-lower arc from posture C to A in *ni chan* (out-reeling).

Do the movements of the reverse-hand pattern 20 times to get a feel of the motion. Pay attention to the lower and upper arcs of the circular motion following the waist, and the waist turning. Be mindful of relaxation at the kua to maintain posture balance. Then repeat the exercise with the left hand (fig. 11.5).

Let us review the right-hand pattern in details tracing through the postures A, B, C, and D (fig. 11.4).

Fig. 11.4 A Start Reverse Hand Silk Reeling

Fig. 11.4 B Count 1 Hand to shoulder level

Fig. 11.4 C Count 2 Shift weight left

Fig. 11.4 D Count 3 Hand to waist level

Count 1 Posture A to B. Start with right bow-stance in posture A. Relax at the waist-groin. Turn waist to right 45 degrees. Hand follows, in-reeling (shun chan) with little finger leading 90 degrees from palm (wrist) facing down to facing front at shoulder level to the side in half of the right-upper arc to posture B. Weight is still on the right.

Count 2 Posture B to C. Be mindful of the relaxation at the waist-groin. Shift weight to left bow-stance, trunk turns 45 degrees to face front. Arm follows and hand continues in-reeling another 90 degrees to complete the upper arc motion, ending with palm (wrist) facing up at the front of chest (posture C).

Count 3 Posture C to D. Relax at the waist-groin. Turn waist to the left 45 degrees. Hand follows, out-reeling with thumb leading 90 degrees from palm (wrist) facing up to facing abdomen at waist level in half of the left-lower arc to posture D. Weight is still on the right.

Count 4 Posture D to A. Be mindful of the relaxation at the waist-groin. Shift weight to right bow-stance as torso turns to face front. Arm follows and hand continues out-reeling another 90 degrees to complete the lower arc motion, ending with the palm (wrist) facing down to the side back to posture A.

As in the cloud-hand silk-reeling, initially, do the exercise a few times tracing through the 4 counts to gain clarity of the *shun chan* and *ni chan*, the change of *shun-ni* orientations, the weight shifting, and the arm motion following the waist. Then let go and relax for the motion to flow smoothly.

Do the left-hand reverse-hand silk-reeling motion, tracing through Postures A, B, C and D (fig. 11.5), paying attention to the same details as in the right hand.

Fig. 11.5 A Start Reverse Hand Silk Reeling

Fig. 11.5 B Count 1 Hand to shoulder level

Fig 11.5 C Count 2 Shift weight right

Fig 11.5 D Count 3 Hand to waist level

Double-Hand Silk-Reeling Patterns

In double-hand silk-reeling, the hands can combine flowing in the same or different patterns. One hand can be doing cloud-hand and the other reverse-hand, or both hands twirling in cloud-hand or reverse-hand, yielding multiple patterns of double-hand silk-reeling.

The double-hand silk-reeling patterns fall into two categories. The first category consists of the hands moving in opposite chansi orientation, that is, if one hand is doing in-reeling (shun chan), the other hand is out-reeling (ni chan). The second category consists of the hands moving in the same chansi orientation—both hands in-reeling or out-reeling together. The double-hand silk-reeling patterns of 1, 2 and 3 below belong to the first category, and those of 4, 5 and 6, the second category.

The coordination of the hands is dictated by the silk-reeling pattern of each hand. That is, do the exercise following the body's rotational motions of the waist, arms, and hands, the in-reeling and out-reeling, and the change. The coordination thus is internally driven.

1. "Hands Waving Clouds" (Yun Shou)

The "Hands Waving Clouds" pattern consists of both hands doing the same cloud-hand silk-reeling, but one hand is in-reeling while the other hand out-reeling. In fig. 11.6, the right-hand motion in postures A, B, C, and D describes the single cloud-hand pattern, and so does the left-hand motion, but with a phase difference of 180 degrees. Do the exercise following the postures in the pictures 20 times to get a feel of the double-hand motion. Keep in mind the pattern of the circular arcs, the arm motion following the waist, and the posture balance. If confused, revert back to the single-hand motion, and then merge in the other hand.

Count 1 Posture A to B. At the start, right bow-stance in posture A (fig. 11.6), the right-hand position is the same as at the start of single cloud-hand (fig. 11.2 A) and the left-hand is at the end of the left-lower arc (fig. 11.3 C). (The hands are 180 degrees off phase.) Turn waist to the right 45 degrees. Right hand follows in-reeling 90 degrees of the lower arc, and at the same time, the left hand out-reels 90 degrees of upper arc, to posture B, weight still on the right.

Count 2 Posture B to C. Right hand palm (wrist) is facing front at waist level, and left hand palm (wrist) is facing chest at shoulder level (posture B). Shift weight to left bow-stance as torso turns to face front. Right-hand continues in-reeling 90 degrees to complete the lower arc, while left hand out-reels 90 degrees to complete the upper arc to posture C.

Count 3 Posture C to D. Right hand palm (wrist) is facing up at front of abdomen, and left hand palm (wrist) is facing down at shoulder level (posture C). Turn the waist to the left 45 degrees. Right hand follows out-reeling 90 degrees of the upper arc, and at the same time, the left hand in-reels 90 degrees of the lower arc, to posture D, weight still on the left.

Count 4 Posture D to A. Right-hand palm (wrist) is facing chest at shoulder level, and left-hand palm (wrist) facing front at waist level (posture D). Shift weight to right bow-stance as torso turns to face front. Right-hand continues out-reeling 90 degrees to complete the upper arc, while left hand in-reels 90 degrees to complete the lower arc back to posture A.

Do the exercise, tracing through the 4 counts for the first few rounds, then let the motion flow smoothly with no breaks. Note that the coordination of the hands flows from the in-reeling and out-reeling chansi motion, the change of shun-ni orientation, and the arm motion following the waist turning and the weight-shifting of the body. Repeat this exercise daily, and let the sweat attest that you are burning calories.

The "Hands Waving Cloud" is a very familiar movement in the Taijiquan form, and it recurs several times in all the routines.

Fig. 11.6 A Start Double Cloud-hand silk Reeling

Fig. 11.6 B Count 1 L hand up R hand down

Fig. 11.6 C Count 2 Shift weight left

Fig. 11.6 D Count 3 R hand up L hand down

2. Front-Back Silk-Reeling (Qian-Hou Lü)

The "Front-Back Silk-Reeling" (*Qian-Hou Lü*) pattern consists of both hands doing the same reverse-hand silk-reeling, but one hand is in-reeling while the other out-reeling, 180 degrees in phase difference.

Note that the right-hand motion in the postures A, B, C, and D (fig. 11.7) is describing the single reverse-hand pattern, and so is the left-hand motion. As in the cloud-hand silk-reeling, the change between in-reeling and out-reeling occurs as the waist turns. Do the exercise following the postures in the pictures as many times as you wish for the body to get a feel of the motion. Keep in mind the pattern of the circular arcs, the arm motion following the waist, and the posture balance. If confused, revert back to single-hand motion, and then merge in the other hand

Fig. 11.7 A Start Double Reverse-hand   Fig. 11.7 B Count 1 L hand down R hand up

Fig. 11.7 C Count 2 Shift weight left   Fig. 11.7 D Count 3 R hand down L hand up

Count 1 Posture A to B. At the start, right bow-stance in posture A (fig. 11.7), the right-hand position is the same as at the start of single reverse-hand (fig. 11.4 A) and the left-hand is at the end of the upper arc (fig. 11.5 C). (The hands are 180 degrees off phase.) Turn waist to the right 45 degrees. Right hand follows in-reeling 90 degrees of half of the upper arc, and at the same time, the left hand out-reels 90 degrees of half of the lower arc, to posture B, weight still on the right.

Count 2 Posture B to C. Right-hand palm (wrist) is facing front at shoulder level, and left-hand palm (wrist) facing abdomen (posture B). Shift weight to left bow-stance as torso turns to face front. Right-hand continues in-reeling 90 degrees to complete the upper arc, while left hand out-reels 90 degrees to complete the lower arc to posture C.

Count 3 Posture C to D. Right hand palm (wrist) is facing up at front of chest, and left hand palm (wrist) is facing down at waist level (posture C). Turn the waist to the left 45 degrees. Right hand follows out-reeling 90 degrees of half of the lower arc, and at the same time, the left hand in-reels 90 degrees of half of the upper arc, to posture D. Weight is still on the left.

Count 4 Posture D to A. Right-hand palm (wrist) is facing abdomen, and left hand palm (wrist) is facing front at shoulder level (posture D). Shift weight to right bow-stance as torso turns to face front. Right-hand continues out-reeling 90 degrees to complete the lower arc, while left hand in-reels 90 degrees to complete the upper arc back to posture A.

Do the exercise, tracing through the 4 counts for the first few rounds, then let the motion flow smoothly with no breaks. Once again, the coordination of the hands flows from the shun chan and ni chan silk-reeling and the change of the shun-ni orientation. Note the arm motions following the waist turning and the weight-shifting of the body. Repeat the exercise to gain fluency of the silk-reeling motion.

The movement, "twist step" (*ao bu*) in the Chen form routine, uses this pattern.

3. Double-hand Rollback (Shuang Lü) Left and Right Sides

In "Double-hand Rollback" (*Shuang Lü*), one hand is doing cloud-hand pattern and the other reverse-hand pattern, but one hand is in-reeling while the other out-reeling, 180 degrees in phase difference. The pattern is oriented on the left or right side.

In the right side rollback (fig. 11.8) the right-hand motion in postures A, B, C, and D is describing the single-hand cloud-hand pattern, and the left-hand motion, the reverse-hand pattern. Note again that the change between in-reeling and out-reeling occurs as the waist turns. The silk-reeling pattern is easier to follow as both hands are moving in lower or upper arcs together. Keep in mind the pattern of the circular arcs, the arm motion following the waist, and the posture balance. If confused, revert back to single-hand motion, and then merge in the other hand.

Fig. 11.8 A Start Double Rollback   Fig. 11.8 B Count 1 Both hands down
Right Side

Fig. 11.8 C Count 2 Shift weight left   Fig. 11.8 D Count 3 Both hands up

Count 1 Posture A to B. At the start, right bow-stance in posture A (fig. 11.8), the right-hand position is the same as at the start of single cloud-hand (fig. 11.2 A) and the left hand is at the end of the upper arc reverse-hand pattern (fig. 11.5 C). Turn waist to the right 45 degrees. Right hand follows in-reeling 90 degrees of half of the lower arc, and at the same time, the left hand out-reels 90 degrees of half of the lower arc to posture B, weight on the right.

Count 2 Posture B to C. Right hand palm (wrist) is facing front at waist level, and left hand palm (wrist) is facing abdomen (posture B). Shift weight to left bow-stance as torso turns to face front. Right-hand continues in-reeling 90 degrees to complete the lower arc, while left hand out-reels 90 degrees to complete also the lower arc to posture C.

Count 3 Posture C to D. Right hand palm (wrist) is facing up, at front of abdomen, and left hand palm (wrist) is facing down at waist level (posture C). Turn the waist to the left 45 degrees. Right hand follows out-reeling 90 degrees of half of the upper arc, and at the same time, the left hand in-reels 90 degrees also of half of the upper arc, to posture D, weight on the left.

Count 4 Posture D to A. Right-hand palm (wrist) is facing chest at shoulder level, and left hand palm (wrist) facing front also at shoulder level (posture D). Shift weight to right bow-stance as torso turns to face front. Right-hand continues out-reeling 90 degrees to complete the upper arc, while left hand in-reels 90 degrees to also complete the upper arc back to posture A.

Do the exercise, tracing through the 4 counts for the first few rounds, then let the motion flow smoothly with no breaks. Once again, the coordination of the two hands flows from the silk-reelings and the change of the shun-ni orientation. Note the arm motions following the waist turning and the weight-shifting of the body.

This pattern of silk-reeling motion is the most prevalent in the Taijiquan form routine. Repeat the exercise of "Double-Hand Roll-Back" on the left side (fig. 11.9).

Fig. 11.9 A Start Double Rollback Left Side   Fig. 11.9 B Count 1 Both hands down

Fig. 11.9 C Count 2 Shift weight right   Fig. 11.9 D Count 3 Both hands up

4. Hand-Crossing Silk-Reeling (Left and Right Sides)

In "Hand-Crossing Silk-Reeling Right Side," the right hand is doing the cloud-hand pattern while the left hand, the reverse-hand pattern, but unlike the "Double Rollback" pattern, both hands are in-reeling or out-reeling together.

Fig. 11.10 A Start Cross hands right side   Fig. 11.10 B Count 1 R hand down L hand up

Fig. 11.10 C Count 2 Shift weight left   Fig. 11.10 D Count 3 R hand up
                                            crosses L down

Count 1 Posture A to B. At the start, right bow-stance in posture A (fig. 11.10), the right-hand position is the same as at the start of single cloud-hand (fig. 11.2 A) and the left hand is at the start of the reverse-hand (fig. 11.5 A), except that the weight is on the right. Turn waist to the right 45 degrees. Right hand follows in-reeling 90 degrees of half of the lower arc, and at the same time, the left hand in-reels 90 degrees of half the upper arc to posture B, weight still on the right.

Count 2 Posture B to C. Shift weight to left bow-stance as torso turns to face front. Right-hand continues in-reeling 90 degrees to complete the lower arc, while left hand in-reels 90 degrees to complete the upper arc to posture C.

Count 3 Posture C to D. Turn the waist to the left 45 degrees. Right hand follows out-reeling 90 degrees of half of the upper arc, and at the same time, the left hand out-reels 90 degrees of half of the lower arc to posture D, right hand crossing outside of left, weight still on the left.

Count 4 Posture D to A. Shift weight to the right bow-stance as torso turns to face front. Right-hand continues out-reeling 90 degrees to complete the upper arc, while left hand out-reels 90 degrees to complete the lower arc back to posture A.

Trace through the postures for "Cross-Hand Silk-reeling Left Side" (fig. 11.11).

Fig. 11.11 A Start Cross hands left side

Fig. 11.11 B Count 1 R hand up L hand down

Fig. 11.11 C Count 2 Shift weight right

Fig. 11.11 D Count 3 R hand down crosses L up

5. Double Cloud-Hand Crossing

In "Double Cloud-Hand Crossing," both the right and left hands are doing cloud-hand pattern, but unlike the "Hands Waving Cloud" pattern, both hands are in-reeling together or out-reeling together.

Count 1 Posture A to B. At start, right bow-stance in posture A (fig. 11.12), the right-hand position is the same as at the start of single cloud-hand (fig. 11.2 A) and the left hand is also at the start of cloud-hand, except weight is on right (fig. 11.5 A). Turn waist to the right 45 degrees. Right hand follows in-reeling 90 degrees of half the lower arc, and at the same time, the left hand also in-reels 90 degrees of half the lower arc to posture B, weight still on the right.

Count 2 Posture B to C. Shift weight to left bow-stance as torso turns to face front. Right-hand continues in-reeling 90 degrees to complete the lower arc, while left hand in-reels 90 degrees also to complete lower arc to posture C, right hand crosses below left.

Count 3 Posture C to D. Turn the waist to the left 45 degrees. Right hand follows out-reeling 90 degrees of half of the upper arc, and at the same time, the left hand also out-reels 90 degrees of half of the upper arc, to posture D, weight still on the left.

Count 4 Posture D to A. Shift weight to right bow-stance as torso turns to face front. Right-hand continues out-reeling 90 degrees to complete the upper arc, while left hand also out-reels 90 degrees to complete the upper arc back to posture A.

Fig. 11.12 A Start Double Cloud hand crossing

Fig. 11.12 B Count 1 Both hands down

Fig. 11.12 C Count 2 Both hands close down

Fig. 11.12 D Count 3 Both hands close up

6. Double Reverse-Hand Crossing

In "Double Reverse-Hand Crossing," the right hand is doing the reverse-hand pattern and so is the left hand, but unlike the "Front-Back Silk-Reeling" pattern (fig. 11.6), both hands are in-reeling or out-reeling together (fig. 11.13). Follow the silk-reeling through postures A, B, C, D. The mechanics of silk-reeling is the same.

Fig. 11.13 A Start Double Reverse hand crossing

Fig. 11.13 B Count 1 Both hands up

Fig. 11.13 C Count 2 Both hands close up

Fig. 11.13 D Count 3 Both hands close down

A Regimen of Silk-Reeling (Chansi) Exercises

Following Zhu Tiancai, we can string together the chansi patterns to form a regimen of chansi motion exercises. Be mindful of in-reeling (shun chan) and out-reeling (ni chan), the shun-ni change, motion of the arms following the waist, and posture balance. Do each pattern 10 to 20 times each, and you will seriously burn some calories.

1. Single Cloud-Hand. Start with right cloud-hand silk-reeling, then switch to left hand.
2. Single Reverse-Hand. Switch the left cloud-hand to left reverse-hand pattern. Then switch to right reverse-hand silk-reeling.
3. Double-hand Front-Back. Bring in left hand to merge into double-hand front-back silk-reeling.
4. Hands Waving Cloud. Change from the front-back silk-reeling pattern to "hands waving cloud" pattern.
5. Double-Hand Roll Back. Switch from "hands waving cloud" to "double-hand roll-back" clockwise direction (the right side). Then change to anti-clockwise direction (the left side).
6. Hand-Crossing Silk-Reeling. Change from the "double-hand roll-back" to "hand-crossing right side" pattern. Then change to "hand-crossing left side."
7. Double Cloud-hand Crossing. Switch from the "hand-crossing left side" to "double cloud-hand crossing" pattern.
8. Double Reverse-Hand Crossing. Switch from the "double cloud-hand crossing" to "double reverse-hand crossing."
9. Bring both hands and leg in to close.

The above set of silk-reeling exercises can be practiced in whole or in part, which can be treated as a regimen for a "Silk-Reeling *Qigong.*" It is convenient to engage in the exercise. Just get into a bow-stance and start silk-reeling, at any time and at any place. Do it daily. It is relaxing and energizing, and brings relief to stress.

Silk-Reeling with Moving Foot Steps

By taking steps forward, backward, left or right, the silk-reeling motion flows from fixed-step to moving-step patterns. Be mindful to maintain posture balance by relaxation. It is easy to unintentionally lean forward or backward when stepping.

1. Side-Step to Left (Hands Waving Cloud)

Practice a few rounds of "Cloud-Hand Silk Reeling" fixed steps (fig. 11.2 A, B, C, D) and then change to moving steps. The weight shifts completely to one leg and the other leg is brought to the side in count 2.

Count 1. Start at right bow-stance posture A (fig. 11.14). Turn waist right 45 degrees, right hand in-reels and the left hand out-reels to posture B.

Fig. 11.14 A Start Double Cloud-hand

Fig. 11.14 B Count 1 L hand up R hand down

Count 2. Shift weight to left bow-stance as torso turns to face front, but continue to transfer weight completely to the left foot and bring the right foot in to the side. Both hands follow silk-reeling; the right hand completes the in-reeling and the left hand, the out-reeling to posture C. The weight is on the left foot.

There is a leg-crossing variation where the right leg crosses behind the left, instead of being brought to the side, as in posture C*.

Count 3. Turn waist left 45 degrees as both hands change shun-ni orientations in silk-reeling to posture D, weight still on left. (Posture D* Legs remain crossed.)

Fig. 11.14 C Count 2 Bring right foot side of leg

Fig. 11.14 D Count 3 L hand down R hand up

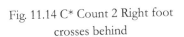

Fig. 11.14 C* Count 2 Right foot crosses behind

Fig. 11.14 D* Count 3 L hand down R hand up

Count 4. Shift weight to right foot as torso turns to face front; transfer weight completely to the right foot, raise left foot and step to the side, landing with the inner heel. Both hands continue silk-reeling; the right hand continues to complete out-reeling and the left hand in-reeling back to right bow-stance (posture A).

Fig. 11.14 E Count 4 Step to left side   Fig. 11.14 A Back to beginning posture

2. Side-Step to Right (Hands Waving Cloud)

Do the exercise as above, but side-step to the right. Start at left bow-stance posture A and follow the postures B, C, and E (fig. 11.15).

Fig. 11.15 A Start Double Cloud-hand left   Fig. 11.15 B Count 1 R hand up L hand down

Fig. 11.15 C Count 2 Bring left foot in
to side

Fig. 11.15 D Count 3 R hand down L
hand up

Fig. 11.15 C* Count 2 Left foot
crosses behind

Fig. 11.15 D* Count 3 R hand down L
hand up

Fig. 11.15 E Count 4 Step to right side   Fig. 11.15 A Back to beginning posture

3. Stepping Forward Double-Hand Rollback (Right Side)

Practice the right-side double-hand rollback motion several times in fixed steps (fig. 11.8 A, B, C, D) and then change to moving steps. The weight transfers completely to the front foot in count 2 and the rear foot is drawn in behind.

Fig. 11.16 A Start Double Rollback   Fig. 11.16 B Count 1 Both hands
right side   down

Fig. 11.16 C Count 2 Shift weight, draw in R foot   Fig. 11.16 D Count 3 Both hands up

Count 1. Start with right bow-stance at an angle of 45 degrees, posture A (fig. 11.16). Turn waist right 45 degrees, both hands follow in half of the lower arc, right hand in-reeling and the left hand out-reeling to posture B.

Count 2. Shift weight to left bow-stance as torso turns to adjust, but continue to transfer weight completely to the left foot and draw the right foot in behind. Both hands follow silk-reeling, the right hand in-reeling and the left hand out-reeling to complete the lower arc to posture C. The weight is on the left foot.

Count 3. Turn waist left 45 degrees as both hands change shun-ni orientations and silk-reel in half of the upper arc to posture D, weight still on left.

Count 4. Shift weight completely to the right foot as torso turns to adjust and both hands continue silk-reeling to complete the upper arc, and raise the left foot to step forward (posture E). Step out at an angle of 45 degrees, landing on the inner heel back to right bow-stance (posture A).

Fig. 11.16 E Count 4 Step forward 45
degrees

Fig. 11.16 A Back to Posture A

4. Stepping Forward Double-Hand Roll-Back (Left Side)

Practice the left-side double-hand rollback motion in fixed steps several rounds (fig. 11.8 A, B, C, D) and then change to moving steps. The weight transfers completely to the front foot in count 2.

Start with left bow-stance at an angle of 45 degrees to the left (posture A) and follow the postures B, C, D and E (fig. 11.17) as below.

Fig. 11.17 A Start Double Rollback left
side

Fig. 11.17 B Count 1 Both hands
down

Fig. 11.17 C Count 2 Shift weight,
draw in L foot

Fig. 11.17 D Count 3 Both hands up

Fig. 11.17 E Count 4 Step forward 45
degrees

Fig. 11.17 A Back to posture A

5. Stepping Forward "Twist Step" (Ao Bu)

In this silk-reeling, the hands are doing reverse-hand "front-back silk-reeling" and the foot steps forward at 45-degree angle, landing with the heel (fig. 11.18).

Fig. 11.18 A Start "Twist Step" R bow-stance

Fig. 11.18 B Count 1 R hand down L hand up

Count 1. Start with right bow-stance at an angle of 45 degrees (posture A). The right hand is at the end of the in-reeling of the upper arc but with the edge of the palm thrusting forward. The left hand is at the end of the out-reeling lower arc. Turn waist to right 45 degrees, and the hands follow silk-reeling in half of the arcs of double-hand "front-back" pattern: Right hand out-reels to the front of abdomen and left hand in-reels to shoulder level (posture B).

Fig. 11.18 C Count 2 Bring left foot front

Fig. 11.18 D Count 3 Step forward 45 degrees

Fig. 11.18 E Count 4 Shift weight to   Fig. 11.18 F Count 5 R hand up L
left   hand down

Count 2. Relax at right kua and twist right foot at heel outward 45 degrees. Transfer weight completely to the front foot and bring rear foot to the front, balanced on right foot, poised to step forward (posture C).

Count 3. Sit into the right kua to keep firm support and step out 45 degrees to the left, with heel landing, hands remaining in the same positions. Weight is still on the right (posture D).

Count 4. Shift weight forward to left bow-stance, and hands continue silk-reeling: Left hand completes in-reeling 90 degrees forward and right hand completes out-reeling 90 degrees to posture E. This is the same as the starting posture but on the left side.

Count 5. Repeat the above on the left side. Turn waist to left 45 degrees, and the hands follow silk-reeling in half of the arcs of double-hand "front-back" pattern: Left hand out-reels to the front of abdomen and right hand in-reels to shoulder level (posture F).

Fig. 11.18 G Count 6 Bring right foot front   Fig. 11.18 H Count 7 Step forward 45 degrees

Count 6. Relax at left kua and twist left foot at heel outward 45 degrees. Transfer weight completely to the front foot and bring rear foot to the front, balanced on left foot, poised to step forward (posture G).

Count 7. Step out 45 degrees to the left landing with the heel, and hands remain in the same positions. Weight is still on the left (posture H).

Count 8. Shift weight forward to right bow-stance, and hands continue silk-reeling: Right hand completes in-reeling 90 degrees forward and left hand completes out-reeling 90 degrees back to posture A.

In essence, in "Twist Step" silk-reeling, the hands move forward aggressively with the advancing footsteps. The left hand follows the left foot forward and the right hand follows the right foot forward.

6. "Arms Twining Backwards" (Dao Juan Gong)

In this silk-reeling pattern, as above, the hands are doing reverse-hand front-back silk-reeling. The steps are taken backwards at 45-degree angle, landing with the toes on the ground, as the hands twine (fig. 11.19).

Fig. 11.19 A Start "Twine Back" R
bow-stance

Fig. 11.19 B Count 1 R hand down, L
hand up

Fig. 11.19 C Count 2 Bring right foot
back

Fig. 11.19 D Count 3 Step backward
45 degrees

Count 1. Start with right bow-stance at an angle of 45 degrees (posture A). Turn waist to left 45 degrees, and the hands follow in half of the arcs of the front-back silk-reeling pattern: Right hand out-reels to the front of abdomen and left hand in-reels to shoulder level (posture B).

Count 2. Relax left kua and turn on the rear heel inwards. Transfer weight completely to the rear foot and draw in the front foot, balanced on the left foot, poised to step backward (posture C).

Count 3. Sit into the left kua and step back at a 45-degree angle to the right landing with the toes, hand positions remaining the same to left bow-stance (posture D). Note that the torso is turned at an angle.

Fig. 11.19 E Count 4 Turn waist to right

Fig. 11.19 F Count 5 R hand up, L hand down

Fig. 11.19 G Count 6 Bring left foot in

Fig. 11.19 H Count 7 Step backward 45 degrees

Count 4. Turn waist to right to align torso in the left bow-stance, and hands continue silk-reeling: Left hand completes in-reeling 90 degrees forward and right hand completes out-reeling 90 degrees to posture E. This is the same as the starting posture on the left.

Count 5. Repeat the above on the left side. Turn waist to right 45 degrees, and the hands follow in half of the arcs of the front-back silk-reeling pattern: Left hand out-reels to the front of abdomen and right hand in-reels to shoulder level (posture F).

Count 6. Relax at right kua and turn on the rear heel inwards. Transfer weight completely to the rear foot, draw the front foot in, balanced on right foot, poised to step backward (posture G).

Count 7. Sit into right kua and step back at 45 degrees to the left landing with the toes, and with the hand positions remaining the same to right bow-stance (posture H). Note that the torso is turned at an angle.

Count 8. Turn waist to left to align torso in the right bow-stance, and hands continue silk-reeling: Right hand completes in-reeling 90 degrees forward and left hand completes out-reeling 90 degrees back to posture A.

Note that in stepping backwards, the hands do not retreat but stay put to maintain peng energy of defense. As the waist turns to align the torso (from posture D to E or H to A), the edge of the palm follows in-reeling forward offensively.

Chansi in Taijiquan Form

The above provides a set of basic silk-reeling patterns where the circles of in-reelings and out-reelings are regular in cycles and sizes. One can devise other patterns of chansi exercises. The key is practice to cultivate fluency of the silk-reeling motions—the series of self and general rotations in sequential order and the change of shun-ni orientations.

The in-reeling (shun) or out-reeling (ni) can change orientations at any time and at either the left or right bow-stances, the hands can coil in varying sizes, and the footsteps can be in different directions. Taijiquan motion is produced by varying the patterns of silk-reeling. The Taijiquan form routine is a symphonic score of silk-reeling motions built on the notes of the basic patterns, changing in orientations, radial sizes, and directions.

For example, the first part of the movement "Buddha Pounding Mortar Board" is primarily a "double-hand roll-back" (shuang lü) silk-reeling motion, but the hands coil in different radii of the cycle. The first half of the cycle is regular, but in the second half, following the left foot stepping out, the left hand out-reels in a smaller arc while the right hand in a larger arc. Thus, the left hand coils more to the front of the chest while the right hand less to arrive over the right knee. Likewise, all Taijiquan movements can be analyzed in terms of chansi cycles. In martial applications, the chansi variations are effected according to the myriad changes in a combat situation.

Shen Long
(Spirit of Dragon)
Calligraphy by Chen Xiaowang

Glossary of Pinyin & Chinese Characters

The meanings of the Chinese characters are as used in the context of the book.

B

bi shi ji xu 避实击虚 "avoid the strength and attack the weakness"

bu 步 "foot-step"

bu dao wei 不到味 "short, not having reached the flavor of the form"

bu diu bu ding 不丢不顶 "neither lax nor resisting"

bu ji 不及 "falling short and not reaching the form"

C

chanfa 缠发 "coiling-methods"

chanrao 缠绕 "coiling"

chansi 缠丝 "silk-reeling"

chansi jin 缠丝劲 "silk-reeling energy"

chen jian zhui zhou 沉肩坠肘 "drop the shoulder and sink the elbow"

chi ku 吃苦 "eating the bitterness"

cong wai dao nei 从外到内 "from the external to the internal"

cong xin suo yu 从心所欲 "the body performing as one wishes"

cui chi 摧齿 "break the teeth"

D

dang yao jin 裆腰劲 "waist-groin energy"

dantian 丹田 "located at three fingers below the navel, and a third of the way inside the abdomen")

dantian hexin de xing cheng 丹田核心的形成 "formation of the central status of the dantian"

dantian neizhuan (丹田内转) "dantian internal rotation"

dantian wei hexin 丹田为核心 "the central status of the dantian"

dantian qi baoman 丹田气饱满 "fullness of dantian qi"

daoyin 导引 "calisthenics to cultivate qi or induce internal energetics"

daoyin tu'na 导引吐纳 "early qigong or practice of qi energetics"

de ji de shi 得机得势 "to take advantage of an opportunity or to put oneself in an advantageous position"

dige 递个 "one by one"

ding 顶 "pushing against the top or an opponent"

ding shi 定势 "practice of stationary postures"

diu 丢 "to lose"

dong jin 懂劲 "comprehension of the gang-rou duality of jin"

dong wu bu dong, jing wu bu jing 动无不动，静无不静 "in motion, no part of the body is not set in motion; in stillness, not a part is set in motion"

duan jin 断筋 "sever the tendons"

duan jin 短劲 "short fajin (arm not fully extended)"

F

fajin 发劲 "explosive release of jin"

fangsong 放松 "letting go to relax"

fu shi huxi 腹式呼吸 "abdominal breathing"

G

gang 刚 "hard"

gao shou 高手 "an expert"

gong fang 攻防 "offense and defense"

gong li 功力 "core strength developed in training"

gong zhuan 公转 "general rotation to describe the motion of the body's CM"

gongfu jiazi 功夫架子 "basic form practice to develop kungfu"

gu 骨 "bones"

guo 过 "going over"

guo le 过了 *"over-extended, having gone past"*

H

hanxiong 含胸 "contain the chest"

hanxiong tayao 含胸塌腰 "contain the chest and settle the waist"

haoran zhi qi 浩然之气 "magnificent and noble qi"

hejin 合劲 "coordinated and unified power"

huan jin 换劲 "change of internal energy"

J

jiang 僵 "stiff, tense, tight"

jiang jin 僵劲 "stiffness or tenseness"

jie jie guanchuan 节节贯穿 "threading through all the joints"

jie li da ren 借力打人 "borrowing the opponent's force to strike back"

jin 筋 "tendons and muscles"

jin 劲 or *neijin* 内劲 "internal strength"

K

kai kua 开胯 "opening the kua"

kou dang 扣裆 "closing inward at the crotch"

kua 胯 "hip joints"

L

li 力 "external force or strength"

li shen zhong zhen, bu pian bu yi 立身中正，不偏不倚 "keep body straight and centered, not leaning"

linghuo 灵活 "lively, agile"

ling kong jin 灵空劲 "empty-space force"

luoxuan 螺旋 "coiling or spiraling"

M

miaoshou 妙手 "magical hands"

N

neijin 内劲 "internal strength or energy"

nei kai wai he 内开外合 "opens from the inside and closes from the outside"

nei lian yi kou qi wai lian jin gu bi 内练一口气外练筋骨皮 "the internal training of the breathing discipline and the external training of the muscles, tendons, bones, and skin" *nei sanhe* 内三合 "Internal Three Unities"

nei wai jie he 内外结合 "uniting the inner and outer"

neng huxi ran hou neng ling huo 能呼吸然后能灵活 "only if one can breathe can one be lively"

ni shi fu huxi 逆式腹呼吸 "reverse abdominal breathing"

P

peng jin 掤劲 "jin of Taiji balance extending from within"

Q

qi 气 "the vital life-force energy"

qi chen dantian 气沉丹田 "qi sinking to the dantian"

qian hou xuan zhuan 前后旋转 "front and back rotation"

qinna 擒拿 "the art of capturing joints to immobilize, and of escape from same"

qing zhong 轻重 "light and heavy"

qu xi kai kua 曲膝开胯 "bend at the knees and open the kua"

quan lian xiao 圈连小 "Train to move in smaller circles"

R

ren ta ju li lai da wo 任他巨力来打吾 "no matter how much force he comes at me"

rou 柔 "soft"

S

sanhe 三合 "three unities"

sanjie 三节 "three sections"

sanluan 散乱 "scattered and confused"

shang zhong xia qing 上重下轻 "top heavy and base light"

shang xia xiang sui ren nan jin 上下相随人难进 "upper and lower in mutual accord, enemy hard to enter"

shao jie ling, zhong jie sui, geng jie cui 梢节领，中节随，根节摧 "the extremity leads, the middle section follows, and the root section drives"

she ji cong ren 舍己从人 "give up self to follow"

shen 身 "body"

shen jin ba gu 伸筋拔骨 "stretching the tendons and the bones"

shenmiao 神妙 "wondrous of the divine order"

shen ming 神明 "divine insight"

shisan shi 十三势 "thirteen postures"

shou 手 "hands"

shou zuo wan 手座腕 "let the hand sit on the wrist joint"

shi 实 "solid, substantial"

Shisan Shi 十三势 "Thirteen Postures"

shuang zhong 双重 "double weightedness"

si liang bo qian jin 四两拨千斤 "four ounces repelling a thousand pounds"

sishao 四梢 "four extremities"

song jian 松肩 "relax the shoulders"

song yao yuan dang 松腰圆裆 "relax the waist and round the crotch"

sui ji ying bian 随机应变 "changes accordingly to the situation"

T

ta quan 大圈 "large circles"

ting jin 听劲 "listening jin"

tou 头 "head"

tou gu 透骨 "pierce through the bones"

tu'na 吐纳 "breathing methods to take in the fresh and expel the stale"

W

wan fa gui yi 万法归一 "the ten thousand techniques flow from one principle"

wai jia quan 外家拳 "external kungfu"

Wai Sanhe 外三合 "External Three Unities"

wei wu wei 为无为 "action without action"

wu chu bu shi quan 无处不是圈 *wu chu bu shi quan* 无处不是拳 "not a part of the body that is not a circle, and not a part that is not a fist"

wuji 无极 "primordial void, nothingness, non-being"

wu quan 无圈 "no circles"

wu zang 五脏 "five internal organs"

wucha 误差 "errors or deviations"

wu shi you tu ao chu 无使有凸凹处 "no part protrusive or depressive"

X

xia gongfu 下功夫 "attained kungfu"

xiao fu bu 小腹部 "small abdomen"

xiao quan 小圈 "small circles"

xin 心 "heart"

xin wei ling, qi wei qi, yao wei dao 心为令，气为旗，腰为纛 "Mind is the commander, qi is the signal flag, waist is the banner (movements filing under it)"

xinyuan 心猿 "the mind of a monkey"

xiong yao zhe die 胸腰折叠 "folding motion of the chest and waist"

xu ling ding jin 虚领顶劲 "point the crown of head up with no tension, as if lifted at the crown with no tension"

xu 虚 "hollow, insubstantial"

xu qi xin shi qi fu 虚其心实其腹 "light is the heart, full is the abdomen"

xu shi 虚实 "insubstantial and the substantial"

xu shi fenming 虚实分明 "clarity of the insubstantial and the substantial"

xu xi fa hu 蓄吸发呼 "breathe in to collect, breathe out to issue"

xue qi 血气 "blood charged with the fullness of qi"

Y

yi 意 "mind/intent"

yi 义 "rightness"

yi dao qi dao, qi dao, shen dong 意到气到，气到身动 "yi initiates, qi follows, and when qi arrives, motion is activated"

yilu 一路 "first routine form"

yi gang wei zhu 以刚为主 "predicated on hardness"

yi nei qi cui wai xing 以内气催外形 "qi drives the motion internally to set the external form"

[*yi nei qi wei tong yu* 以内气为统驭 "qi is the driver of motion"] deleted this from use.

yi qi guan tong 一气贯通 "qi extending throughout and engaging the whole body as one"

yi qi jun lai gu rou chen 意气君来骨肉臣 "yi and qi are the sovereign, bones and muscles follow as subjects"

yi rou ke gang 以柔克刚 "the soft to overcome the hard"

yi rou wei zhu 以柔为主 "predicated on softness"

yi shao jie ling jin 以梢节领劲 "extremity leads the jin"

yi shou ling jin 以手领劲 "the hand leading the jin"

yi yi dao qi, yi qi yun shen 以意导气，以气运身 "use mind-intent to guide qi, with the qi move the body"

yin jin luo kong 引劲落空 "leading force to emptiness"

yong yi bu yong li 用意不用力 "use mind/intent not force"

yuan huo 圆活 "round and lively, agile"

Yundong Guilu 运动规律 "Principle of Motion"

Z

zha zhou 乍肘 "spread elbow out to leave a space between the rib and elbow"

zhan nian lian sui 沾连黏随 "stick, connect, adhere, follow"

zhe die 折叠 "folding motion"

zheng qi 正气 "qi of morality or righteousness"

zhi cheng ba mian 八面枝撑 "propped up and guarded in the eight directions"

zhong quan 中圈 "medium circles"

zhou shen xiang sui 周身相随 "whole body in mutual accord and support"

zhuan yao kou dang 转腰扣裆 "turn the waist, close the groin inward" *zhuzai* 主宰 "control center"

zhuo li 拙力 "clumsy strength"

zi zhuan 自转 "self-rotation to describe spinning motion"

ziran huxi 自然呼吸 "natural breathing"

ziru 自如 "natural and spontaneous"

zuo you xuan zhuan 左右旋转 "left and right rotate

End Notes

1
Allure of Taijiquan

1   Wolf SL, Barnhart HX, Kutner NG, Mcneely E, Coogler CE, Xu T. Reducing frailty and falls in older persons: an investigation of Tai Chi and computerized balance training. Atlanta FICSIT Group. Frailty and Injuries: Cooperative Studies of Intervention Techniques. J Am Geriatr Soc. 1996; 44(5):489-497.

2   Thompson, James C. *While China Faced West: American Reformers in Nationalist China.* Thomson describes the Nanking Decade (1928-1937) as "a brief period of excitement, hope, creativeness, and promise. But it gave way to tragedy and to more violent collision which continues today, with no end in sight."

3   Buried in the footnotes of history of the 1936 Berlin Olympics, the new Chinese National Anthem, "Three Principles" was named the best national anthem of the Games.

4   Fu Shu-Yun (1916-). A brief biography. http://www.chinesemartialarts.eu/ FU%20SHU-YUN.html. Fu describes that Hitler honored the team with a private audience and expressed to her that Taijiquan would be the kind of exercise he would like to take up.

5   As of writing, wushu is in the short list to be selected an Olympic event in time for the 2016 Games.

6   Kang Gewu (1995). *The Spring and Autumn of Chinese Martial Arts – 5000 Years.* Plum Publishing, California. The reader can find a concise and panoramic view of Chinese Martial Arts in the book.

7   Luo Guanzhong. *Three Kingdom.* Trans. Moss Roberts. Foreign Language Press, Beijing, China, 1995.

8   Li Tianji (1913-1996) was the first of the wushu careerists. He graduated from Shandong Martial Arts College as a wushu instructor in 1931 and held several teaching coaching positions. In 1990, he was honored as one of the "Ten Greatest Wushu Masters of Renown in China" (*Zhongguo Shi Da Wushu Ming Shi*).

9   Lee Martin, etc. (1996). *The Healing Art of Tai Chi: Becoming One with Nature*. New York Sterling Pub Co Inc.

10   Chen, Pan Ling (1998) *Chen Pan Ling's Original Tai Chi Chuan Textbook*. Blitz Design, New Orleans, p. 8.

11   Astin JA, Pelletier KR, Haskell WL, Hansen E, Marie A. A Review of the Incorporation of Complementary and Alternative Medicine by Mainstream Physicians. Arch Intern Med. 1998;158:2303-2310.

12   The Health Benefits of Tai Chi, Harvard Women's Health Watch May 2009, Harvard Health Publications, Harvard School of Medicine. http://www.health.harvard.edu/ newsletters/Harvard_Womens_Health_Watch/2009/May/The-health-benefits-of-tai-chi?print=1

13   The Arthritis Foundation website: http://www.arthritis.org/tai-chi.php

14   Horstman, Judith, Lam, Paul (2002). *Overcoming Arthritis*. Dorling Kindersley.

15   Li Deyin (1938 -), a nephew of Li Tianji of the 24-Form Taijiquan, led the Committee in choreographing the Competition Routine in 1989.

16   Wang Zongyue. *Taijiquan Classics*. One of the five classical canonical texts of Taijiquan.

17   The biographical notes posted by Wu Tunan's (1884-1989) followers describe him as a student of Wu Jianquan and Yang Shaohou, and a highly accomplished Taijiquan master who "could exert his inner strength on a person from the distance of one meter, causing that person to fall a few yards away." More can be found in a feature article, Tai Chi Magazine, April 2007, and http://wutunantaijigong.com/wutunan.htm.

18   Hong Junsheng (1989). *Practical Boxing Method of Chen Style Taijiquan*. Shandong Science and Technology Press.

19   Kuo Lien-Ying, Trans Guttmann (1994). *The T'ai Chi Boxing Chronicle*. Berkeley, CA, North Atlantic Books.

20   The local press carried the news of this challenge, which Kuo also fondly recalled in an interview in the San Francisco Chronicle Feb 22, 1972.

21   To name a few of the disciples: Cui Yishi, Wu Huichuan, Fu Zhongwen, Chen Weiming, Li Yaxuan, Dong Yingjie, Niu Chunming, and many others. The list is not intended to be complete or exclusive.

2
Evolution of the Major Schools

1   Chen Dehu's house still stands today, a popular place of visit by Taijiquan visitors.

2   Wile, Douglas (1983). *Tai Chi Touchstones: Yang Family Secret Transmissions* Brooklyn, New York. Sweet Chi Press. The author cited Xu Zhen's note, "... the master (Chen Changxin) was so impressed that he not only transmitted the art to him (Yang Luchan) but bought his freedom for fifty ounces of silver and returned him to Yongnian." Translator's Note, p. v.

3   Yang Luchan had three sons born in Yongnian, the first Fenghou died early, the second Banhou was born in 1837, and the third, Jianhou in 1839. So the earliest date of Yang's first return would be 1836. It is said that he came back to the Village three times to advance his skills.

4   YeYoung Culture Studies, *The Origins of Tai Chi*; the Chen Camp, http://www.literati-tradition.com/chen camp.html. The subsection, *Intriguing new evidence in Taijiquan Development*, provides a well-referenced article on a recent study of a Li Family Genealogy which is shedding some light on Wang Zongyue. The genealogical record reveals a relationship between the Chen Family and the Li Family, and Chen Wangting as a cousin by marriage. The Li's recalled that Wang Zongyue was a school teacher from Shanxi Province, and had studied the art from them.

5   Assuming Zhang Sanfeng was an adult when Song Emperor Huizong (1101-1125) summoned him, and he survived to the reign of Ming Yongle Emperor (1402-1424) who purportedly also sought him, he would be over 300.

6   Wile, Douglas (1996). *Lost Tai Chi Classics from the Late Ching Dynasty* State University of New York Press, Albany, New York. The book and Ibid 2 cite the research works by Tang Hao (1897-1959), Xu Zhen (1898-1967) and Gu Liuxin (1908-1991). The reader can also find a research of this in the YeYoung Culture Studies at: http://www.literati-tradition.com/zhang sanfeng camp.html

7   Ibid 6. Translation of the Epitaph p. 26.

8   Henning, Stanley. Ignorance, Legend and Taijiquan. Journal of the Chen Style Taijiquan Research Association of Hawaii, Vol. 2, No. 3, pp. 1-7. Copy available at http://seinenkai.com/articles/henning/il&t.pdf.

9   Ibid 2, pp 25-26.

10   Bing YeYoung The Origins of Tai Chi: Zhang Sanfeng Camp. YeYoung Culture Studies. http://www.literati-tradition.com/zhang sanfeng camp.html

11   Ibid 6 p. 33.

12   Sun Lutang (1921). *The Study of Taijiquan*. Cartmell, Tim (2003) Translation, North Atlantic Books, Berkeley, California.

13   Director Yuen Wo Ping (2003) *Taiji Master* (Taiji Zong Shi) Hong Kong TV miniseries, starring Jack Wu as Yang Luchan. The dual can be viewed in http://www.youtube.com/watch?v=jYdl9DX25Rc.

14   After the fall of the Manchu rule, Quan You's son adopted the Han surname of Wu, a different character from the Wu of Wu Yuxiang.

15   The troops of eight nations, Austria-Hungary, Britain, France, Germany, Italy, Japan, Russia, and the United States entered Beijing in August 1900, ransacked and looted the Forbidden City, forcing the emperor to flee to the Palace in Xi'an.

16   This amounted to each Chinese paying one tael, as the population was estimated at 450 million in 1900. 1 tael is equal to 1.2 troy ounces. It also tested the ingenuity of the private banking system to finance the debt.

17   The core texts in the Yang family came from the Wu family's collection.

18   Ibid 2. p. 153. Yang Chengfu recounts in the Preface of his book a conversation he had with his grandfather, Yang Luchan, which was a clearly a concoction as he was born only after his grandfather's death.

19   Ibid 6. p. 41

20   Davis, Barbara (2004). *The Taijiquan Classics: An annotated translation*. North Atlantic Books, Berkeley, California.

21   Chen Xin (1933). Illustrated Explanations of Chen Family Taijiquan (Chen Shi Taijiquan Tushou). Shanghai Books Publication, Shanghai, China.

22   Chen Panling (President of Henan Province Martial Arts Academy), Han Zibu (President of Henan Archives Bureau), Wang Zemin and Bai Yusheng of Kaiming Publishing House, Guan Baiyi (Director of Henan Provincial Museum) and Zhang Jiamou, together raised 800 yuan to publish the book.

23   Chen Zhenglei (1998). *The Art of Chen Family Taijiquan (Chen Shi Taijiquan Shu)*. Shanxi Technology Publication, China. pp. 677-685.

24   Ibid 24. p. 673.

25   Tian Guilin. Veritable Record of Taiping Army Attacking Huaiqing County (Taiping Jun Gong Huaiqing Fu Shilu); Ye Zhiji. Daily Records of Huaiqing Defense (Shou Huai Rizhi). http://www.chinafrominside.com/ma/taiji/xiaojia.html. Also in the Chen Family records.

26   The vibrational power of the long pole is evident in the demonstration by Chen Zhenglei in http://www.youtube.com/watch?v=kQoWDLmXuvY

27   Chen Kesen. *My Father, Chen Zhaopi*. A commemorative essay by his son, http://www.taiji-bg.com/articles/taijiquan/t48.htm.

28   Chen Zhenglei. *In Memory of Chen Zhaopi*. T'ai Chi Magazine. Fall 2012.

3
Historical & Cultural Perspective of Taijiquan

1   Zhou Dunyi (1017-1073). *Taijitu Shou.* The Taiji diagram first appeared in the essay, in a revival of Taoism during the Song Dynasty (960 - 1279).

2   Wang Zongyue (attributed author). *Taijiquan Classics.* One of the Five Canons of Taijiquan (chapter 2).

3   The yao-lines of yin and yang are depicted in the oracle bones of the Shang Dynasty (c. 1562 - 1066 B.C.). It is said that the legendary ruler Fuxi circa 2800 B.C. invented them.

4   Wilhelm, Richard, Baynes Cary. Translation (1950). *The I Ching* Princeton University Press 1990 reprint. Table taken from the book.

5   The post-birth arrangement of the bagua is credited to King Wen (1099 - 1055 B.C.), and the pre-birth arrangement to the legendary Fu xi. Fuxi invented the bagua octagon, inspired by the design of a tortoise shell. Steve Moore's *Trigrams of Han,* discusses the two arrangements. http://www.triplexunity.com/docs/background1.htm.

6   The Five Chinese Classics are: I-Ching, Book of History (Shujing), Book of Odes (Shijing), Book of Rites (Lijing), and Spring and Autumn Annals.

7   Ibid 4 p. 348.

8   These two books were the predecessors of *Yi (Change) of Zhou,* which later would be called *I-Ching (Yi Jing).* They were named after the Xia Dynasty (c. 2200-1600 B.C.), the Shang Dynasty (c. 1600-1046 B.C.), and the Zhou Dynasty (1045-256 B.C.).

9   Ibid 6. *Shijing* is one of the Five Chinese Classics.

10   Szuma Chien (Sima Qian), trans. Yang Hsien-yi and Gladys Yang. *Records of the Historian (Shiji).* The Commercial Press, Hong Kong. 1985.

11   The Three Rulers and the Five Emperors, the Sanhuang Wudi (c. 2850 - 2200 B.C.), which include the Yellow Emperor and the model emperors, Yao and Shun.

12   Sima Qian (c.145-90 B.C.) is the author of *Shiji (Records of the Historian).* His compilation has been the richest source of ancient Chinese history, spanning over two thousand years, from the Yellow Emperor to his time, the Han Wudi (156-57 B.C.). His influence is so extensive that it is hard to find a historical writing of early Chinese history without reference to him.

13   Ibid 6, *Book of History (Shujing)* is one of Five Chinese Classics.

14   The seven states contending for hegemony were Chu, Han, Qi, Qin, Wei, Yan and Zhao. The Qin State began its annexation in 230 B.C. with the conquest of Han, then followed by Wei (225 B.C.), Chu (223 B.C.), Yan, and Zhao (228 B.C.), and finally Qi (221B.C.).

15   Sima Qian, the Grand Historian describes six contentious schools of philosophy: Yin-Yang School (Yin-Yang Jia), School of Names (Ming Jia), School of Mozi or Mohism (Mo Jia), School of Legalists (Fa Jia), School of Tao or Taoism (Daode Jia), School of Confucianism (Ru Jia).

16   The 36.4-kilometer waterway runs north-south, connects the Yangtze and the Pearl River systems. As the Great Wall kept out the barbarians, the Lingqu canals served to link the north and south in transportation and economy. Though less well-known than the Great Wall, its sentimental significance is conveyed in the saying, "In the north there is the Great Wall, in the south there is the Lingqu canal."

17   Cotterell, Arthur (1981). *The First Emperor of China*. Holt, Rinehart and Winston, New York. The book describes the richest archaeological finds of the terracotta sculptures of soldiers, charioteers and horsemen in Mount Li, discovered in 1974.

18   Lin, S. *Changes in mind/body functions associated with Qigong practice.* (2004) J. Altern. Complement. Med. 10: 200. More publications in http://mindbodylab.bio.uci.edu/

19   The drawing was found in the Mawangdui excavations between 1972 and 1974, one of the major archaeological finds of the Western Han in China. http://www.hnmuseum.com/ hnmuseum/eng/whatson/exhibition/mwd 2 2.jsp

20   Maoshing Ni (1995) trans. *Yellow Emperor's Classic of Medicine*. Shambala, Boston.

21   Ibid 15

22   Eva Wong. *Seven Taoist Masters, A Folk Novel of China,* Shambala Classics, Boston, 2004. This is an easy-to-read story book about Taoist beliefs.

23   Despeux, Catherine. *Gymnastics: The Ancient Tradition.* Also in Livia Kohn ed. *Taoist Meditation and Longevity Techniques.* The University of Michigan, 1989.

24   An iconic figure of longevity, Peng Zu was a high official of the Shang Dynasty (c. 1600 - 1046 B.C.), who was reputed to live for 800 years.

25   There is a tomb in Wakayama (Japan) dedicated to Xu Fu, with the inscription of "Tomb of Xu Fu of the Qin Dynasty (221 – 206 B.C.)."

26   Qiu Chuji founded the White Cloud Monastery in Beijing, which still stands today. He was one of Wang Chongyang's seven disciples. Wang Chongyang was a prominent figure in the pantheon of famous Taoists and the founder of the Quanzhen Sect.

27   Lin Zixin, Yu Li, Guo Zhengyi, Shen Zhenyu, Zhang Honglin, and Zhang Tongling. *Qigong Chinese Medicine or Pseudoscience?* Prometheus Books, 2000. This book gives an account of the qigong craze in the period.

28   Ting, Leung. *Skills of the Vagabonds*, 1983, Leung's Publications, Kowloon, H.K.

29   Mainfort, Don, Sima Nan: *Fighting Qigong Pseudoscience in China*, CSICOP Skeptical Brief, 1999 Vol 9 March Issue. There are numerous newspaper articles on Sima Nan: New York Times, Nov 20, 1999, The Wall Street Journal, Aug 30, 1999, and The Nation, Nov 20, 2000.

4
Synthesis of Taijiquan

1   Kang Gewu, The Spring and Autumn of Chinese Martial Arts – 5000 Years. Plum Publishing, Santa Cruz, CA, 1995.

2   The reader can enjoy a cartoon version of this story in *Stories of Honour*, Asiapac Books, 1999.

3   Ibid 1, p. 30

4   Big Scholar Tree still stands today at Guhuai Park in Hongdong County, Shanxi, and is a popular tourist attraction.

5   Chenbuzhuang still stands today.

6   Chen Family Genealogy (*Chenshi Jiapu*) and Gazetteer of Wen County.

7   The painting was found in an ancestral altar in Chen Village in the 1930s by Tang Hao, the martial arts historian conducting field research then.

8   It was reported that Li Zicheng's general took as spoils the favorite concubine of Wu Sangui. Wu was torn between loyalty to the fallen Ming and mistrust of the rebels. Li Zicheng feared Wu's standing army, and set out to battle him, forcing Wu's hand.

9   Chen Wangting. *Song of Classic Boxing (Quanjing Zongge)*. Tang Hao found the poem in Liang Yi Tang at Chen Village during his field work.

10   I am indebted to Grandmaster Zhu Tiancai for explaining the poem, and for the many long hours of exposition of Taijiquan theory.

11   A classical book in neidan, the Taoist alchemy of internal energetics.

12   David Gaffney and Davidine Sim (2002). *Chen Style Taijiquan*. North Atlantic Books, Berkeley, CA. Chapter 7. Chen Xiaowang (2008). *Chen Family Taijiquan*. Anecdotes, p. 284. The stories are recounted in many Chinese texts on Chen Family Taijiquan.

13   Jarek Szymanski. *Brief Analysis of Chen Family Boxing Manuals* www.chinafrominside.com/ma/taiji/chenboxingmanuals.html, 2000

14   Chen Kong (1943). Tai-chi Hand Form, Broadsword, Two-edged Sword, Spear and Sparring. Excerpted in Douglas Wiles (1983). Tai Chi Touchstones: Yang Family Secret Transmissions. Secret Chi Press, Brooklyn, NY. Translator's Note p. i.

15   Sima Qian (c. 145 B.C. – 86 B.C.) was the famed Han historian and author of *Records of the Grand Historian*.

16   Kennedy, Brian & Guo, Elizabeth (2005). *Chinese Martial Arts Training Manuals A Historical Survey*. North Atlantic Books, Berkeley, CA. The book has a brief biography of Tang Hao by Gu Liuxin. p. 38.

17   Stanley Henning. *Ignorance, Legend and Taijiquan*. Journal of the Chen Style Taijiquan Research Association of Hawaii, Vol. 2, No. 3, 1994. pp. 1-7. http://seinenkai.com /articles/henning/il&t.pdf

18   Stanley Henning. *On Politically Correct Treatment of Myths in the Chinese Martial arts*. Journal of the Chen Taijiquan Research Association of Hawaii, Vol. 3, No 2, Summer 1995. http://seinenkai.com/articles/henning/politicallycorrect.pdf

19   C.P. Ong. *Chen Xiaowang, Carrying the Burden of Taiji Legacy*. Kungfu Qigong Magazine, 2003. The event was organized by Pat Rice, in Winchester, Virginia.

5
Neijin Phenomenon

1   Wong Zongyue. *Taijiquan Classics*. One of the Five Canons of Taijiquan.

2   http://www.youtube.com/watch?v=W6e01Gb-2h4 posted by Robert Smith, student of Cheng

3   http://www.youtube.com/watch?v=ldH40uF_f28.

4   http://www.youtube.com/watch?v=rZf4taeqht0. Asia's strongman pushing Chen Xiaowang.

5   C.P. Ong. *Chen Xiaowang, Carrying the Burden on Taiji Legacy Chen Xiaowang*. Kungfu Magazine, Sep/Oct 2003. An account is given in this article. (http://ezine.kungfumagazine.com/ezine/article.php?article=380.)

6   Chen Xiaowang (2008). *Chen Family Taijiquan*. Ren Ming Tiyu Chu Banshe, Beijing, China. p. 47.

7   This news article can be accessed in http://query.nytimes.com/gst/abstract.html?res=9C07E7D7173CE533A25751C2A9649D946195D6CF.

8   LIFE photo by Francis Miller taken from (Google Images) http://images.google.com/hosted/life/9b86fd33188aa461.html

9   Penner, Raymond. *Physics of Golf.* Reports on Progress in Physics 66, 131-171 (2002).

10   Tiger Woods. *Instruction Tip,* Golf Digest, May 2005.

11   A demonstration in YouTube: http://www.youtube.com/watch?v=3UCvZQVlmn0

12   http://www.youtube.com/watch?v=7IbLoMusajM. Demonstration of the same genre by Shaolin monks, but more dramatic.

13   Willey, David G. *The Physics Behind Four amazing Demonstrations.* Skeptical Inquirer, Vol 23, No 6 Nov/Dec 1999.

14   Halliday, David, Resnick, Rober, Walker, Jearl. *Fundamentals of Physics.* John Wiley & Sons, Inc, New York, 1993 (Calculation Problem 13-8, p. 369).

15   Feld, M.S., McNair, R.E., Wilk, S.R. *Physics of Karate.* Scientific American 240, 150-158 (1979).

16   Video recording of physics students breaking boards in class. http://www.physics.pacificu.edu/KarateMovies/karatemovies03/karatemovies03.html. Dr. Juliet Brosing, Physics Department, Pacific University, Forest Grove, Oregon.

17   In YouTube, http://www.youtube.com/watch?v=H1ZozmX6Pck.

18   In YouTube, http://www.youtube.com/watch?v=59MyUtwph1k.

19   Dictionary, www.Zhongwen.com

20   C.P. Ong. *Kungfu-Qigong Magazine,* Jan-Feb, 2001 issue, p 66. The event was also recounted in this article.

21   Chen Yu is the son of Chen Zhaokui, and a grandson of Chen Fa'ke. The author is privileged to learn from Chen Yu during in his occasional visits to Beijing.

6
Force of Neijin

1   Wile, Douglas (1983). Tai-chi Touchstones: Yang Family Secret Transmissions, Sweet Chi Press, Brooklyn, NY. Trans. Oral instructions of Yang Chengfu recorded by Chen Weiming. p. 12.

2   Dong, Paul & Raffill, Thomas (2006). *Empty Force: The Power of Chi for Self-Defense and Energy Healing*, Blue Snake Books, Berkeley, CA. There are many other presentations of ling kong jin on the internet.

3   Committee for Skeptical Inquiry. *Skeptical Inquirer*, a magazine that publishes claims of paranormal abilities and of debunking them. (http://www.csicop.org/).

4   There are many demonstrations of empty-space force posted on YouTube, for example, http://www.youtube.com/watch?v=e1kTE8vUl5Y and associated links.

5   Knierim, James. *Chapter 1, Motor Units and Muscle Receptors, Neuroscience Online*. Department of Neuroscience, The Johns Hopkins University. http://neuroscience.uth.tmc.edu/s3/chapter01.html

6   Nave, Carl R. *HyperPhysics Instructional Materials*. Department of Physics and Astronomy, University of Georgia, Atlanta. A very good summary of Fundamental Forces of Nature in a chart-form in http://hyperphysics.phyastr.gsu.edu/hbase/forces/funfor.html#c1

7   Slow-twitch muscle fibers generate a small force, but can sustain the force for a long period without being fatigued, and are found more in muscles that maintain posture and balance, example, the red meat of the chicken leg. Fast-twitch ones generate a strong force, but fatigue easily, so are used for a surge of power, such as in sprinting.

8   Branch, John. New York Times article 3/3/2009, and statistics from NBA.com. http://www.nytimes.com/2009/03/04/sports/basketball/04freethrow.html?pagewanted=all

9   *Song of Thirteen Postures*, one of the Five Canonical Texts of Taijiquan.

10   Wu, Yuxiang, *Elucidation of the Thirteen Postures*, one of the Five Canonical Texts of Taijiquan.

11   Keith L Moore and Arthur F Dalley. *Clinically Oriented Anatomy*. Lippincott, Williams & Wilkins. Details described here are taken from this text but are available in any anatomy text.

12   Wang Zongyue. *Taijiquan Classics* one of the Five Canonical Texts of Taijiquan.

13   One of the Five Classical Canons of Taijiquan Ibid 2.

14   Panek, Richard (2011). The 4 Percent Universe, Dark Matter, Dark Energy and the Race to Discover the Rest of Reality. Houghton Mifflin Harcourt, New York.

7
Taiji Balance

1   The essay contains the essence of Chen Family Taijiquan practice. The literature is independent of the Five Classical Canons of Taijiquan discussed in chapter 2. The essay is

found in Chinese books on Chen Family Taijiquan, for example, by Chen Zhenglei, Chen Family Taijiquan Theory (1998), Xi'an Science Technical Publication.

2   Wolf, S. L., Barnhart, H. X., Ellison, G. L., and Coogler, C.E. (1997) *The effect of Tai Chi Quan and Computerized Balance Training on Postural Stability in Older Subjects*. Physical Therapy, 77, 371–384. One of the earliest studies, and cited frequently.

3   In the context of mass distribution, center of gravity is the center of mass. Both concepts are defined in textbooks on physics, for example, Halliday, Resnick, & Walker, *Fundamentals of Physics*.

4   Chapter 8, section *Taijiquan's Waist-Power Action* studies the mechanics of waist power.

5   Chen Xin (1919). *Illustrated Explanations of Chen Family Taijiquan (Chen Shi Taijiquan Tushou)*. Shanghai Books Publication, Shanghai, China.

6   Chen Xiaowang (2008). *Chen Family Taijiquan*. People's Publication, China. p 308.

7   C.P. Ong. *Chen Xiaowang, Carrying the Burden of Taiji Legacy*. Kungfu Taichi Magazine. Sep/Oct 2003 http://www.kungfumagazine.com/ezine/article.php?article=380.

8   Ibid 10, p 314.

9   Grandmaster Zhu Tiancai is one of the "Four Great Jingangs (Gems)" of the Chen Style Taijiquan. The author has sponsored his workshops over many years in Washington, D.C.

10   Dr. Herbert Benson is the Director Emeritus of the Benson-Henry Mind Body Institute at Massachusetts General Hospital, Boston (http://www.massgeneral.org/bhi/) and Associate Professor of Medicine, the Mind Body Medical Institute at Harvard Medical School.

11   Picture of Andy Pettitte of the New York Yankees, by Frank Gunn, *The Associated Press*.

12   Zhang Zhijun was a student of Chen Zhaokui. I had the honor and opportunity of studying and traveling with him for a few weeks when he toured the United States in 2002, as well as in China a year later. He has a following in China, and is based in Zhengzhou, Henan.

13   The anecdote of Chen Jixia is also recounted in the books by Zhu Tiancai (1994) *Chen Village Taijiquan*. Percetakan Turbo Sdn, Petaling Jaya, Malaysia. (Chinese) p.308, by Chen Zhenglei (1999) *Chen Family Taijiquan*, (Chinese). Xi'an Science and Technology Publications, and others.

14   Wells, Marnix (2005). *Scholar Boxer Chang Naizhou's Theory of Internal Martial Arts and the Evolution of Taijiquan*. North Atlantic Books, Berkeley, CA. The book relates the Chen Jixia connection in p. 38.

8
Theory of Chansi Jin

1 The point of an object where its entire mass is represented, which in the context of gravity, is the center of gravity. Chapter 7. Ibid 3.

2 Halliday, David; Resnick, Robert; Walker, Jearl. *Fundamentals of Physics*. Fourth Edition. p. 335.

3 Chen Xin. *Chen Shi Taijiquan Tu Shuo*. Shanghai Books Publisher. 2001 Chinese ed. p. 74 *Taijiquan's Theory of Chansi*. The book was completed in 1919, but published only in 1933. It is regarded as a most comprehensive work on Taijiquan. Translation (2007) by Alex Golstein, *The Illustrated Canon of Chen Family Taijiquan*. INBI Matrix Pty Ltd, PO Box 775, Maroubra 2035, NSW, Australia.

4 Zhang Zhijun (2005). *Chen Shi Taijiquan Xin Tan* (New Exploration of Chen Taijiquan).

5 Ibid 3. *Taijiquan's Theory of Chansi*. p. 74.

6 Ibid 5.

7 Ibid 3. *Taijiquan's Theory of Chansi*. p. 72.

8 Gu Liuxin (1984). *Chen Style Taijiquan*. Hai Feng Publishing Co. The essay, *The Origin, Evolution and Development of Shadow Boxing*, is in the book.

9 Chapter 7. *Dantian and Internal Balance at the Kua*.

10 Rendered images of Asdrubal Cabrera (Chuck Crow—*The Plain Dealer*) and Roger Federer (Alastair Grant—*Associated Press*).

11 Zhang Sanfeng. *Taijiquan Treatise*, one of *The Five Classical Canons of Taijiquan* (chapter 2).

12 Chen Changxin. *Yong Wu Yao Yan* 用武要言 *(Essential Words on Taijiquan Applications)*.

13 Ibid 3. p. 120

14 Chen Xiaowang's fajin action is captured on YouTube, albeit not the same as seeing it in person, http://www.youtube.com/watch?v=zxxebP0u31g, and Chen Yu, http://www.youtube.com/watch?v=j_vcWq2GYXs

15 Chen Xiaowang. *Chen Family Taijiquan*. p. 308. Also instructions in class.

16 Ibid 12.

17   Wang Zongyue. *Taijiquan Classics*. One of the *Five Classical Canons of Taijiquan*.

18   Ibid 16.

19   Ibid 10.

20   Ibid 16.

21   Cheng Manching (1902-1975), a disciple of Yang Chengfu, was instrumental in spreading the Yang Style Taijiquan to Taiwan, South-East Asia, and the United States.

22   Mike Sigman studies "the practice and methodology of traditional internal strength." He is the owner-moderator of the QiJin Forum.

23   *Song of Push-hands*, one of the Five Classical Canons of Taijiquan.

24   Chapter 6. *Discerning Imbalance as Jin Errors*.

25   A stanza in *Song of Push-hands*.

26   Ibid 12.

9
Methods of Taijiquan Kungfu

1   Zhu Tiancai (1994). *Zhen Zhong Chenjiagou Taijiquan* [Authentic Chen Village Taijiquan]. Percetakan Turbo, Petaling Jaya, Malaysia. p. 20

2   Among the many postings, the following shows the various push-hand patterns (by Chen Zhenglei and his son) http://www.youtube.com/watch?v=adJwzXfCufE, and the next shows Chen Xiaowang and his son http://www.youtube.com/watch?v=B8kx7pW_T18.

3   Chen Changxing *Essential Words on Taijiquan Martial Applications* (*Taiji Yong Wu Yao Yan* 太极用武要言).

4   One of the Five Classical Canons of Taijiquan. Chapter 2.

5   Chen Xin (1919). *Chen Shi Taijiquan Tushuo (Illustrated Explanation of Chen Family Taijiquan)*. Shanghai Shiji Publication, 1986. p. 132. (English Translation Copy available by INBI Matrix Pty Ltd, Maroubra, NSW, Australia.)

6   Wang Zongyue. *Taijiquan Classics*.

7   Yang Yang, *Interview of Grandmaster Feng Zhiqiang*. T'ai Chi Magazine, June 2000. Yang Yang is a student of Feng who is a disciple of Chen Fa'ke. Yang Yang also elaborates on the eight energies in his book, *Taijiquan, The Art of Nurturing, The Science of Power*, Zhenwu Publications, Champaign, IL, 2005, p. 122.

8   *Elucidation of Thirteen Postures*. One of the Five Classical Canons of Taijiquan.

9   C.P. Ong, *Peng Jin*. Tai Chi Magazine, Oct 2002.

10   Douglas Wile, *Tai Chi Touchstones: Yang Family Secret Transmissions*. Sweet Chi Press, Revised Edition (1983) p. 28.

11   Chapter 8. *Dantian Internal Rotation (Dantian Neizhuan)*

12   Ibid 10, p. 29

13   Ibid 5.

14   Ibid 1. p. 23.

15   Ibid 5.

16   Ibid 1, p. 19.

17   Ibid 10, p. 33

18   Chapter 3. *Bagua (Eight Trigrams)*

19   Barbara Davis *The Taijiquan Classics, An Annotated Translation, Including Commentary by Chen Weiming*, North Atlantic Books, 2004, p. 99 or Chinese text of *Taijiquan Lun*, p. 157

20   Ibid 10. p. 132 Translation of Yang Chengfu's *Self-Defense Applications of Tai Chi Chuan*.

21   Ibid 5.

22   An excellent translation of Chen Xiaowang's essay by Tan Le-peng can be found in http://www.shou-yi.org/taijiquan/5-levels-of-skill-in-chen-taijiquan.

23   Ibid 1. p. 283.

10
Breathing & Meditation of Taijiquan

1   Grandmaster Zhu Tiancai adds that according to Taoist beliefs, the saliva generated during the exercise is an "essence of life-fluid" to be swallowed to rejuvenate the body.

2   Zhu Tiancai (1994). *Zhen Zhong Chenjiagou Taijiquan* [Authentic Chen Village Taijiquan]. Percetakan Turbo, Petaling Jaya, Malaysia. p. 30.

3   Ibid 2. p. 31.

4   Chen Changxin's *Principle of Three Unities.* Chapter 7.

5   The many studies of Dr. Herbert Benson are listed in the website: http://www.relaxationresponse.org/

6   Chen Changxin's *Principle of Four Extremities.* Chapter 7.

7   Chen Xin (1919). *Chen Shi Taijiquan Tushuo (Illustrated Explanation of Chen Family Taijiquan).* Shanghai Shiji Publication, 1986. p. 69.

8   The author was most fortunate to have spent parts of several summers in the early 1990s at the Saddhamaransi Monastery, Yangon, Myanmar, practicing meditation under the guidance of the Saddhamaransi Sayadaw.

9   Nyanatiloka, *The Word of Buddha.* A small tract that gives an outline of the teaching of the Buddha in the words of the Pali Canon. The book is available at http://www.wisdom-books.com/Author.asp?AUTH=Nyanatiloka+Mahathera

10   The reader can find an essay of Taoist Meditative Practice in the YeYoung Culture Studies, http://www.literati-tradition.com/meditative_practice.html

11   Chapter 3. *Taoist Practice and Early Qigong.*

12   Ibid 10.

13   *Vipassana* (Insight) meditation is a Theravada Buddhist practice. It is also taught in many meditation centers in non-religious setting.

14   Master Chen Xiaowang has been conducting Taijiquan workshops throughout the world since the 1990s.

15   Sunzi. *The Art of War* Sun Tzu, trans. Lionel Giles, chap 11, no 29. Google eBook

16   Chen Xin. *Illustrated Chen Family Taijiquan* (Chinese). On danbian posture p. 173. Shanghai Books Publisher. 2001 ed. A translation appears in *Peng Jin*, Tai Chi Magazine Oct 2002, by the author.

11
Silk-reeling Exercises

1   In 1983 the Singapore Wushu Association specifically requested for a Chen Village master to teach Taijiquan and Zhu Tiancai was sent.

2   Chapter 8. Section: *Orientations of Shun and Ni.*

About the Author

C.P. Ong is a 20th generation Chen Family Taijiquan disciple of both Chen Xiaowang and Chen Zhenglei. Since 1998, he has helped the two masters, as well as Zhu Tiancai, organize their annual workshop tours in the United States.

He first began his Taiji studies in 1972 learning the Guang Ping Yang Style from Master Y.C. Chiang in Berkeley, CA. He is also a student of *vipassana* (insight) meditation and has attended several intensive meditation retreats in Buddhist monasteries in Yangon, Myanmar.

He grew up in Malaysia and attended the University of Western Australia, Perth, under a Colombo Plan Scholarship. After graduating with First Class Honors (1968), the university awarded him a Hackett Studentship to pursue graduate studies in University of California, Berkeley, where he received his Ph.D. in Mathematics in 1973.

www.cpTaiji.com
cpTaiji@gmail.com

25348128R00201

Printed in Great Britain
by Amazon